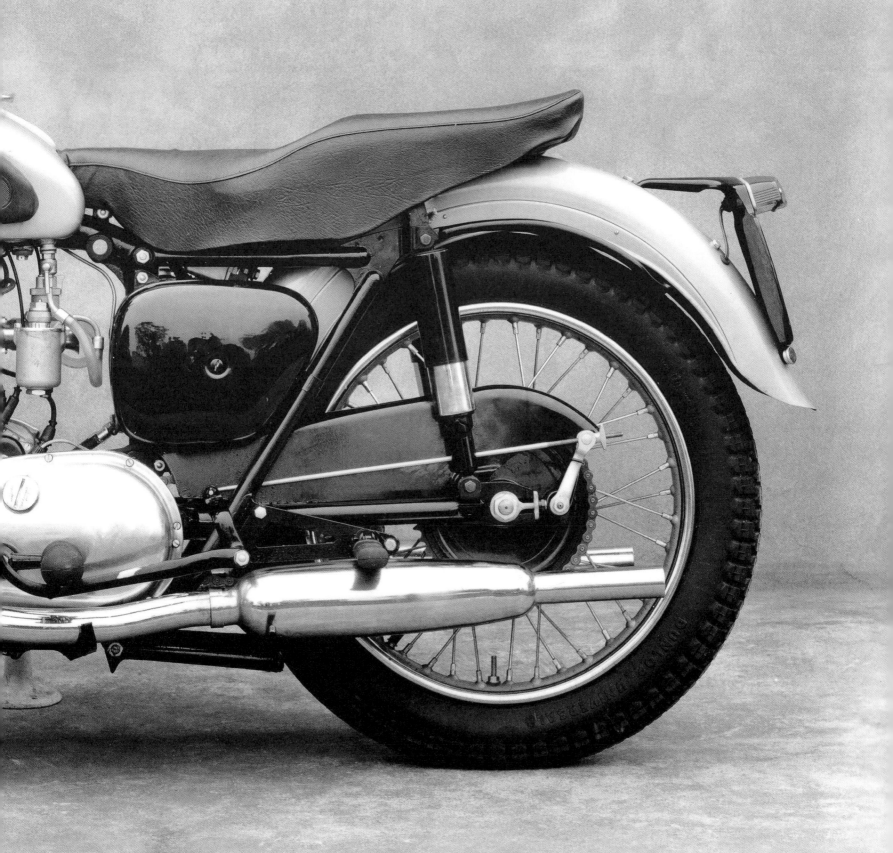

Brimming with creative inspiration, how-to projects, and useful information to enrich your everyday life, Quarto Knows is a favorite destination for those pursuing their interests and passions. Visit our site and dig deeper with our books into your area of interest: Quarto Creates, Quarto Cooks, Quarto Homes, Quarto Lives, Quarto Drives, Quarto Explores, Quarto Gifts, or Quarto Kids.

10 9 8 7 6 5 4 3 2

ISBN: 978-0-7603-5328-8

Library of Congress Cataloging-in-Publication Data

Names: Brooke, A. Lindsay, author.
Title: Triumph motorcycles in America / Lindsay Brooke and David Gaylin.
Description: Minneapolis, MN, USA : Motorbooks, an imprint of The Quarto Group, 2018. | Includes index.
Identifiers: LCCN 2017030126 | ISBN 9780760353288 (hc)
Subjects: LCSH: Triumph motorcycle--History. | Motorcycle industry--United States--History. | Motorcycles--United States--History.
Classification: LCC TL448.T7 B76 2018 | DDC 629.227/5--dc23
LC record available at https://lccn.loc.gov/2017030126

Acquiring Editor: Zack Miller
Project Manager: Alyssa Bluhm
Art Director: Brad Springer
Cover Designer: Brad Norr
Layout: Simon Larkin

On the front cover: Illustration by Brad Norr
On the back cover: Brooke archive
On the endpapers: Brooke archive (front), David Gaylin archive (back)
On the frontis: Brooke archive
On the title page: Ken Grzesiak collection; Brooke photo

Printed in China

MIX
Paper from responsible sources
FSC
www.fsc.org   FSC® C008047

TRIUMPH
MOTORCYCLES IN
America

The Most Exciting Motorcycle Ever!

TRIUMPH

Thunderbird

TRIUMPH ENGINEERING CO. LTD, Meriden Works, Allesley, COVENTRY, ENGLAND.

Lindsay Brooke and *David Gaylin*

Foreword by Peter Egan

motorbooks

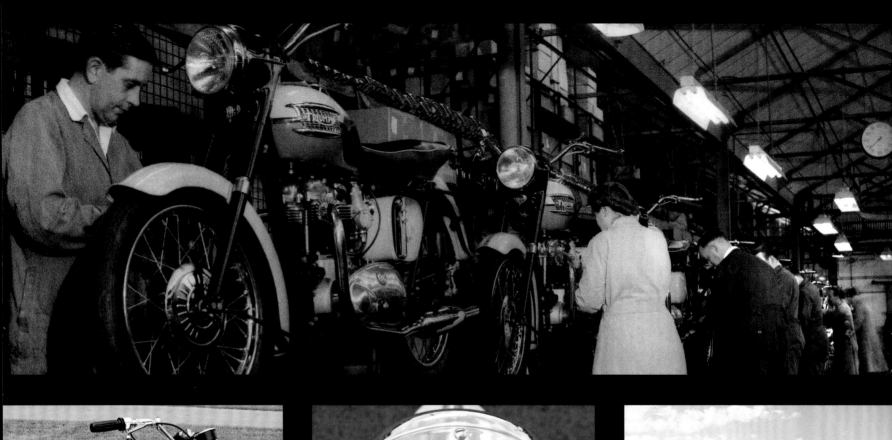

Bonneville 120

TRIUMPH

CONTENTS

ACKNOWLEDGMENTS

The original edition of this book published in 1993 required an entire page to credit the dozens of friends and contributors who helped us by providing interviews, key information, photographs (all analog prints, film transparencies, and hard copy in those days), period correspondences, contacts, and access to motorcycles.

Sadly, quite a few of the former Triumph executives, employees, dealers, racers, and tuners who graciously shared their memories and historical files with us have passed away in the intervening years. Some others have fallen out of contact. Quite a few, however, have continued to provide insights into Triumph's American story, and they deserve our thanks (in alphabetical order): Bill Baird, Randy Baxter, "Wild Bill" Betz, Mick Duckworth, Don Emde, Ed and Suzie Fisher, Ken Grzesiak, Tom Gunn, John and Tom Healy, Michael Lock, Dan Mahony, Keith Martin at Big D Cycle, Eddie Mulder, Bob "Ozzie" Oswald, Ted Rivard, Gene Romero, Mike Vaughan, and Craig Vetter.

For this latest edition, valuable contributions of original period photography came from Jon Blonk, Eddie Boomhower, Piet Boonstra, Scott Campbell, John Byrne Cooke, Ed Cunningham, George Hack, "TV Tommy" Ivo, Joe Lachniet, Norman Mayersohn, Ron Rae, Tim Remus, Bob Sholly, and John S. Stein.

John Hubbard saved Bob Leppan's collection of original 35mm slides taken in the 1950s and 1960s from a burst water pipe that nearly destroyed them. Triumph PR man Garrett Carter gave us access to modern-era images and information.

Information and images related to Triumph's Canadian history were enthusiastically provided by Greg Williams, himself an award-winning author of the Nicholson Bros.' history, and veteran historian Allan Johnson.

Thanks to the following enthusiasts who gave access to motorcycles and Triumphabilia for photography: Joel Alderman, Hermy Baver Jr., John Bishop, Graham Cousens, Bill Hoard, Mike Iannuccilli, John Lacko, John Melniczuk Jr., H. C. Morris, Jerry Romano, Paul Rye, Mike Selman, Steve Tremulis, Drew Winter, and Katy Wood. Other contemporary images were graciously provided by Randy Birkey/Bonneville Performance, Jim Davies, Johnny "Ton-Up" Greene, Jeff Hackett, Russell Hightower, Keith May, and Mark Mederski.

UK-based Charles Rising graciously opened his obsessive research on the T120C and TT Special. Triumph Owners Club stalwart Roy Schilling and American super-collector Wayne Hamilton provided their views on collectible Triumphs. Author Kevin Cameron shared numerous email anecdotes and insights from his days as a Boston dealer.

Triumph–Detroit dealer Dave Canu, Bonneville Performance boss Bill Gately, and Triumph's chief engineer Stuart Wood broadened our understanding of the Hinckley enterprise. Globetrotter and Guinness record-setter Danell Lynn gave us permission to show her astride her prized Bonneville.

A special tip of the flat cap to Peter Egan for contributing his thoughtful foreword, and to Nick Berard for his photos of Peter. And we're indebted to Bill Milburn, whose deep knowledge of AMA dirt and road racing history and racing Triumphs in general is unsurpassed.

This book is dedicated to the late Larry Klein, proprietor of GT Motors, raconteur, motorcycle book connoisseur and retailer, and ardent supporter of the updating and re-publication of this volume.

FOREWORD BY PETER EGAN

A geneticist and a behavioral psychologist could probably have a spirited debate as to whether those of us who have spent our lives infatuated by English motorcycles were born that way or if we might have, say, fallen off a second-floor porch—as I actually did when I was three—and hit our heads a little too hard on the pavement below. Faulty genes or a harsh environment? It's the old nature versus nurture debate.

Whatever the cause, something strange kicked in almost overnight when I was about thirteen years old. First, I inexplicably became fascinated by motorcycles—which no one else in my family was—and, second, I looked around at the machines available then and decided that the new Triumph Twins of the early '60s were simply the best-looking bikes in the world.

You could walk all the way around them and not find one wrong shape, false line, or muddled styling cue on the entire bike. Everything looked right, whether it was the flare of the "Delta head" cooling fins, the heart shape of the timing cover, the sweep of the exhaust pipes and mufflers, the streamlined gas tank, or the rear taper of the tidy bench seat. These bikes seemed a perfect collection of highly evolved shapes all distilled into one light and beautiful package.

But there was more there than great looks. Triumphs also enjoyed competition success in virtually every category. Bill Baird, one of my personal high school heroes, won the National Enduro Championship twelve years in a row on a nearly stock Triumph Trophy 500. Meanwhile, Buddy Elmore and Gary Nixon won back-to-back Daytona 200s on Triumph 500s in 1966 and 1967. And in 1966, Bob Leppan's Triumph-powered Gyronaut X-1 set a new world speed record of 245.66 miles per hour at Bonneville, bettering Johnny Allen's 1956 record—which had given the mighty Triumph Bonneville its name. Triumph Twins were the kings of speed.

They dominated desert racing, enduros, AMA flat track, TT, road racing, and hill climbs, piloted by such legendary champions as Romero, Nixon, Mulder, Mann, Scott, Van Leeuwen, Ekins, White, Tanner, Burnett, Kretz, Castro, and scores of others.

It's nice when your favorite bikes look great and win races, but it's even better when you can buy similar or identical models at a local dealership and ride them around on the street. It was this do-everything versatility that made Triumphs (at least in my world) the very essence of cool during the '60s, and the single most desirable material object a person could possess.

I don't think there was a time all though my high school, college, and military service years when I did not have a Triumph picture or brochure tacked on the wall of my bedroom, dorm room, or bunker in Vietnam. I folded and re-folded a sweat-soaked brochure of a 1968 Trophy T100C so many times when I was in the army that it finally fell apart.

Years later, I bought one of these very bikes, but at the time I couldn't afford a Triumph. I had to content myself with used Hondas—which were all outstanding motorcycles, by the way. But I wanted a Triumph. All my heroes had them, whether winning races, crashing near Woodstock, or jumping fences in *The Great Escape*.

Unfortunately, by the time I could afford a new Triumph, the British bike industry was in serious decline, Triumph Twins had been "modernized" in ways that didn't appeal to me, and the bikes were no longer world leaders in performance. What they had needed much more than restyling was upgraded engineering and reliability, and the Meriden factory finally shut its doors in 1983.

So, I stopped seeing Triumphs as versatile "only bikes" and began to view them as secondary hobby bikes, purchased

for their beauty and history, restoring a succession of them in my workshop—1968 Bonneville, 1969 Daytona 500, 1967 TR6-C, 1968 Trophy T100C, and a 1969 TR6 Tiger. They were beautiful to look at in the garage and fun to ride on the weekends, but I never ventured too far from home on any of them.

Then—miracle of miracles—an Englishman named John Bloor revived Triumph in the late 1980s, building a new factory in Hinckley and introducing a whole new, thoroughly engineered line of bikes. This was not some underfunded exercise in nostalgia, but a well-financed foray into the modern competitive motorcycle market—done with a determination to end forever the flickering headlight and oil leak jokes. Bloor wisely produced several years of fast, utterly reliable modern bikes before going retro with a new line of Bonnevilles and Scramblers.

Since then, I've owned two of the new Hinckley Bonnevilles and one Scrambler, all good, solid, reliable standard bikes that I've enjoyed a lot. With reservations. I thought all of them could use a little more power, taller gearing for the road, and slightly better suspension—along with an unbent exhaust system on the otherwise lovely Bonnevilles.

Well, this year Triumph introduced an all-new water-cooled 1200cc T120 Bonneville. Thoroughly modern but subtly restyled to look even more accurately "old," with ABS, heated grips, traction control, and much improved power, suspension, and component quality. I took a demo ride and ordered a red and silver one immediately. I've had it now for a full summer, and it's one of the finest bikes I've ever owned.

So, at the age of sixty-eight, I'm finally exactly where I want to be, Triumph-wise. These bikes have been a recurring theme in my life, like a musical refrain that runs through the soundtrack of a movie, and this latest strain is easily the new favorite in my small stable. I guess at heart I'm just basically a lifelong Triumph guy.

And, of course, so is Lindsay Brooke, a good friend and the author of this much-expanded version of one of my favorite and most well-thumbed books. We chat on the phone often and are clearly on the same wavelength about Triumphs and many other things. Our shared sense of values could be genetic, I suppose, traceable back to some common ancestor in the British Isles or elsewhere, but then I haven't asked Lindsay if he ever fell off a porch.

INTRODUCTION

This book marks the third step in uniquely telling Triumph's eighty-year North America story. The first edition, published in 1993, rapidly sold out, as did the three print runs that followed. The book then went out of print not long after the twenty-first century began. According to Motorbooks, our publisher then and now, *Triumph Motorcycles in America* was their bestselling motorcycle title that wasn't about Harley-Davidsons. We were quite proud of that.

If you needed a copy in the intervening years, you were faced with paying escalating prices on the online used-book market. Co-author Brooke witnessed a conversation in the Mid-Ohio swap meet around 2006: A parts vendor had a dog-eared copy of *Triumph* among his table full of assorted literature and early Honda Scrambler bits. A customer spotted the book, priced at $100, grabbed it, and told the vendor, "I want this book more than I want that CL160 gas tank, but only have cash for one. I'll take the Triumph book now and come back later for the tank."

Enthusiasts clearly couldn't get enough of Triumph's America history. So, around 2012, we decided it was time to tickle the Amals and stomp on the kickstarter again.

Motorbooks' editor, Zack Miller, a bike guy himself, agreed. There was a broader tale to tell. In the years since the original edition hit the street, we had acquired additional period images, literature, and ex-TriCor and JoMo memoranda. And we'd talked to more people who'd been involved in Triumph's rise, fall, and resurrection.

We were saddened, however, by the passing of so many Triumph heroes and friends whom we interviewed for the first edition, among them top US executives Don Brown, Pete Colman, and Earl Miller; Meriden chief engineer Doug Hele; dealers Jack "Big D" Wilson, "Saginaw Sam" Hawley, and Bob Myers; racing legends Gary Nixon, Bud Ekins, Ed Kretz Sr. and Jr., Cliff Guild, and Pat Owens; and key observers, including Gordon Jennings, TriCor's Davy Jones, JoMo's Clyde Earl, Eddy Mercer, Marge Coates, former AMCA president Mort Wood, and Flat Track Motorcycle Museum founder Dan Rouit.

This new edition brings Triumph's US and Canada saga up to 2017. We hope you enjoy the ride.

Lindsay Brooke—*Plymouth, Michigan*
David Gaylin—*Baltimore, Maryland*

THE TRIUMPH "SPEED TWIN"

01

TRIUMPH IN THE NEW WORLD
PRE-1938 PIONEERS

The first motorcycles marketed with a "Triumph" tank emblem in the US were launched in 1907—and manufactured in America. In fact, Triumphs from two different US makers existed decades before the first British Triumphs were officially imported.

ABOVE: **Reggie Pink outside his New York City shop circa 1930, with a Velocette KTT and a 500cc Ariel Model G in the foreground.** *Gaylin archive*

LEFT: **Brochure artwork created by Triumph for its North American distributors prior to World War II took some strange liberties with the US state borders in the map behind the 1940 5T. But it made the point that Triumph's new twin was available across the continent.** *Brooke archive*

Chicago's Excelsior Automobile Supply Co. was the first to use the Triumph name, on a machine powered by a 2¼-horsepower Thor single; the engine itself was designed by the Hendee Mfg. Co., which made Indian. It is unknown how many bikes were produced. Five years later, the startup Triumph Manufacturing Co. appeared in Detroit, acquiring the Triumph name and trademark from Excelsior and launching its Models A, B, and C, the latter with two-speed gearing.

The Detroit Triumph company allegedly produced over 1,000 machines before it ceased manufacturing in 1913. None of their motorcycles are known to have survived, according to the Antique Motorcycle Club of America.

One of the first accounts of a British-made Triumph in the US was documented in the April 20, 1916, issue of the American magazine *Motorcycle Illustrated*, when C. A. Shaw road-tested the 30.25ci Model H. In his story, entitled "Experience with an English Mount," Shaw expressed his delight with the bike throughout a virtually incident-free 7,400-mile trek. He also offered his opinion of the apparent superiority of the Triumph's belt drive versus a chain final drive, then the US industry standard.

At the beginning of his story, Shaw revealed why foreign motorcycles in general were so scarce in America: "I bought the machine like a pig in a poke, never having seen it, and when it at last arrived by freight, it took some ingenuity to figure out the controls." No dealers and no support—a Triumph buyer was a pioneer in every sense of the word.

Of course, the odd "Limey" bike would trickle in across the Canadian border. As a member nation of the British Commonwealth, Canada benefited from unfettered trade in British-made goods. If an American wanted to test ride a BSA, Ariel, or Douglas, he had only to go north.

A few early entrepreneurs did try to set up shop in the US, banking on the British bikes' more manageable size as a sales advantage. During the early 1920s, Jonas B. Oglaend opened a shop in New York City and offered BSA motorcycles, bicycles, and rifles. His operation was really an "agency," in that he had only a few sample models on hand to show customers, selling primarily from a catalog.

A potential customer ordered the motorcycle of his or her choice and paid installments while it was en route from England—which could take up to eight months. Under these conditions, nobody lined up to buy BSAs or the BSA franchises Oglaend offered in his ads. How many bikes he actually sold is unknown, but certainly it wasn't many.

REGGIE PINK AND AMARANTH RED

Like any motorcycle dealer, Oglaend knew the value of racing and staged stunts in advertising. He hired one of New York's most capable and enthusiastic riders, Reggie Pink, to demonstrate BSA's fuel economy and performance. Pink was well known to motorcyclists in the eastern states, having successfully competed in nearly all forms of two-wheel sport. As a sixteen-year-old, he had sold and wrenched Reading-Standard motorcycles for an area dealer and was best known as a hill-climb champion, riding a Douglas opposed twin.

Pink couldn't get enough of British motorcycles. In 1926, he opened his own British bike shop in New York City. Oglaend helped Reggie set up, as he was then eager to exit the motorcycle business. Initially, Pink ran his operation much as Oglaend had, keeping a few sample models on the floor and taking orders. But he soon branched out, and entries in his 1927 ledger note that he was selling AJS, Ariel, BSA, Douglas, and Levis machines.

In every way, Pink was more serious than Oglaend about exposing Americans to foreign motorcycles. In 1928, he sailed to England, where he visited the London Motorcycle Show as well as many of the factories he represented. From this trip, Pink gained knowledge about his products and established relationships with marques he wasn't selling. By 1930, Pink had added Velocette, Dunelt, Scott, New Imperial, Calthorpe, and OK Supreme to his Bronx showroom. He also began wholesaling to dealers and offering Reg Pink franchises.

Business was surprisingly good, considering that the Depression was then ravaging America. In fact, by 1935

1937 Tiger 90 500cc sports singles like this one shown in an October 1936 magazine ad helped Reggie Pink launch his pre–World War II Triumph franchise. The Tiger singles were offered with either raised or low roadster-type exhaust systems. *Gaylin archive*

A 1940 Speed Twin correctly restored by New Jersey Triumph specialist Mike Benolken shows Triumph's nouveau Amaranth Red paint along with the overall lithe proportions of the machine. *Jeff Hackett*

Pink had added JAP, Norton, and even Indian to his line. Pink represented as many as nineteen different motorcycle brands at once, making him the all-time champ of US motorcycle dealers in terms of variety. But lack of capital prevented him from maintaining large stocks of machines for ready purchases; Pink remained mainly a mail-order motorcycle agent.

Because he had already established a US outlet for Ariel, Pink was also able to handle the parent company's other products. When Ariel's owners, led by Jack Sangster, took over the manufacture of Triumph motorcycles in 1936, Pink was in an excellent position to become the US Triumph distributor. He immediately advertised himself as the sole importer for this exciting new brand. It is unlikely that he brought over more than a few sample models in 1936, but by 1937 Pink was importing significant numbers of Tiger singles into America.

The overhead-valve 500cc Tiger 90 and 350cc Tiger 80 were restylings of earlier designs by legendary British motorcycle engineer Val Page. Although their performance was typical of contemporary British singles, their finishes were exquisite— every bit as attractive as the beautiful Ariel Red Hunter. This was no accident, as both works of art were from the same master, Edward Turner.

By 1938, Pink's sales brochure highlighted Triumph above all other marques. That year, Turner unleashed his 500cc OHV Speed Twin on an unsuspecting world. The 5T Speed Twin had the clean, graceful lines of the Tiger single, but with an extra cylinder. More importantly, it was much smoother than a single of the same displacement and performed even better.

To the sporting motorcyclist seeking an alternative to the huge American bikes, the Speed Twin was seductive indeed. It was slender and compact, weighing just 365 pounds wet.

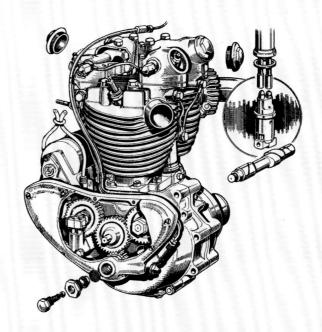

From a 1939 Johnson Motors advertising flyer, this was the first detailed drawing to be published, originally in *Motor Cycling* magazine, of the new Tiger 100 engine. Shown is the spring-loaded pressure valves fitted into the timing case; its shape differs from the Speed Twin's. Note arrangement of the piping to the pressure gauge and the overhead rocker assemblies. Inset: one of the camshafts and tappet assemblies. *Brooke archive*

ABOVE: **John Esler was a pioneering American Triumph dealer who began selling the brand in 1939. His Grand Rapids, Michigan, British bike shop also sold Vincent, Ariel, and Norton before World War II. After the war, Esler grew his Triumph franchise, supported by TriCor, into one of the most successful in the US. Parked on the street in this 1940 photo, left to right, are a Tiger 100, Speed Twin, and Ariel Square Four.** *Brooke archive*

Starting was easier than it had been with a single, with no decompresser required. The new parallel-twin engine was more tractable too; early road tests noted that, by retarding the spark, the Triumph could be slowed to 12 miles per hour in fourth gear without any chain snatch. Furthermore, top-gear acceleration was described as "delightful," and the bike would "zoom from 30 miles per hour to 60, 70, or 80 at the will of the rider," according to an October 1937 road test in *The Motor Cycle*.

In standard trim, the Speed Twin produced 26 horsepower—just one horsepower less than Harley-Davidson's over-the-counter race bike, the 750cc WLDR. And Turner's brainchild offered excellent speed tuning potential. It would rev safely to 6,000 rpm without a valve float, something that was astronomical to American riders accustomed to flathead V-twin sloggers. Like the Tiger singles, the 5T's four-speed, foot-change gearbox and hand clutch made it easy to ride fast on twisty roads. Top speed was about 90 miles per hour.

The engine was basically the only new piece in the package, as it was designed to fit into the existing Tiger 90 chassis. Edward Turner had performed this engineering trick once before at Ariel, when he designed his revolutionary 1931 Square Four to fit the frame of Ariel's big, sloping single of the previous year. It's challenging enough to create a world-beating design on a clean sheet of paper, but Turner did it within existing dimensions.

"The Speed Twin was consciously designed to be simple and inexpensive at every point," observed *Cycle World*'s technical

OPPOSITE: **A pair of 1940 Tiger 100s restored by Mike Benolken show the two fender paint schemes available that year—the optional black with silver center stripe (foreground) and standard silver with black stripe on the background machine.** *Jeff Hackett*

Rod Coates's original shop in Rochester, New York, was typical of the humble beginnings of many American motorcycle dealers prior to World War II. A Harley Knucklehead shares the sidewalk with two early Speed Twins; the bike on the right is equipped with raised exhaust and a then-new Goulding Rocket sidecar, made in Saginaw, Michigan. *Gaylin archive*

editor Kevin Cameron in 2011. "Raising the performance bar wasn't enough; big 1,000cc Twins from Brough, BSA and others had already done that. What also had to happen was the planned union of higher performance with affordable price." Turner succeeded, even embracing the then-exotic technology of forged-aluminum connecting rods. Hundreds of thousands of examples of his original design were sold over six decades. The significance of Triumph's new powerplant and its impact on the motorcycle industry cannot be overstated.

Perhaps in an attempt to mask the fact that the Speed Twin's engine was the only new item, Turner decided at the eleventh hour to finish the entire machine in the brownish-red color then being used on the De Luxe model (non-Tiger single) fuel tanks. The color, Amaranth Red, successfully projected the new model as not only a departure for Triumph—known for its silver-and-black Tigers—but as a step away from the conservative motorcycle industry.

Only four Triumph models were offered by Reggie Pink in 1938: the Speed Twin ($446.46), Tiger 90 ($423.94), Tiger 80 ($386.39), and the 250 De Luxe ($315.04). A host of accessories, including a rear fender luggage rack, deeper-radius fenders, and an engine skid plate were offered too. Orders for the new Triumphs, especially the Speed Twin, quickly dominated Pink's ledger books. Some early franchise dealers included Rod Coates in Rochester, New York, and two Pennsylvanians: Earl Martz in McSherrystown and Al Shire in Allentown.

Pink began to concentrate on Triumph in 1939. He was then offering all thirteen of the factory's models, including the new Tiger 100 ($480.26). The Tiger was the sporting version of the Speed Twin; from the moment of its announcement, it was preferred by American riders. Its engine was "breathed on" by the factory, with polished ports and internals, 8:1 compression, forged pistons, and a 1-inch Amal carburetor.

The T100 gave a claimed 34 horsepower at 7,000 rpm—8 more horsepower than the 5T. Buyers were issued a test card showing their bike's power curve from when the engine was run up on the Coventry factory's brake. This was Triumph's first production street bike genuinely capable of 100 miles per hour, though riders usually found 95 to 98 miles per hour to be more realistic—unless the muffler end caps were removed, which created bona fide megaphones. For those wishing to race their new Tiger, a bronze cylinder head ($31.50) was available. Triumph claimed this component aided top-end cooling under extreme load conditions. Standard finned front brake drums offered improved cooling.

The Tiger 100 looked as good as it performed. Its chromed fuel tank was highlighted with Silver Sheen panels outlined in blue pin striping. Combined with silver fenders (black with a silver center stripe were also available), gloss black frame, oil tank, and tool box, and just the right amount of buffed aluminum, a resplendent machine was created.

The Tiger 100's fuel tank grew to carry nearly one gallon more gasoline than the Speed Twin, though it maintained its slim width in the leg area. Triumph offered the prewar twins with three different front fenders and two different rear fenders. The narrow sports fenders were preferred by US customers, while fenders with deeply valenced, 6-inch cross sections (the latter with welded-in side panels, popular with wet-weather riders) were more popular in Canada. The touring fenders came either valenced or non-valenced.

A 1940 Export Trade List booklet obtained by the author from Rod Coates and marked "Strictly Confidential" revealed more features in the pipeline. These included the patented rear "sprung hub" (which finally arrived after World War II), an optional 5-inch-diameter speedometer, and a Tiger 85 sports 350 twin that never made it to production.

Triumph's sensational new 500cc twin was a natural for modification and instantly began showing up in winner's circles. During a challenging 1938 hill climb in western New York, a Speed Twin was the only motorcycle to reach the summit. In California, prewar riders Ted Evans, Bud Lowrie, Vern Gardner, Bruce "Boo Boo" Pearson, Felix Passot, and others consistently rode their Triumphs to dirt track victories. In Canada, Chuck Stockey was the man to beat in road racing and TT events (see Chapter 3).

And at the Daytona 200 itself, at least thirteen Triumph riders competed on the beach course between 1939 and 1941, according to the authors' research. The Coventry factory was struggling to satisfy demand; it continued to ship new machines to North America, even after World War II began in September 1939. Remarkably, in May 1940—just weeks before the Battle of Britain—Triumph's Export Department dispatched a special race-prepped Tiger 100 to Indiana racer Rody Rodenberg. Original factory invoices later published by "Vintagent" Paul d'Orleans show it was equipped with a bronze head, special 8:1 pistons, TT carburetor, BTH racing magneto, works-type open megaphones, and rear-seat footpegs.

The Tiger survived the sea journey across the U-boat–infested Atlantic, but the war years put a hold on Rody's racing plans. After World War II, it was campaigned through the early 1950s and still survives as of 2017.

America discovered the Triumph twin with Reggie Pink's help. But his lack of capital kept him from exploiting the vast US market, and he never advanced much beyond a pay-as-you-go dealer. From 1936 to 1940, Reggie Pink imported only about 100 Triumphs.

Triumph's Canadian distributors were also making inroads to the US market. By early 1941, though, the Coventry factory had completely switched over production to British military bikes and all exports were halted. Pink held out with Indian until their full output also changed to army machines. He had little choice but to sign a deal with Harley-Davidson a few years later, thus ending all his British dealings.

This was of little consequence to the Triumph Engineering Company: they had already set up shop in California with a gentleman who possessed deeper pockets.

An unknown rider gets some last-minute streamlining—a sheet of Lucite or Plexiglas acrylic plastic—fitted to his race-prepped Tiger 100 on the Daytona beach, pre–World War II. At least thirteen Triumph riders competed in the 200-miler during 1939 to 1941. Note the large-diameter "works-type" open megaphones fitted to this machine and the rider's sweater showing his "BSMC" club logo, along with leather pants and boots typical of the period. *Gaylin archive*

02
HOW THE WEST WAS WON
THE RISE OF JOHNSON MOTORS INC.

As a thirty-one-year-old attorney vacationing in Hawaii, William E. Johnson wasn't looking for anything but a bit of sand, surf, and relaxation from his California law practice. But the moment he saw a little motor scooter on a Honolulu street, his professional life changed—and the seeds of Triumph's first official factory distributorship were sown.

ABOVE: Johnson's second store was at 1240 West Pico Boulevard. in Los Angeles from 1940 to 1945. A new Speed Twin is displayed in the center window and an Indian Four is on the right. *Gaylin archive*

LEFT: JoMo founder Bill Johnson, dressed in hat and coveralls, watches the Catalina Grand Prix in an impromptu grandstand. At his right in sunglasses is Triumph managing director Edward Turner. JoMo service and racing manager Pete Colman is in the white logo sweater. Between Johnson and Colman is *Motorcyclist* magazine editor Bill Bagnall. Burbank, California, Triumph dealer Bill Martin is on the far right. *Brooke archive*

A sight to make motorcycle collectors today wish for a time machine! Johnson's Pico Boulevard showroom, 1940. A Speed Twin is on the stand at right and a Tiger 100 graces the back window. Lined up on the floor are an Ariel Square Four, Ariel Red Hunter, various Indian Chiefs, Scouts and Fours, and a Tiger 100 behind the Square Four. *Gaylin archive*

The tiny machine that caught Johnson's eye that day in 1936 was a Salsbury Motor Glide. Immediately he was intrigued—"It occurred to me that it had real sales possibilities," he recalled in a 1951 guest editorial in *Motorcyclist*. Upon his return to Pasadena, Johnson purchased a new Motor Glide. Until then, he'd never ridden a powered two-wheeler and was admittedly frightened by some of the Bay Area motorcyclists he had seen on local roads. He knew little about Indian and Harley-Davidson, America's two surviving motorcycle giants.

But none of that mattered. Bill Johnson was a gearhead at heart, a talented amateur machinist who collected scale-model trains, expensive German cameras, and firearms. The Salsbury scooter kicked off a new obsession: motorcycles. Johnson learned all he could by reading *Motorcyclist*—then the major American monthly bike magazine—*The Motor Cycle*, and *Motor Cycling*. The two British weeklies mesmerized him with the 1,000cc Ariel Square Four, arguably the most sophisticated motorcycle of the late 1930s.

Johnson ordered a new Square Four from Bill Gibson at British and American Motors in Pasadena. It was a huge leap from his first little scooter.

"I was most impatient for its delivery and in the meantime I had read the specifications so many times that I could repeat them chapter and verse," he later recalled in the *Motorcyclist* article. Owning the big Ariel convinced Johnson that the American market was ripe for powerful, high-quality, beautifully finished foreign motorcycles.

Edward Turner agreed. The two men had begun corresponding regularly after Johnson wrote to the Triumph managing director praising his Ariel. At the time, Turner had been scouting for an official American distributor for Triumph's machines; he sensed potential in Johnson. Their letters started a close personal and business relationship that lasted until Johnson's death in 1962.

Clearly, Johnson wanted into the motorcycle business, but he needed a partner. He found one in Wilbur Ceder, an accountant friend who worked next door to his law firm. Ceder was older than Johnson and had a solid financial background. In 1938, after some negotiations, the new partners purchased Bill Gibson's modest British and American Motors shop, which was up for sale.

E. W. "Pete" Colman, Gibson's salesman and mechanic, told the authors that, in order to clinch the sale, Gibson had assured Johnson that the profit he would make from the Coca-Cola machine alone would pay the rent on the building!

Johnson and Ceder initially kept the British and American Motors name. They agreed that Johnson would be president and director and Ceder would serve as secretary/treasurer. From the start, the business was on shaky ground: they lost the Indian franchise when the factory transferred it to a nearby dealer, and they also had trouble securing financing to purchase new motorcycles.

"When Wilbur and I approached bankers and finally mentioned 'imported motorcycles,' the gleam of human kindness in their eyes changed to astonishment—and the answer was 'NO,'" he later recalled in *Motorcyclist*. In 1938, after considerable searching, Johnson and Ceder found a bank willing to back them. Cash flowed so that they could order the sensational new Triumph Speed Twin and a smattering of Ariels, BSAs, and spare parts.

Bankers weren't their only skeptics. Established Indian and Harley dealers believed Johnson to be an affluent playboy running a "hobby" venture. Looking back years later, Johnson

loved to tell this story: one day, not long after the business opened, he was cleaning up the shop, clad in overalls, when he heard someone banging on the door.

Two men were outside: Dudley Perkins, the famed San Francisco Harley-Davidson dealer, and Hap Alzina, the California Indian distributor who would later become BSA's Western distributor. Obviously Perkins and Alzina were snooping on their new competition. But neither man recognized Johnson in his "worker's" clothes.

"I went on with my job," Johnson explained in the article, "but couldn't help overhearing their conversation. The gist of it was that this chap Johnson 'will never make a success of this business' as it has been tried before in a small way, without success."

Johnson and Ceder spent most of the next two years promoting Triumph and Ariel, mainly in Southern California. Shortly after acquiring British and American Motors, they

D-Day was three weeks away when Triumph aimed this May 1944 ad in *The Motor Cycle* at the thousands of US servicemen then in Britain preparing for the Normandy Invasion, as well as the army air force aircrews based there. Among them were many future Triumph owners! *Brooke archive*

A bare-armed Ted Evans slides his 1939 Tiger 100 racer around the Ascot Park half-mile in Los Angeles in 1940. Note the upswept pipes with large-diameter megaphones, a typical Triumph racing modification. *Gaylin archive*

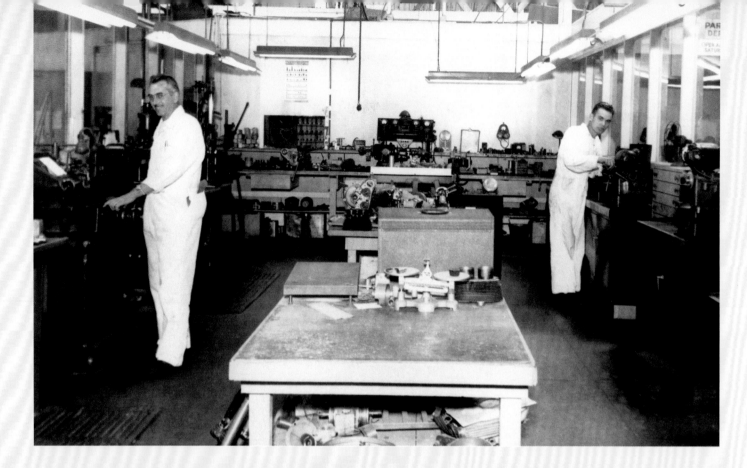

JoMo service manager Bud Felker (left) and chief mechanic and race tuner Cal Makela in the machine shop at Colorado Boulevard, late 1940s. The Service Department featured six hydraulic lifts for bike repairs and was one of the best-equipped motorcycle shops in North America. *Gaylin archive*

Early on, Johnson and Ceder saw the benefit of advertising in national magazines that were popular with young men. *Brooke archive*

hosted a weekend motorcycle exposition in their showroom and invited the public to attend the event free of charge. In addition to a display of new Ariels, BSAs, Calthorpes, and Salsbury scooters, Johnson pulled a radical move—he invited his competitors to display their new Harley-Davidsons and Indians! Some dealers thought that Johnson was crazy. Many predicted he'd soon be out of business.

Some 15,000 people attended the three-day show. Pete Colman remembered it as a great success, he told the authors, though Johnson did not yet have a new Speed Twin to display. Alzina, who'd brought some Indians to the open house, was so impressed with Johnson's spirit and promotional abilities that he offered him the Indian franchise for central Los Angeles.

Johnson and Ceder went "professional" in 1939 and hired their first sales manager, Andy Anderson, a rider popular with area motorcyclists. Joining on as a mechanic was "Iron Man" Ed Kretz, the 1937 Daytona 200 winner. That same year, Johnson received his first new 500cc 5T Speed Twin. Americans called it a "thirty-fifty," referencing its engine displacement in cubic inches (500cc equals 30.50 ci). Then came a batch of Tiger 90 500cc singles, followed by the Tiger 100 sports twin, which quickly became the hot ticket for West Coast dirt track and TT racers and discerning road riders.

As the 1930s ended, so did the Great Depression. The storm clouds of World War II brought huge aircraft plants, shipyards, and countless new jobs to Southern California. Money became more available and Johnson saw another opportunity: Triumph racing successes bred new bike sales.

From the very beginning, Johnson and Ceder supported all forms of motorcycle competition. "Without exception," Johnson noted in *Motorcyclist*, "every Sunday [from 1939 to 1941] we attended whatever race meet was scheduled and entered a Triumph T100." Press recognition of Triumph's new California base gained momentum in late 1940, after Bruce "Boo-Boo" Pearson and his tuned Tiger 90 and Tiger 100 cleaned house in California competition, winning thirty-two of thirty-six events that season. Johnson and Ceder's constant promotion at competition events began to pay off in sales and brand recognition.

In 1940, Johnson finally accepted Hap Alzina's long-standing offer of an Indian franchise. He and Ceder moved their shop to 1240 West Pico Boulevard in Los Angeles. There they changed the name to Johnson Motors Inc. (JoMo). Edward Turner came over from Britain to visit for the first time during this period of American neutrality prior to Pearl Harbor. While there, he granted Johnson direct sales rights for Southern California—Triumph's first official "factory" foothold in the US.

With Triumph Speed Twins ($448.51) and Tiger 100s ($488.11) sharing their showroom with Indian Fours, Chiefs, and Scouts, along with Ariel Red Hunters and Square Fours, Johnson and Ceder dropped BSA and Calthorpe. They now offered an excellent selection of high-quality, high-performance domestic and foreign motorcycles. At last, Johnson Motors seemed poised for success—until World War II intervened.

Remarkably, while the British bike industry shifted over to military production, Triumph continued to ship small quantities of new bikes and spares to Johnson Motors and other select US customers, despite the U-boat threat in the Atlantic and the priority of war materiel as cargo. Through Turner's direct influence, Triumph sent transmission gears and other key parts to its new California outlet while Hitler's panzers raced across Europe. Such "back-door" commerce ended in November 1940, when a massive 400-plane air raid on Coventry demolished Triumph's Priory Street works. A temporary plant was set up for army bike production, while a new "greenfield" plant between the villages of Allesley and Meriden was constructed. Triumph was fully back in business by late 1942, but America's entry into the war had already put all civilian motorcycle trade on hold.

From 1939 through 1941, Johnson Motors had sold around 300 new Triumphs and Ariels, Ed Kretz told the authors. To stay afloat during the war, Johnson and Ceder transformed the business into a tool-and-die shop that served the aircraft industry while handling a trickle of motorcycle repairs. In the meantime, Johnson and Turner maintained close contact via letters and cablegrams. In 1944, as the Allies neared victory, the two friends discussed the opportunities of the postwar US motorcycle scene.

Since the mid-1930s, Harley-Davidson and Indian had battled each other within a stagnant market. They did little to attract younger riders into the sport. New bike production in the US hovered between 12,000–17,000 machines per year, many destined for police forces. Cars were becoming ubiquitous for everyday transportation. Turner and Johnson reckoned that Triumph's sporting middleweight twins were perfect for expanding the market.

The annual 500-mile Greenhorn Enduro started in front of Johnson Motors in Pasadena and ran north to Greenhorn Mountain. JoMo supplied the coffee and donuts to all entrants before the race, in addition to hosting various customer events through the year. Decades later, the Colorado Boulevard facility reverted back to a high-end automobile dealership; in 2017 it was home to Resnak Audi. *Gaylin archive*

Turner predicted that, within a year after the war's end, Triumph could be selling a minimum of 1,000 new motorcycles per year in the US. While he blew hot and cold on racing—he complained about its cost but loved it when Triumphs won—Turner often politely suggested that Johnson not overemphasize racing as a sales tool. And he cautiously questioned how Harley and Indian would react to a postwar British motorcycle invasion. No doubt about it, Turner was serious about developing the US into a major, if not *the* major, export market for his products. But, fearing a tariff backlash, he also expressed a reluctance to take on America's two remaining motorcycle giants.

During October 1944, Triumph was approached by Alfred Rich Child, Harley-Davidson's Asian sales agent since the 1920s. Child had boosted Harley sales dramatically in Japan and China and had even set up a factory in Japan to produce Harley twins (Japanese Rikuos) under license. He now pitched Triumph to become their exclusive factory-authorized importer in the US. Turner and Jack Sangster, Triumph's chairman, were impressed. They especially liked the fact that Child already had an East Coast base. But Turner's strong friendship with Johnson and the early success of Johnson Motors determined Triumph's decision to stick with the Californian.

Late that year, Johnson agreed to become the official US distributor for Triumph and Ariel motorcycles. *Motorcyclist* reported in its January 1945 issue that postwar plans for a nationwide dealer network were under way and that Bill Johnson was accepting applications for Triumph and Ariel franchises. By that time, Johnson Motors had moved back to Pasadena to a new location, 267 W. Colorado Street (later Boulevard). The building formerly housed an auto dealership and Johnson and Ceder immediately invested $85,000 (more

PETE COLMAN MADE IT HAPPEN

In a remarkable Triumph career that spanned three decades, E. W. "Pete" Colman did it all. His reputation as a member of America's undefeated 1936 to 1937 Class A Speedway team and top-notch technical credentials landed him a job as JoMo's on-the-road salesman in 1948. Colman rose through the company ranks, from parts and service to general management, before switching hats in 1965 to run BSA's western US operations. Four years later, he was promoted to vice president of engineering for the US Triumph-BSA combine, a post he held until leaving a terminally ill Norton-Triumph Inc. in 1974.

Colman (in white logo sweater) steadies the JoMo sidecar rig during filming at the Catalina GP. His many duties included race promotions and prepping new machines for magazine road tests. *Bill Bagnall/Brooke archive*

Colman was the heart and soul of JoMo's Service and Racing departments. Like his TriCor counterpart, Rod Coates, with whom he had a prickly relationship, Colman helped many western states dealers become successful race sponsors. Working with Meriden's Ernie Nott, Colman pushed to get the popular Speed Kit produced and onto US racetracks. He and JoMo service mechanic Cal Makela prepared powerful Triumph twins for a cast of star riders, including Blackie Bullock (five AMA speed records), Johnny Gibson (Pacific Coast dirt-track championship), Jimmy Phillips (Peoria TT victory), and Bill Johnson (230-mile-per-hour world speed record). Walt Fulton, Billy Meier, Bill Tuman, Don Hawley, Dick Dorresteyn (countless Ascot TT wins), and Sammy Tanner were other riders associated with the brand.

Colman's friendship with independent tuning wizard Tim Witham resulted in Witham's magic touch applied to many JoMo-sponsored racing machines. It also ensured that Witham's superb S&W valve springs became a JoMo catalog part and were eventually fitted at the factory. The S&W springs were just one of a long list of Colman-approved goodies sourced from Webco, Harman & Collins, MCM, Bates, Norris, Wenco, Morris, and other famous names in California's thriving speed-parts industry.

In 1964, Colman joined the AMA Competition Committee, bolstering Triumph's influence within the "Iron Triangle" of companies (along with BSA and Harley-Davidson) that set much of US racing policy. A die-hard Californian who, according to many who knew him, unabashedly stoked Triumph's West-versus-East fires, Colman assembled and directed (with chief mechanic Danny Macias) the powerful 1970 to 1971 BSA-Triumph teams that won back-to-back AMA national championships. He also pushed a reluctant Meriden to develop the 750cc T140 twin for 1973 production.

than $1.1 million in 2017 dollars) to revamp the entire place, including six new hydraulic lifts for the Service Department and a beautiful neon sign on the façade.

The spacious showroom had floor-to-ceiling windows providing a full view of the motorcycles on display. This was important because Johnson Motors continued to retail new bikes as well as distribute them to dealers. Offices were on the second floor, the Parts Department entrance was at the back of the showroom, and Service had a separate entrance at the rear of the building. The place was top class in every regard, far beyond even the best US motorcycle agencies. Only the Nicholson Brothers' facility in western Canada could compare with Johnson's in terms of its clean, modern customer service amenities.

Despite warnings from the old Harley-Indian school that such a fancy place would scare away "traditional" motorcyclists, Bill Johnson wanted an attractive store—not a "motorcycle shop"—where respectable people interested in motorcycles would feel comfortable. His goal in pioneering the acceptance of British motorcycles in the US, he told *Motorcyclist*, was to "lift the motorcycle business to a higher plane than anyone else."

"Everything had to be meticulous," recalled Pete Colman, who hired into Johnson's Sales Department in 1948. "The showroom floor tiles were buffed every day by our janitor. He kept the drip pans under the bikes spotless; there was never any oil in them."

JoMo, as the operation was known by employees and customers alike—was a reflection of Johnson himself. Highly

Long before he was American Honda's service manager and masterminded Dick Mann's 1970 Daytona win on the 750 Four, Bob Hansen raced a prewar Triumph twin on midwestern dirt tracks. Note the reinforced girder fork, open primary, and single carburetor on Hansen's Tiger 100, shown here at Davenport, Iowa, in 1946. *Brooke archive*

articulate and well groomed, a wearer of tailored double-breasted suits, Johnson commanded the respect of every employee. As the business grew, he directed the company's overall operations and left the daily management to Ceder—particularly as alcoholism took its toll in later years. He rode every bike he sold, but favored his Cadillac convertible or svelte Jaguar XK120 roadster, the latter purchased with the help of Edward Turner.

Johnson dropped the Indian franchise when the store moved to Colorado Street to better concentrate on distributing Triumph and Ariel products. He also picked up the new Mustang, a locally built motorcycle/scooter hybrid. In a logical business move, Johnson Motors secured exclusive national distribution of Lucas electrical parts, Amal carburetors, Dunlop and John Bull tires, and Renold chain.

Under its contract with Triumph, Johnson Motors initially had to sell a minimum of twelve new Triumphs per year—an easy target, considering the shiploads of servicemen returning to the US. World War II had nearly bankrupted Britain and its postwar government sent an "Export or Die" edict to British industry. The motorcycle makers set their sights on the ripe US market, which had been untouched by war. By the late 1940s, many were shipping half of their production to the States; but only Triumph possessed a decade of vertical-twin experience and thus charged back to America with a competitive edge.

A telescopic fork with two-way hydraulic damping and a 350cc ("21-cubic-inch") overhead-valve twin were Triumph's big news for 1946. The Speed Twin and Tiger 100 were little

Triumph's 350cc 3T De Luxe was available in the US for six years beginning in 1946, but American riders and dealers preferred the more powerful (and profitable) 500s. *Factory photo/Brooke archive*

While his reputation at the Meriden factory was often that of a tyrant, Triumph supremo Edward Turner could turn on the British charm during his annual visits to Southern California. Bill Johnson's connections with Hollywood enabled Turner to rub elbows with many celebrities, including screen star Rita Hayworth in this 1947 photo, taken on the Columbia Pictures sound lot. Snazzy shoes, nice bike, knockout passenger! *Gaylin archive*

changed from prewar specs, other than their forks. The new 3T De Luxe was billed as a scaled-down, lighter (335 pounds dry), and lower-priced Speed Twin. But with a claimed 19 horsepower at 6,500 rpm and 70 mile-per-hour top speed, the new 350 twin didn't resonate with American riders, who preferred the extra snap of the 500s. Nor was it popular with dealers, who made more profit on the larger bikes. Few 3Ts were imported by Johnson Motors during the bikes' six-year production run. They are scarce in the US today.

Triumph's optional-at-extra-cost sprung hub rear suspension appeared in America in 1948, two years after its debut in Britain. The "Spring Wheel," as JoMo advertised it, had been designed by Edward Turner in the late 1930s and was first slated for production on 1941 models. The hub weighed an extra 17 pounds and moved in a vertical plane, about 2 inches of travel, while the rear wheel spindle was fixed in place. As an engineering solution, it was not as effective nor as robust as the latest swinging-arm rear suspensions. But it was Turner's low-cost alternative.

Turner had incorporated stiff, undamped springs, fitted under considerable compression above and below the wheel spindle, inside a bolted-up spring box. Naive Triumph owners who, for whatever reason, took their sprung hubs apart without using a special workshop tool were sometimes injured, as the guide member could virtually explode when the springs were released.

It was "worse than defusing a bomb," recalled *Cycle World*'s Henry Manney in 1981.

With minimal springing and no damping, a sprung hub-equipped Triumph on bumpy roads was a handful. Handling seriously deteriorated as the cup-and-cone ball bearings on each side of the guide member wore—which they tended to do quickly. In late 1949, after AJS and Matchless introduced swinging arm frames and began advertising their "Unequalled Spring Frame Comfort"—a boon for California desert racers—JoMo announced Triumph's redesigned Mark II sprung hub. The Mark II incorporated sealed ball bearings for reduced wear. It stayed in the lineup through 1955, even after Triumph's first swinging arm frame was introduced.

Demand was great for the postwar Triumphs. New riders without allegiance to Harley or Indian who test rode a Speed Twin or Tiger 100 were often sold on their easy handling. And the perfectly proportioned, unmistakable "Triumph look" often sold the machine. John Brooke, the co-author's father, was one rider seduced by the Triumph's lines. "It was the combination of that slender tank and those twin, down-swept exhaust pipes that got me," Brooke explained about his 1948 Tiger 100, purchased for $907 from Rod Coates's Pluckemin, New Jersey, shop. His Tiger came with a little card from Triumph that recommended keeping the standard mufflers in place, for the public interest. "The neighbors used to compliment me on my 'quiet motorcycle,'" Brooke said.

By 1946, roughly a dozen shops scattered across the US handled Triumphs. Most of those sold just a few bikes each year and provided spotty service at best. Johnson Motors' challenge was to establish a true nationwide dealer network. As it had done before the war, JoMo took out full-page magazine ads and often bought the back cover of *Motorcyclist*. The ads showed the Triumph models, trumpeted racing success, and displayed JoMo's swoopy, British-looking logo. They also mentioned "A Few Choice Dealerships Available."

Searching out and signing on new dealers was the big task facing JoMo. Sales manager Andy Anderson frequently traversed the entire country by himself, towing a trailer full of new Triumphs and calling on established motorcycle shops, or any other likely prospects. However, this was hardly an efficient way to build a large dealer organization.

So in 1948, Wilbur Ceder appointed Pete Colman as JoMo's "road man." Colman and Anderson worked the showroom during the winter, then hit the road, splitting the US up into North and South sales territories. Each man had half the nation to cover, coast to coast.

Colman scoured the country with a $500-per-month expense account and a Mercury sedan that "leaked water like a sieve." Prospective dealers were typically hundreds of miles apart, and covering such massive territory required endless hours of driving. Colman noted that, in 1948, when he and Anderson crisscrossed the US, they visited nearly every established motorcycle dealer.

"Harley had a policy against any 'dualing' with 'foreign' makes," noted Colman. "Their dealers simply weren't interested in talking about 'Limey' motorcycles, let alone becoming a dealer. Some were even hostile about being approached by a Triumph representative." Indeed, in late September 1949, the Federal Trade Commission charged

The first Triumph Grand Prix production racer to arrive at Johnson Motors, photographed in the shop area, autumn 1947. This is a Mark I model with 4¼-gallon chrome-and-painted fuel tank, long megaphones, and steel wheel rims, all unique to the first production batch. Note the unusual gear change linkage, 8-inch brakes, and Vokes remote oil filter canister in the scavenge line between gearbox and crankcase. Lack of a kick-start lever, required under AMA rules, indicates this bike is fresh out of the crate. *Brooke archive*

Period image of a stock 1948 Tiger 100 sans the optional sprung hub purchased new by the co-author's father shows the 4-gallon fuel tank, 19-inch wheels, and two-section rear fender. Compared with the Speed Twin, the Tiger featured higher (8:1) compression and more sporting final drive ratio. *Brooke archive*

Harley-Davidson with making illegal exclusive-dealing contracts with its dealers and unlawfully enforcing them. The FTC charged that Harley had been threatening to cut off new bike and parts shipments to its dealers unless they agreed not to sell British motorcycles.

Indian dealers seemed more receptive, though. Some, like Ed Kretz (who had left JoMo during the war) in Monterey Park, California, applied for Triumph franchises, even though Indian was about to launch its own line of 440cc (later 500cc) British-influenced parallel twins, aimed right at Triumph.

A prospective Triumph dealer had to put up about $2,000—a lot of money in those days—for franchise rights. Then they haggled with JoMo over terms for buying new motorcycles, spare parts, tools, and equipment. Many famous Triumph shops opened in the late 1940s, including Pete Dalio's in Ft. Worth, Texas, where ace speed tuner Jack Wilson worked, and Roman's Triumph in Youngstown, Ohio.

Johnny Roman recounted his 1948 opening: "Johnson Motors would send us the leftover bikes, the ones they couldn't sell at retail," he told the authors. "In 1948, they sent

Daytona Beach, 1948 and the proud owner of this personalized Speed Twin has displayed it for racegoers to admire. Lavish chrome plating, Flanders handlebars and risers, sheepskin seat cover, a rear cargo rack, and the ever-popular fringed leather saddlebags are custom touches that never seem to go out of style with American motorcyclists. *Brooke archive*

A freshly built Tiger 100 dirt track racer for one of JoMo's sponsored riders soaks up sunshine on the Colorado Boulevard sidewalk in 1948. The Mustang fuel tank was wildly popular with American racers and customizers. Many Triumphs in this configuration were also run in speed-record events on California's dry lakes. *Brooke archive*

me three Triumphs—three for the entire year! Later, I took on Ariel and Mustang. But in the early days we had to take what we could get."

For 1949, that meant new styling in the form of Turner's classic headlamp nacelle on the T100, 5T, and 3T, which phased out the old tank-top instrument panel and added an optional parcel grid.

The 1949 Triumph model range grew to five with the introduction of the TR5 Trophy. "Intended for off-the-highway events, such as trials, scrambles, and endurance runs," read JoMo's TR5 ad copy. "The high ground clearance and exceptionally good steering characteristics enable the rider to choose his course over the roughest terrain." It was true. Based on the factory Triumphs that won gold medals in the 1948 International Six Days Trials, the 500cc Trophy was the world's first genuine "dual-purpose" twin. It could be ridden to events, raced, and then ridden home. Packing 25 horsepower and 300 pounds, it was perfect for field meets, eastern enduros, and just plain trail riding. Its rigid frame was shorter than Triumph's roadsters and the bike came standard with a high-level, siamesed exhaust and block-pattern "Trials" tires—20 inches front and 19 inches rear. The sprung hub was an option.

The original TR5 engine combined the Speed Twin's lower end assembly with the "square fin" aluminum barrels and cylinder head used in the Grand Prix production racer. Its mild state of tune (6.0:1 compression) made the bike competitive with most big singles, except in lengthy western desert events like the 500-mile Greenhorn Enduro, where AJS and Matchless thumpers ruled in the early days.

As Johnson Motors marked its first decade in business, the company had signed over 100 Triumph dealers in the US—fantastic growth, but more of an indication of how American motorcycling had been revitalized by the "British invasion." Triumph itself had raised its annual production to nearly 12,000 bikes, and was exporting over 60 percent of them. JoMo was selling at Turner's envisioned sales rate of 1,000 Triumphs a year, and the order list was growing fast.

Johnson Motors kick-started Triumph's success in the US, but it wasn't the only British motorcycle importer thinking "big." Rich Child had gone to BSA's executives as soon as Triumph turned down his pitch for the US distributorship and was selling Beezas nationwide from New York when the war ended. In December 1949, Child effectively created a BSA stronghold in the West when he handed over eleven western states to Hap Alzina, Johnson's old Indian rival. BSA now had two main US distributors—Child's in the East and Alzina's in California—and was adding dealers faster than JoMo.

Turner, Johnson, and Ceder realized that a similar "two-coast" strategy was needed for Triumph. In the fall of 1950, Johnson Motors and Triumph negotiated the creation of an eastern distributorship to be wholly owned by the factory. The Triumph Corporation (TriCor) opened for business January 1, 1951, in Baltimore Maryland.

Triumph called out its new-for-1949 headlamp nacelle in period advertising and sales literature. Note the "New Harem" typo in the text—British copywriters muffed the names of US states and towns (in this case New Haven) in more than one magazine ad. *Brooke archive*

03

OH, CANADA!

MAPLE LEAF TRIUMPH PIONEERS

Long before Bill Johnson uncrated his first Tiger single in California—
and years prior to Reggie Pink opening shop in New York City—
Triumphs were being imported in Canada. In 1911, the Toronto Police
Department purchased its first motorcycles: a four-bike fleet of Triumph
3½-horsepower belt-drive singles. The 500cc machines featured
Triumph's innovative Free-Engine Clutch, which enabled the rider to start
the bike while in the saddle—a benefit for cops. They were tasked with
enforcing the 15 mile-per-hour (24 km/h) speed limit and often wore
business suits to surprise the city's speed violators.

ABOVE: Bernie Nicholson launches up a Saskatoon hill on his modified 1939 Speed Twin. *Nicholson Bros. Archive, courtesy Greg Williams*

LEFT: The beauty of the Canadian wild beckons in this evocative cover art on the 1955 Nicholson Bros. catalog. *Brooke archive*

Hard-charging Chuck Stockey won the 100-mile race at Wasaga Beach in 1939 on his T100 with optional bronze cylinder head. On the same bike he placed second in the 1940 Daytona 100-miler and raced countless dirt track events in Ontario and the northeastern US. *Brooke archive*

As a dominion of the British Empire, Canada had been a favored trading partner of Britain and so enjoyed no import duty on English machines. But trade with its southern neighbor was different. From 1913 to World War II, the two nations rode a roller coaster of trade liberalization followed by tariffs, depending on prevailing economic trends. Soon after the Great Depression began, the US Tariff Act of 1930 dealt an immediate and sharp blow to the Canadian economy and helped precipitate worldwide protectionism. Canada responded by raising tariffs on US goods twice during 1930 and 1931; included were a 40 percent duty on American luxury cars and a 33 percent tariff on American motorcycles.

For a short period, this situation benefited British bike sales to the detriment of Harley-Davidson and Indian. But by 1936, a steady decline in US–Canada trade barriers and closer economic ties began as World War II loomed. From 1928 to 1938, exports of new British bikes of all makes to Canada totaled 2,667 units—over four times greater than the 579 machines shipped to the US during the same period, according to Canadian scholar Steve Koerner in his 2012 book, *The Strange Death of the British Motorcycle Industry.* After 1938, however, the establishment of Johnson Motors as Triumph's official US distributor and the arrival of the new parallel twins began turning the export tide in the US's favor.

Before the war, motorcycle sales in Canada "were pretty much a sideline to bicycles and sporting goods," observed Ontario-based motorcycling historian Allan Johnson, and those selling them "were often a small one-man-and-a-boy type of shop." Sales were conducted in various ways, he noted, including direct importation by individuals who had corresponded with British factories, as well as importation by "dealers franchised as distributors or retailers to sell particular makes."

Americans who were looking to sell Triumphs, including Rod Coates (now in Rochester, New York), and John Esler in Grand Rapids, Michigan, set up their own arrangements with Canadian importers to bring machines into the US.

The "import/export agent" shipping method meant that the factory received payment for the motorcycles when they arrived at the shipping agent's door in Britain, who then owned and insured the machines until they were delivered to the distributor or retailer in Canada. Even in the 1970s, Norton was shipping Commandos to Canada this way, Johnson explained. Such a de-centralized strategy differed significantly from how Triumph tackled the US, with demarcated eastern (wholly owned) and western (independent) distributors. For the relatively small motorcycle sales volumes in Canada during the 1930s and 1940s, however, having separate wholesale distributors for the vast and sparsely populated nation was not financially feasible.

As in the US, competition events were vital for raising a marque's public profile. Enthusiasts in the Toronto area founded the British Empire Motor Club in 1928 to organize a scrambles event; the group (still going strong in 2017) became a magnet for all types of motorcycle sport. The BEMC promoted its first road race in 1931 on a 1.5-mile closed-road circuit in what is now midtown Toronto. By 1935, it was organizing races on the sand at beautiful Wasaga Beach on Lake Ontario's Georgian Bay. The beach races—preceding Daytona by three years—drew big crowds. Race programs from the period show Triumphs, likely tuned Mark 5/10 500cc singles, listed among the entries.

However, the brand lacked the visibility of Norton and BSA until the arrival of the Speed Twin in 1938. Triumph's status was given a boost when Britain's King George VI and Queen Elizabeth toured their North American Dominion in 1939; the Canadian government had a small fleet of Triumph's new 500cc twin ready for escort duty. Race wins by Chuck Stockey on his Tiger 100, the hill-climb standout J. B. "Bernie" Nicholson on his tuned Speed Twin, and others helped the early dealers promote Triumphs as reliable machines that could be easily modified to win races.

Triumph "distributor" Brown's ad in the 1940 Wasaga Beach races flyer. *Brooke archive*

New machines in Nicholson Bros.' showroom, 1939. From left: mechanic Glen Chappell on an Ariel Square Four; Bernie Nicholson on a Tiger 100; brother Lawrence on a Speed Twin; and office staffer Ellen Lathey on an Ariel Red Hunter. *Nicholson Bros. Archive, courtesy Greg Williams*

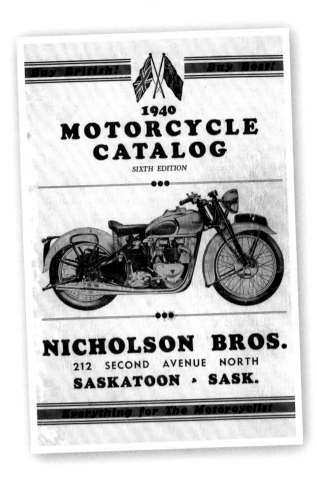

Photos of the Nicholsons' Tiger 100 with optional deep-valanced fenders graced both their catalog and a page in the *Modern Motorcycle Mechanics* book. *Gaylin archive*

The Nicholson Bros.' first purpose-built facility opened in Saskatoon in 1946. Its modern, elegant showroom measured 40x26 feet. *Nicholson Bros. Archive, courtesy Greg Williams*

STAKING OUT SALES TERRITORY

During the pre–World War II years, an advertising battle raged among Canada's motorcycle dealers who sold Triumphs. The ads, placed in newspapers and race programs, targeted the country's most populous eastern provinces, particularly Ontario. Many dealers boasted that they were "distributors" for the marque when, in fact, Triumph had yet to name one for Canada. A photograph of the 1932 British motorcycle exhibition in Toronto shows a white sign proclaiming Walter Andrews to be the Triumph and Harley-Davidson "distributor," even though Andrews and others involved in the event were only retail agents. An ad in the 1936 Belleville 200 Mile Canadian Championship flyer proclaimed J. E. Watson of East Toronto to be "Sole Distributor of Triumph-Levis-Excelsior."

Nearly four years later, these and other dealers were still staking illegitimate claims. A half-page ad with a drawing of a Tiger 100 in the May 1940 Wasaga Beach race program touted Brown's Sports & Cycle Co. Limited, Toronto, as Triumph's "Eastern North American Distributors." Brown's was still retailing Triumphs into the 1960s, at which point the eastern Canada Triumph distributorship was held by Raymond Burke, an operation that did not have a retail outlet.

In French-speaking Montreal there was Sammett & Blair; in the late 1930s, this dealership applied to Triumph for a distributorship and was granted official non-exclusive rights across a broad swath of Canada—and a massive chunk of the US as well! They wasted no time printing US promotional materials, including a four-page flyer covering Triumph's 1940 models. The flyer, part of the author's sales-literature collection, shows "Sammett & Blair, P.O. Box 75, Detroit – Michigan, Importers and Distributors of Outstanding British Motorcycles" boldly typeset under the Triumph logo on the front page.

NICHOLSON BROS. *Motorcycles*

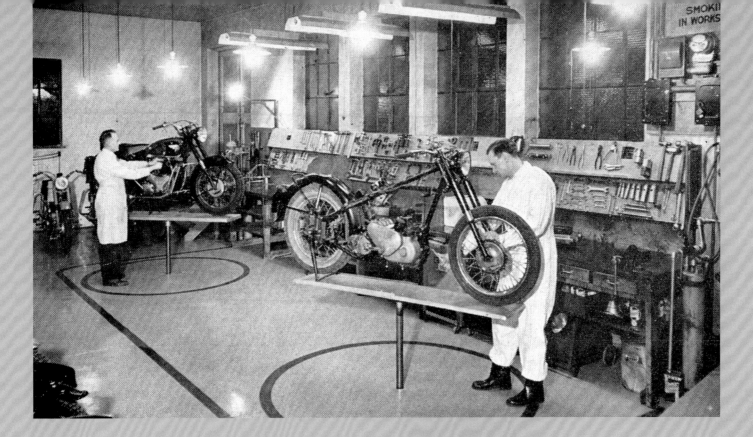

Inside the Nicholson Bros. service area in 1955. An Ariel Square Four is on the hydraulic lift in foreground. *Brooke archive*

When that flyer appeared, Triumph Managing Director Edward Turner was working to clarify the boundaries of his latest North American outlet. Was Sammett & Blair overstepping the terms of their contract? In a November 13, 1939, letter to Bernie Nicholson, whose official Triumph-Ariel distributorship for central and western Canada had already been established, Turner wrote the following:

We take this opportunity of making specific reference to alterations in our agency arrangements for Eastern Canada. We have appointed Messrs. Sammett & Blair of Montreal, on an open agency basis, together with certain other agents, to pursue Triumph business wherever possible. Unfortunately, Messrs. Sammett & Blair, in order to lose no time, have sent out a circular which may give cause for misunderstanding, and to remove any ambiguity to what the position is, we are enclosing herewith a copy of our contract with them.

A scan of the letter was provided to the authors by Greg Williams, whose essential 2010 book, *Prairie Dust, Motorcycles and a Typewriter*, recounts the history of Nicholson Bros. Motorcycles. The letter specifies that Sammett & Blair's contract covers "certain territories of Canada and the US excluding British Columbia, Alberta, Saskatchewan and Manitoba." It also gives the Montreal agents sales rights to the US except for California, Washington, Oregon, Nevada, Utah, and New Mexico—six states reserved exclusively for Johnson Motors.

"As you will see, your interests have been adequately protected," Turner assured Bernie Nicholson. With World War II already underway in Europe and the war's outcome far from certain, Turner was laying the ground for his company's North American distribution network, one brick at a time.

ENTER NICHOLSON BROS.

While Bill Johnson and Wilbur Ceder were establishing Triumph's US West Coast beachhead, two young Canadians were working almost in parallel in Saskatoon, in the north-central province of Saskatchewan. This prairie city of less than 44,000 residents was about 450 miles north of Bismarck, North Dakota. For motorcyclists, Saskatchewan's wide-open spaces and long distances between remote towns seemed to favor the heavy, low-revving American V-twins and inline fours.

Bernie and Lawrence Nicholson believed that British machines could thrive there too. They proved it by building Nicholson Bros. Motorcycles (NBM) into a unique and successful business. NBM was famous for its global mail-order-parts operation and its motorcycle distribution and sales, with Triumph the flagship brand. Equally famous was Bernie's *Modern Motorcycle Mechanics and Speed Tuning*, the legendary motorcycle service "bible" he wrote and updated for thirty-two years. The book was published through seven editions with over 100,000 copies sold.

The Nicholsons grew up on a farm and were attracted to machinery at an early age. Their first exposure to the British weekly bike mags, *The Motor Cycle* and *Motorcycling*, lit their fuse of enthusiasm. The magazines provided an exciting window into the industry, its products, and motorcycle sport. With money saved from their newspaper delivery route, Lawrence and Bernie in 1932 took delivery of their first bike, a 148cc, three-speed Dot lightweight. They put 3,000 miles on the little two-stroke, sold it for a profit, and quickly plowed their earnings into a new 350cc Douglas twin. They briefly rode the Douglas before selling it, too, for a profit.

Next came a 500cc Ivory Calthorpe and sidecar, then more Douglases and AJS singles, all paid for by bank check and sold at profit soon after arrival. They also began servicing Harleys and Indians. The brothers' father Alfred helped them build a small wooden shop for bike storage, service, and repair. Bernie began a two-year Motor Engineering and Machining course at the local technical college. As Saskatoon's economy rose slowly out of the Great Depression, orders for new bikes increased. At seventeen and fourteen years old, respectively, Lawrence and Bernie were in the motorcycle-import business.

In 1935, the brothers and their parents traveled to Britain on an extended trip to visit family. There Lawrence and Bernie rode a borrowed Sunbeam single to visit various motorcycle factories and parts-making companies such as Lucas, Lodge, Renold, and Amal. They cut supply deals at nearly every stop. Upon their return to Canada, they published their first price list of Douglas and Calthorpe machines along with parts, accessories, and their own repair services.

The Nicholsons worked relentlessly, plowing all but a fraction of their profits back into the business. Their dedication, and some strategic loans from their parents, enabled them to move into a succession of larger, more substantial shops. Their reputation for honest, dependable service grew, as did the list of motorcycles and parts they carried. By 1936, their price list had expanded to an eight-page booklet as the energetic siblings added the Royal Enfield and Ariel brands, then Panther and even Indian. They also imported their first new 600cc Ariel Square Four, the high-performance status machine that was captivating Bill Johnson around the same time.

On September 9, 1939, the brothers made their biggest leap yet. They mailed a letter to Triumph's export manager stating their interest in distributing the company's products in Saskatchewan. Enclosed was a £15 deposit (about $200 today) on one new Tiger 100, which then cost about $530 Canadian.

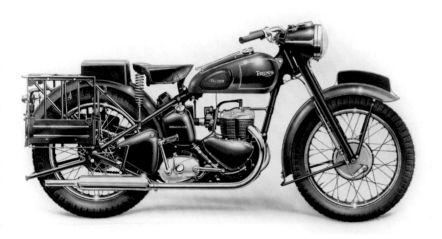

Triumph's flathead 500cc TRW produced from 1948 to 1969 was popular with the Canadian Army. Some of the bikes were kept in storage in nearly new condition and auctioned off in the 1990s. *Brooke archive*

An affirmative reply came thirteen days later via telegram from Thomas Whitworth at the Coventry factory. In his three-page letter, Whitworth assured the Nicholsons that he would notify Triumph's "friends" at Northwest Cycle & Motor Supply of the news. Located in Winnipeg, nearly 490 miles (782 km) across the prairie to the southeast of Saskatoon, Northwest Cycle was already selling Triumphs when the Nicholsons were granted their territory.

Regardless of the great distance between the two agencies, Whitworth had the courtesy to alert Nicholson's closest competitor that its sales landscape was about to shrink. Northwest Cycle continued to sell Triumphs alongside Harley-Davidsons for years after World War II.

"Superb proportioning, providing adequate strength with minimum weight, together with an almost absolute absence of initial faults, rank it as a masterpiece of motorcycle design and engineering," wrote Bernie Nicholson of the Triumph twin, in the 1974 edition of *Modern Motorcycle Mechanics*. First distributed during the war to widespread industry acclaim, the book actually helped "introduce" the Nicholsons to Edward Turner. It so impressed Triumph's chief that he wrote Bernie, which in turn sparked ongoing correspondences between the two. Both were contemplating postwar motorcycling and envisioning what type of machine riders would want.

American riders' desire for faster, more powerful machines is not unique in the motorcycle world, including Canada. An illuminating letter to Edward Turner, dated August 12, 1944, shows that Canadian riders also wanted motorcycle engines that better fit their nation's roads and riding conditions. The writer, Bernie Nicholson, knew that the vast expanses of Canada posed a challenge for smaller-displacement machines under extended operation. His prescient and well-considered letter to the Triumph boss, revealed for the first time by author Greg Williams, lays out what Bernie believed to be the ideal motorcycle spec for Canadian customers: a low-compression (7.5:1) 750cc overhead-valve parallel twin, with gear-type oil pump and an aluminum cylinder head with integrally cast rocker boxes.

"Despite the very excellent performance of your prewar Tiger 100, there is a need for something more powerful," Nicholson reasoned. "Many on this continent look for a machine rather more suited to carrying two and considerable accessories on trips of 500–600 miles in a day." Such a 750cc twin "will really be necessary to compete with the larger American models for fast cruising over long distances."

Turner's September 29 response called the idea of a 750cc parallel twin "very interesting." But such a development would have to wait for the "post-postwar" period because it would not sell in Britain and would require dedicated tooling for production. Six years later, Turner delivered the 650cc Thunderbird at Johnson Motors' request. It took another twenty–three years for Bernie Nicholson's vision to be realized in the T140.

CANADA'S 'GOLD' STANDARD

The Nicholsons' success as Canada's premier Triumph importer in the early years can be credited to the high standard of quality Lawrence and Bernie insisted upon in every facet of their business. As Greg Williams's *Prairie Dust* explains, the brothers were careful to expand their business in stages, always allowing their capital investment to keep pace with sales. Being motorcyclists gave them a keen sense of the market, of why people rode and loved bikes.

And as the Nicholson Bros.' business grew, their successive facilities reflected an attention to detail that echoed those of Johnson Motors. Clean and attractive showrooms, spacious and well-lit service bays, ample parts storage and fully equipped machine shops were the rule both in Saskatoon and in Pasadena. In the 1940s, hydraulic lifts were still a rarity in many automobile garages, yet both Nicholson Bros. and Johnson Motors had them in their service departments. These pioneers set the industry's "gold" standard for Triumph

distribution, sales, and service. Their facilities, customer relations, and "class" approach to daily business were later emulated by every major motorcycle importer who followed, including Honda.

As Triumph's Canada retail network spread from Montreal to Vancouver in the 1950s and 1960s, the Nicholson Bros. catalog was already the star of the mail-order motorcycle parts business. While providing a reliable pipeline of spares and accessories for diverse British, European, and, increasingly, Japanese bike brands, it sometimes also served as a lifeline for American Triumph parts and service managers when TriCor or JoMo were out of stock. Sadly, the Nicholsons' Triumph franchise was cancelled by Peter Thornton's BSA Inc. regime in 1970 amid falling bike sales in Canada's prairie provinces. They continued to sell leftover machines through 1972 while further expanding their mail-order parts business.

Trophy TR6SS models were officially sold in Canada, and some trickled in to the US when TR6SRs were sold out. This 1963 example was expertly restored by Paul Rye. *Brooke photo*

04
THE EASTERNERS
THE RISE OF THE TRIUMPH CORPORATION

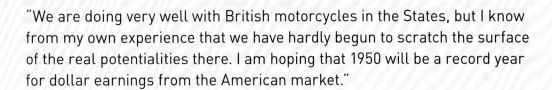

"We are doing very well with British motorcycles in the States, but I know from my own experience that we have hardly begun to scratch the surface of the real potentialities there. I am hoping that 1950 will be a record year for dollar earnings from the American market."

Edward Turner revealed these thoughts to the British weekly *Motor Cycling* in December 1949. By that time, Bill Johnson had been Triumph's sole US distributor for more than four years. But Turner was becoming increasingly anxious that Johnson Motors' West Coast–based efforts to penetrate the American market were woefully inadequate. Although he had established several small warehouses in the East, South, and Northwest, all paperwork still had to be run through Pasadena.

Competition was growing. BSA had its own A7 500cc twin in production and, by 1949, Britain's bike-making giant was carving significant inroads into the US market through the efforts of Rich Child in the East and Hap Alzina in California. The same year, Indian launched its own parallel twin, a move Turner had predicted in a 1944 letter to Bill Johnson. Fortunately for Triumph, the 440cc and 500cc Scout and Warrior twins—as well as a shaft-drive inline four-cylinder, also prototyped—were a short-lived, costly failure that helped sink the Indian Motorcycle Co.

The UK government was exerting its own pressure. British manufacturers had to guarantee that 75 percent of their production would be exported before they were allotted precious raw materials in the austere postwar years. Even so, the number of British machines arriving in the US was actually in decline by 1949. The total represented only half of the 8,500 units shipped during 1946, although Johnson Motors was bringing in about 1,000 machines a year.

England was exporting all right, but mostly to its dominions. For example, with only a fraction of the US population, Australia imported 25,107 British motorcycles during 1949, while the US brought in only 4,275 machines the same year. Despite Bill Johnson's visionary head start, America's vast motorcycling potential was yet to be discovered.

Turner had been making annual visits to the US since the war's end. These trips were usually made in late winter to correspond with the Daytona Beach races that signaled the upcoming riding season in the States. In February 1949, a foreign car and motorcycle show took place at the 69th Regiment Armory in New York. The show was only a fraction of the size of England's Earls Court

LEFT: As a wholly owned subsidiary of the Triumph factory, TriCor briefly added US distribution of Daimler cars in 1959. Showing off the new Baltimore signage are (left to right) TriCor president Denis McCormack, Triumph managing director Edward Turner, TriCor financial boss Earl Miller, and Meriden's chief stylist Jack Wickes. *Brooke archive*

Show, but it was still significant enough to attract the major US bike importers, including Johnson Motors and five others.

On display at the JoMo stand were the new "nacelled" Triumph street bikes and one of the new Tiger 100 Grand Prix models (see Chapter 2). Fewer than 200 complete Grands Prix were built, and Triumph intended them only for qualified racers who might bring the company some publicity. Any New York Show visitor hoping to buy the exotic GP sitting on the Armory floor would have been disappointed to learn that it was already promised to Daytona-bound Rod Coates.

RECRUITING FOR THE EASTERN FRONT

Edward Turner and Bill Johnson both attended the Armory show; Turner used this visit to begin making plans for a distributorship in the eastern US. The Triumph Engineering Co contracted the Market Research Corporation of America (MRCA) to determine US market demographics and sales potential. Turner also sought MRCA's counsel on where the new headquarters should be located.

Unlike Johnson Motors, the new eastern distributor would be wholly owned and under the direct control of the Meriden factory although authors Harry Louis and Bob Currie, in their book *The Story of Triumph Motorcycles*, suggested that

Triumph in America had no greater advocate than the energetic Rod Coates. TriCor's long-serving service manager and racing boss was an avid competitor, winning the Sandy Lane Enduro before World War II and the 1950 Daytona 100. His early Cub racer, "Pappy's Popper," was full of tuning tricks. *Brooke archive*

this route was taken because a suitable independent (such as JoMo) couldn't be found. Baltimore, Maryland, was chosen for its Eastern Seaboard location, superior road and rail access to the rest of the country, and its favorable cost of doing business at the time.

Critical to the whole scheme would be finding the right person to head it up. Turner and Johnson didn't have to look far. Denis McCormack, a forty-eight-year-old mechanical engineer who happened to be vice president of MRCA, clearly possessed the right stuff. Coventry-born, his family had emigrated to America during McCormack's childhood and he became a naturalized citizen. His technical background included employment at industrial-machine companies Vickers and the Friez Co. (later Bendix-Friez), where he was granted two patents.

Beyond mere competence, though, Turner wanted someone who would continue the same stainless, prestigious image so carefully cultivated by Bill Johnson. McCormack also fit the bill here: Triumph sales rep Jack Mercer recalled in the May 1976 *K and K Quarterly Newsletter*, "If Denis did nothing else, he added class to the whole motorcycle business in the postwar period. Until the advent of the Triumph Corporation, motorcycle dealers could not be distinguished from their customers, except perhaps that they looked a bit more soiled. They were, for the most part, wrench-benders-turned-businessmen and they needed help."

Mercer added that, soon after McCormack got Triumph's new operation established, its eastern US dealers "began to look like members of the Junior Chamber of Commerce."

THE THUNDERBIRD ARRIVES

Activities at the Triumph factory were moving at a furious pace. In September 1949, it introduced the first motorcycle model made by a foreign manufacturer expressly for the North American market. The 650cc 6T Thunderbird looked no different than the Speed Twin, but its extra 150cc (10 ci) of displacement delivered the added muscle that US and Canadian riders wanted. Speed tuners and hot rodders were raising the Tiger 100's performance, but the appetite for "more cubes" was unabated.

The new 650cc top end delivered 7 more brake horsepower and a wider torque curve than the 500. The power unit shared the same cycle parts that gave a much-improved power-to-weight ratio. But when the first US-market Thunderbird to arrive in America was uncrated at JoMo, the staff was not impressed. Pete Colman recalled the motorcycle as being downright sluggish—it was a "cast-iron snail," he told the authors. The problem was traced to the inadequate one-inch-bore Amal 276 carburetor fitted to the new machine.

When the carburetor bore was enlarged to 1¹/₁₆ inches during the Thunderbird's first year of production, the bike's overall performance improved significantly. *Cycle* magazine's

TRIUMPH
SETS NEW
DAYTONA
RECORD

Rod Coates Wins 100 Mile

Amateur Classic

AVERAGES
81.26 mph

SEE THE TRIUMPH • ARIEL EXHIBIT
AT THE

BRITISH AUTOMOBILE and
MOTORCYCLE SHOW

GRAND CENTRAL PALACE, NEW YORK CITY
APRIL 15-23, 1950

In his second year at Daytona on the Triumph Grand Prix, Coates came from tenth place to beat Ed Kretz Jr., whose Indian ran out of oil on the final lap. *Brooke archive*

Trained at Meriden, Englishman Davey Jones was TriCor's first "factory" service mechanic—and a mean racer himself. He's seen here before winning the 1953 Laconia 25-mile road race, part of Triumph's "hat trick" victory at Laconia that year. *Ed Fisher collection*

April 1950 inaugural issue carried a road test of the 1950 6T, finding it to be nearly faultless (given the scrutiny and objectivity of that era's bike journalism). But the machine's somber gray-blue paint color caused editor Harry Steele to comment: "Painted a slate blue (the catalog calls it Thunder Blue) and trimmed with chrome and polished aluminum in a minimum of places, led me to believe that the lightning had been left out, leaving only the thunder remaining."

The T-bird's color proved to be so unpopular that it was changed in the 1951 model year to a much more appealing shade of metallic blue. The new livery transformed the bike into one of the most attractive Triumphs ever offered. Steele concluded his report: "The riding characteristics leave nothing to be desired and if it's acceleration you crave, there are very few stock, fully equipped machines that could jerk your cork if you're on a Triumph Thunderbird."

The name "thunderbird" came from Native American lore, a giant eagle-like bird capable of unleashing thunder, lightning, and rain. Turner is credited with giving the model its intriguing new name, but how he came upon the idea is not very romantic. In February 1949, after attending the New York Armory show and laying plans for the Triumph Corporation, he began the long drive south to the Daytona races. Dealer Rod Coates and his wife Marge accompanied Turner; Rod would be riding the Grand Prix model in his first 100-mile amateur race on the beach.

The journey took them along the East Coast and, while passing through South Carolina, Turner noticed the Thunderbird Motel, which had a thunderbird figure atop a huge totem pole in front. Marge Coates remembered the resulting conversation in Florida about how appropriate the "Thunderbird" name would be for Triumph's newest motorcycle. The Ford Motor Co. later adopted the name for its 1955 sports car, but only after reaching a legal agreement with Triumph.

In April 1950, the Triumph Engineering Company itself chose to participate in New York's British Automobile and Motorcycle Show, now held at Grand Central Palace and dwarfing the previous year's event. Turner attended, of course, and Jack Sangster joined him in order to complete the final legal arrangements for Triumph's new US organization.

THE TRIUMPH CORPORATION

After the Triumph leaders' US visit that spring, developments began to move quickly, if covertly. McCormack did not want to alert competitors or arouse Harley-Davidson. Earl Miller, soon to be the company's treasurer, recalled that activities were kept "very hush-hush. That's why not much was heard of [McCormack] within the trade" until the new company was officially announced.

McCormack rented space in the Muncey Building in downtown Baltimore and began to assemble his team. It included Phylis Fansler, his personal secretary at Bendix-Friez, who later became his right hand and a key link to the field reps and sales force. It was through a Fansler relative that Miller came to work for Triumph. He was Johns Hopkins University graduate and a CPA whose accounting firm also had an office in the Muncey Building. The fact that Triumph's eastern distributor remained solidly "in the black" from 1950 to 1970 was largely due to the efforts of the fiscally disciplined Miller.

Asked by co-author Gaylin how the company was able to show a profit even in its first year, Miller explained, "We didn't have terrible expenses and managed to control our costs. They [Triumph] said, here's X dollars to start with. We never went back for more money. We never had any borrowing. Now if I got embarrassed, I'd drag my feet on paying them for their bikes, what the hell. But we had no 'godfather.' "

McCormack wasted no time in setting up TriCor; the cablegram abbreviation soon became the company's popular nickname. He signed a five-year lease on a 14,000 square-foot building on Joppa Road in Towson, a northern suburb of Baltimore. On October 1, 1950, "We moved in hundreds of cases of spare parts that had cleared customs by that time," Miller recalled about TriCor's first day.

In January 1951, the Triumph Corporation announced its existence in two-page-spread magazine advertisements in *Cycle*, *Motorcyclist*, *Buzzzz*, and *American Motorcycling*. The establishment of TriCor effectively cut Bill Johnson's market in half. JoMo's sales realm now consisted of the nineteen western states—all the territory west of the eastern border of Texas, straight north to the Canadian border. It included all of Texas, Oklahoma, and North and South Dakota. Geographically, this was 38 percent of the US, with 30 percent of the total population and far fewer major marketing areas than TriCor's territory. California, with its year-round riding season and motorsports culture, was JoMo's crown jewel.

While Johnson had invested considerable time and expense into developing the US dealer network as it existed in 1950, he had little choice in the decision to create the factory-owned eastern distributor. To compensate for JoMo's loss, Turner named Johnson a vice president at TriCor. Although it was just a title, with no operational input, it did include a minor financial stake.

Pete Colman remembered the division coming as somewhat of a relief to his boss.

"I think that Bill felt that trying to cover the entire US was a pretty difficult task," Colman explained in 1993. "It required a lot more money than Johnson Motors had." The deal undoubtedly eased sales rep Colman's burden—before the advent of TriCor, he was solely responsible for covering the entire southern US!

McCormack inherited all the Triumph dealerships east of Texas's eastern border, plus those in Wisconsin, Minnesota, Iowa, Missouri, and Arkansas. Despite the company's erroneous claim of operating "East of the Mississippi" in some

A personalized 1951 Thunderbird outside TriCor's Joppa Road facility, fitted with Flanders high-rise handlebar mounted on risers and upswept Buco exhaust, made by the Joseph Buegeleisen Co. in Detroit and sold by TriCor. *Gaylin archive*

advertising, TriCor covered the lion's share of the US market in terms of land area and, more importantly, population.

A few of the eastern Triumph shops, including those run by Coates and John Esler in Grand Rapids, Michigan, had been dealers during the prewar Reggie Pink era. Most were mom-and-pop operations, or shops managed by motorcycle racers seeking a way to support their track efforts. Increasing numbers of Indian dealers were also jumping from what they considered to be a sinking ship into the arms of this new "Limey" father. Such defectors included Herb Reiber in Washington DC and Frank Kiss in Pottstown, Pennsylvania, both of whom became highly successful with the Triumph brand.

In all, McCormack started with fewer than one hundred eastern sales outlets in 1951. This number swelled to 308 within just seven years, partially due to Indian's demise but largely because of Triumph's fast-growing popularity, its desirability as a business franchise, and the hard work of McCormack's relentless sales force.

Early in 1951, Jack Mercer became TriCor's first traveling sales rep, or "road man." When McCormack discovered him at the preshow cocktail party in New York City, Mercer was selling British books and magazine subscriptions as well as writing freelance for several motorcycle publications. He had previously sold BSAs for Rich Child. McCormack hired him on the spot and gave him the entire eastern United States sales territory. Mercer's jovial and satirical outlook made him a favorite of all who knew him.

One month later, Rod Coates joined the TriCor team as service manager. The thirty-five-year-old Coates was perfectly suited for the job. A practical engineer who had attended Lehigh and Northeastern universities, he was also a fierce competitor in enduros and hill climbs before World War II.

When the war broke out, Coates was working for Eastman-Kodak's Engineering and Design Department while selling and servicing Reggie Pink–supplied Triumphs in his own small motorcycle shop then in Rochester, New York.

Although the decision to hire Coates seemed obvious, McCormack needed prodding to pursue him, according to Mercer. Indeed, Coates had closed his New Jersey Triumph shop the year before and was working at the Child-BSA distributorship in Nutley as a retail sales manager. McCormack's hesitation was understandable, given Turner's don't-rock-the-boat philosophy.

Because of Coates's tuning and racing expertise—he won the 1950 Daytona 100-mile race on his Grand Prix model—McCormack placed him in charge of racing at Triumph-Baltimore, as TriCor's Competition Department became known to distinguish it from the racing camp at JoMo. Setting up a formal race shop seemed to contradict Turner's limited factory-racing policy. But ever since Ernie Lyons's 1946 Manx Grand Prix victory, the Triumph boss was coming to realize that winning on Sunday sold new motorcycles on Monday. He saw that race success was vital to Triumph's American growth. Now, with TriCor's Coates and JoMo's Colman, he had two ardent competitors with winning in their blood.

By early 1951, TriCor's management structure was close to complete. The only elements lacking were the mechanics to perform the service, warranty, and inevitable development work on the motorcycles themselves. While there was no shortage of "wrenches," TriCor needed skilled mechanics who had an intimate knowledge of the machinery and factory-correct procedures.

More importantly, Turner wanted someone in Baltimore who was "works-trained"—someone who would do it Triumph's way! Coates could not leave his management duties, so Turner searched within the Meriden factory walls for someone who would fit the bill.

David Jones had been with Triumph's Experimental Department since the famed Freddie Clarke days during the war. Jones had never been to America, so when Turner approached him, he jumped at the chance, as he recalled to co-author Gaylin. But when he learned the overseas assignment would be for a minimum of twelve months, Jones's enthusiasm to visit the States was put to the test. Ultimately, Jones, also a keen racer, decided to make the move. He ended up staying at Triumph-Baltimore for the next four years. Jones, along with Howard Carter and Kenny Dransfield, became the core of an expert Service Department that was critical during TriCor's infancy.

There was no service school/dealer meeting during TriCor's inaugural year (1951), so it was decided to use the Daytona race week to meet with the new eastern dealers. A banquet was held at Daytona Beach's Bath and Tennis Club, and more than 200 dealers from across the nation attended, as well as some from JoMo's territory. Turner and other factory

TRICOR'S BENCHMARK SERVICE SCHOOLS

For Triumph's distributors, an important aspect of dealer relations was service training. Once Davy Jones was in place, Rod Coates established TriCor's service schools. These three-to-five-day meetings were held each year at the Baltimore headquarters. Launched in 1952, the schools were designed primarily to instruct dealers and their mechanics on proper factory service procedures. Technicians were also updated on any new factory service information and supplied with the latest bulletins.

Turner astutely ensured that someone from the Meriden plant would always be on site for these meetings, if for no other purpose than to reassure dealers of their concerns and make the factory seem a little closer.

John Nelson, Triumph's service head; Jack Wickes, the chief designer and stylist; and Turner himself were frequent participants. Their presence gave the eastern US dealers and mechanics the envied opportunity to meet top factory

men in person. But the Baltimore meetings were more than just mechanics' workshops. Classes were given on sales strategies, showroom display, parts-and-inventory forecasting, marketing, and many more topics. McCormack wanted these meetings to transcend the idea of simple "tech" seminars and classroom work. He saw the opportunity to create a "Triumph team" enthusiasm across his retail network. The atmosphere was intentionally relaxed and franchise holders were often invited to bring their wives, many of whom helped run their husbands' businesses. As a bonus, the wives were treated to day trips to nearby attractions.

As a result, many of TriCor's dealers looked forward to the annual service schools and revisited them faithfully for the next two decades. The meetings worked so well that the format was soon emulated by Johnson Motors, where Pete Colman emceed the technical workshops along with John Nelson; the meetings were also copied by Honda.

Edward Turner revs up the eastern states' dealers and mechanics at TriCor's 1958 Service School. *Brooke archive*

In the 1950s, an unopened stretch of new highway was the perfect venue to tune open-megaphoned racing motorcycles. Prior to Daytona, Rod Coates (in trenchcoat) brought three new Tiger 100s to the nearly completed Interstate 83 near Baltimore with TriCor mechanics (left to right) Howard Carter, Davey Jones, Kenny Dransfield, and local Triumph dealer/racer Jacques DuPont. *Gaylin archive*

heavies spoke, and the occasion was used to update the dealers on Triumph's plans for the entire US.

During the Q&A, a New York dealer expressed his concerns about the availability of machines in the now-expanding dealer network. Turner was quick to respond, as reported in the May 1951 *Buzzzz*.

"We will have enough machines for you in 1951," he assured the man. "We will have enough in 1952. No sensible person will commit himself beyond that period. Triumph's new branch in this country is proof that we have faith in both our ability to produce, and in you chaps' ability to sell them."

HARLEY CRIES FOUL

Triumph made a big splash in Daytona Beach in 1951, calling attention to its new two-fisted attack on the American market—Johnson Motors from the "left coast" and the Triumph Corporation from the right. Clearly, Edward Turner's wartime concerns about keeping a low profile to avoid arousing Harley-Davidson's anger were now over. Advertisements of Triumph's new factory branch seemed to be everywhere.

To say the bosses in Milwaukee were alarmed at this strategic incursion into "their" market would be a gross understatement. In June 1951, after orchestrating an intense letter-writing campaign from its dealers, Harley petitioned the United States Tariff Commission for higher import tariffs on all foreign motorcycles.

In its complaint, Harley stated that it was being chased out of business by less-expensive imported products. The British imports, Harley claimed, had not really created a new market, but had simply stolen customers away from the existing one. Company officials and their attorneys argued that price was the only criterion of people who buy motorcycles and that the foreign makers had an unfair price advantage.

Harley noted that, since the British pound's September 1949 devaluation, English machines were selling at prices 25 to 30 percent lower than the closest Harley-Davidson model. Never mind that H-D had no comparable model to the 350, 500, and 650cc Triumphs. Price alone, Harley asserted, was the only reason for the British bikes' booming popularity. Harley's lead attorney, Martin Paulsen, suggested that the current import tariff of 10 percent be increased to 40 percent. He also advocated for British motorcycle imports to be regulated and prohibited from exceeding more than 10 percent of the number of machines produced domestically—in other words, Harley's production.

Not only was Harley-Davidson's argument untenable, but, as the October 1951 *Buzzzz* reported, "The Harley faction appeared a bit taken aback with the array opposing them, both in quality and quantity." Harley had been confronted not only with an army of importers, but also by domestic producers Mustang (which made lightweights) and Indian, now the distributor for AJS, Matchless, Norton, and other British makes.

Denis McCormack had been in charge of the Triumph Corporation for only a few months, but already he was faced with a serious threat to his company's future. If he lost this fight, McCormack knew that he'd probably be looking for another job. So he pulled no punches. Joining McCormack on the defense side were JoMo's Bill Johnson, BSA's Rich Child, and Hap Alzina, along with Fred Stote, president of the Indian Sales Corporation. Ironically, most of Indian's US sales volume now consisted of British machines!

In the plaintiff's corner to testify on behalf of big, bad Harley were veteran dealers, including Dudley Perkins of San Francisco, Earl Robinson of Detroit, and Reggie Pink—yes, *the* Reggie Pink. The pioneer British motorcycle importer had become a Harley dealer and was called to testify for Milwaukee.

The tariff hearings opened on September 18; during that first week, the Harley group laid their case before the commission. The final four days were devoted to the British importers' side of the story. They argued that Harley was losing market share due to the simple fact that they were not making motorcycles that the American public wanted. Reporting on the hearings in the October 1951 *Motorcyclist*, Rosemary Arctander relayed the British defense:

> **The Harley-Davidson Motor Company, having no real competition from other American motorcycle manufacturers in the past twenty years, has not met the demands of the American rider. It offers them either a Cadillac (a 61ci or 74ci) or a Crosley (a 125cc), and no satisfactory all-purpose sports machine in between. Thus, most imported motorcycles are not competitive with H-D models, but fill the lack in its line.**

> **The Harley-Davidson Company is being injured not by competition, but by its own lethargy in failing to improve its obsolete models—the 45 was introduced in 1929 and the 74, in the mid-Thirties—and both have remained virtually unchanged since then.**

It seemed that even the motorcycling press had turned against H-D. This is remarkable, given that *Motorcyclist* had protected Harley and Indian interests by "burying" and outright suppressing any racing results in which a foreign motorcycle figured among the winners. Its newfound fairness was rooted in market reality: the buying public liked the British products and the growth in magazine advertising was almost entirely related to import brands.

To graphically demonstrate to the Tariff commission the differences between the Harley and the British offerings, Coates suggested a display of the machines right on the hearing room floor. So, one by one, the "evidence," including a new 6T Thunderbird and a Vincent twin, were wheeled into an elevator and lifted to the building's third floor. Laughter broke out across the hearing room, no less among Tariff Board officials, when they learned that the mammoth Harley Knucklehead was the only bike that had to be disassembled to fit in the elevator!

Testimony upon testimony drove home the differences between the British machines and the Harleys. But the house really came down when Charles Pusey, a Washington DC Triumph dealer, read a letter from one of his customers:

> **When I was struggling with the Harley and asked a certain well-known Harley enthusiast for some advice in 'mastering the monster,' his answer was, 'These machines separate the men from the boys.' Shortly after that, I was separated.**

The motorcycle tariff hearings concluded on September 27, although legal summations continued through December. The commission rendered its decision on June 15, 1952. The Tariff Board agreed with the importers that Harley-Davidson's claimed hardships did not exist, and that Harley should go home, stop crying, and build a middleweight motorcycle. The result was already in development: the 750cc K model. The flathead "45-incher," still 100 pounds heavier than most British bikes and slower than Triumph's 650, was a clear reaction to the popularity of the British middleweight twin in America.

The end of this serious threat gave Triumph's US distributors the green light they'd been waiting for. From scratch, General McCormack has assembled an eastern army ready for battle, and his soldiers included the best of the best. Johnson's troops weren't quite as well organized, but that situation would soon change. The 1950s in America would belong to Triumph.

John Esler (at left) was one of Triumph's key US dealers for nearly five decades. He was a kingpin on AMA racing committees and highly respected by Edward Turner. Esler hosted the Triumph chief at his Grand Rapids, Michigan, home many times. *Brooke archive*

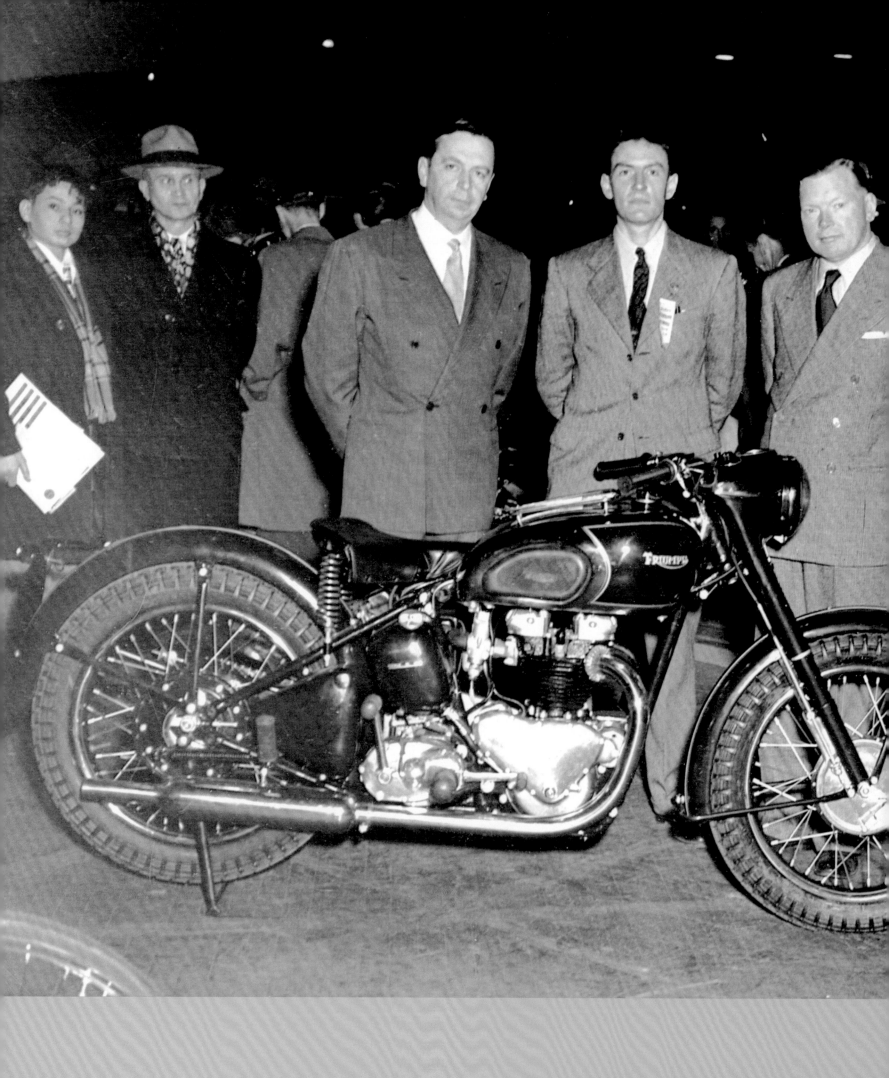

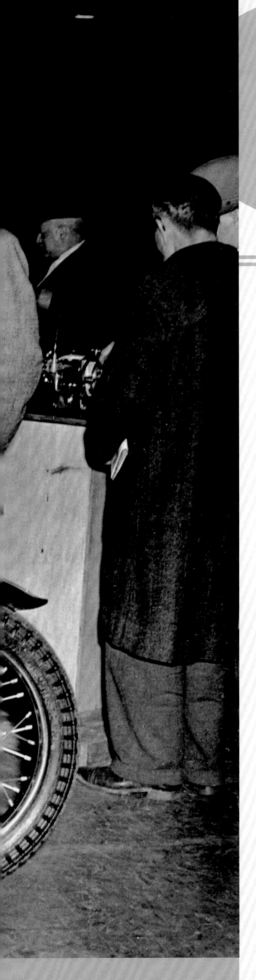

05

TRIUMPH TAKES OFF
GROWTH, SUCCESS & LEADERSHIP IN THE 1950S

The May 1951 issue of *Buzzzz*, a monthly motorcycle magazine published in Chicago, carried a news blurb about a seemingly insignificant (at least to Americans) business transaction. The item announced that the BSA Group had purchased the share capital of the Triumph Engineering Co., in effect absorbing them. It is believed that Jack Sangster, then Triumph's owner, sold out to BSA because of his concern over Britain's punishing inheritance tax.

ABOVE: US Triumph legend E. W. "Pete" Colman shows a newly uncrated 1952 6T Thunderbird to *Cycle* magazine publisher Floyd Clymer. Colman dubbed the first T-bird JoMo received as a "cast-iron snail" and quickly developed a performance kit for dealers and customers. *Gaylin archive*

LEFT: Triumph supremo Edward Turner (at right) joins two Americans who were vital to his company's early US success—Bill Johnson on the left and Rod Coates at center, behind a new 1949 Speed Twin—at the British Automobile and Motorcycle Show at New York's Armory. A few weeks earlier, Coates and his Grand Prix model had debuted in the Daytona 100-miler, a race he won in 1950. *Gaylin archive*

Whatever the motivation, this singular move, finalized on March 15 that year, haunted Triumph in the coming decades and ultimately helped lead to the company's demise. Independently owned Johnson Motors was unaffected by this change and had not been listed in the news article, but, curiously, neither was the Triumph Corporation.

In America, the Triumph invasion had begun in earnest, and was now advancing from both coasts. The numbers showed the impact of the new Baltimore distributorship. In 1950, Johnson Motors imported around 1,000 machines. By the end of the following year, Triumph's exports to the US had almost tripled to 2,730 units, with a value of almost $2 million (in 1951 dollars). Even with its startup costs, TriCor showed a small profit in its first year of operation.

JoMo's Pete Colman told the authors that Denis McCormack was personally involved in recruiting new dealers for Triumph products during the early years of TriCor's existence. But McCormack ran into typical resistance from Harley-Davidson, which reportedly even tried to bar Triumph field representatives from entering their dealers' showrooms.

Triumph, on the other hand, required no such monogamy from its agents. In a memo to all eastern dealers, dated May 1, 1951, McCormack wrote,

It has always been Triumph policy in the US, and has been on several occasions made clear by the Managing Director of the Triumph Engineering Company Ltd., Mr. Edward Turner, and by the writer, that we do not make it a stipulation that in order to be a Triumph dealer no other motorcycles may be handled. We have always found that where Triumphs are given equal display and fair representation alongside their competitors, both imported and domestic, the merit of our product insures for it its fair share of the business.

Besides the grand opening of the Baltimore factory branch, the product highlight of 1951 was the introduction of a die-cast aluminum cylinder barrel and head for the 500 twin. These replaced the square-barrel (generator) top end on the Trophy model and the iron head and cylinder on the Tiger 100. Along with enhancing performance and lowering weight, the alloy top end, with its closely pitched cooling fins, was very attractive; many believe the 1950s TR5 and T100 to be the prettiest motorcycle engines ever made.

In announcing the 1951 model range, Turner tossed a bone to competition-minded dealers and owners still lamenting the loss of the purpose-built Grand Prix: a new racing kit. Its purpose, he noted, was "to prevent our Works from being

Triumph pioneered the postwar "dual-purpose" machine with its nimble 1951 TR5 Trophy, shown here in the paddock of a Michigan half-mile dirt track. The TR5 engine used the same die-cast aluminum top end as the Tiger 100. *Brooke archive*

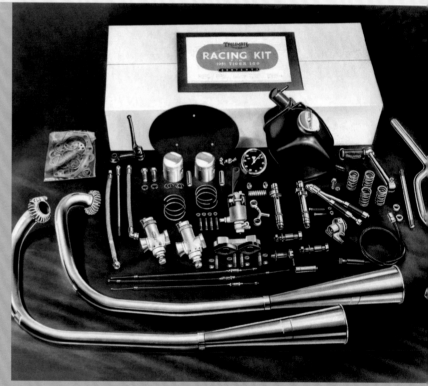

Triumph's factory "Speed Kit" packed $300 worth of go-fast goodies into a $154 package. The kit briefly filled the gap between the Grand Prix and late-1950s production racers. *Brooke archive*

Triumph stunned Harley-Davidson and Indian by winning the prestigious 1952 Langhorne (Pennsylvania) 100-mile National, sweeping first through forth places. Shown in victory circle (from left) No. 46 Dick Beaty, sponsored by TriCor, who placed third; race winner No. 76 Rick Fisher, sponsored by Philadelphia Triumph dealer/tuner Blaine Rhodes (in white shirt behind Fisher); and second-place finisher Gene Smith on the No. 98 Tiger tuned by Ft. Worth, Texas, Triumph legend Pete Dalio. *Brooke archive*

called upon to produce racing machines and it should be understood we must refuse to take orders for machines in racing condition."

While this "no race bikes" policy would not stand for long, the "Speed Kit," as Americans called it, was a low-investment way for Triumph to feed its speed-hungry customers. The kit retailed for $154.38, while parts purchased separately were worth over $300. It had been requested by Johnson Motors' Pete Colman and was based on a similar package that JoMo was already selling through its dealers to hop up the rather staid 650 Thunderbird.

The neat wooden box full of go-fast goodies is a top Triumph collectible today if original, complete, and intact. Packed snugly inside were twin 1-inch Amal Type 6 carburetors with dual inlet manifold and fuel lines; remote float chamber; twin-rotor twist grip; dual throttle cables; 8:1 compression pistons and rings; a pair of Triumph's newly introduced E3134 camshafts; racing valve springs; a one-gallon oil tank with quick-release filler cap; Smith's 8,000 rpm tachometer, drive, and cable; 1.5-inch exhaust pipes and 4-inch racing megaphones; folding kick-starter and foot rests; dropped handlebars; number plates; and a twenty-eight-page booklet, *Tuning the 1951 Triumph Tiger 100*.

A close-ratio four-speed gear set and lightweight aluminum mudguards were available separately. According to a 1993 *Classic Bike* feature, Turner approved the production of 100 racing kits in conjunction with the new alloy 500 twin's launch. It was offered through 1953, with and most shipped to

the US. The kit was used by tuners Tim Witham and Fred Ford on Jimmie Phillips's Tiger 100, which placed third in the 1952 Daytona 200.

A favorable road test of the T100 in both its "street clothes" and in race-kitted trim appeared in the November 1951 *Cycle*. As editor Bob Greene put it rather optimistically, "A gentle Little Miss in stock form capable of a hundred. Then we installed the racing kit and saw a snarling 120mph threat." Triumph's sprung hub, however, was berated for its lack of travel when the testers traversed the broken terrain around California's Rosamund dry lake bed. But no fault was found with the hub when testing the bike on the road.

The Triumph twin's ability to perform superbly under extreme conditions was proven again in 1951 when Walt Fulton won the inaugural Catalina Grand Prix on a 1950 Thunderbird prepared by George Butler, a San Bernardino dealer. The July 1951 issue of *Motorcyclist* carried details of Fulton's winning machine that, aside from high-rise handlebars and upswept pipes, was mostly stock.

"No magic was called on," the article stated, explaining that a standard 6T was received from Johnson Motors, uncrated, set up, and run on the highway to break it in. The engine was then completely dismantled and inspected for tight spots. The head was polished and a hotter camshaft and slightly larger carburetor fitted. That was it: an instant Catalina GP winner, right out of the box.

In accordance with Triumph's "low chrome" policy, begun in 1950 when the factory switched from plated fuel tanks to

The new Tiger 110 arrived in the US in late 1953, bringing Triumph's first sports-tuned 650cc engine and first application of the new swinging-arm frame and vented front brake. The machine in this factory photo is fitted with UK market handlebar. *Brooke archive*

Built for the 1953 season only, the Tiger 100C (C stood for "convertible") was the club racer's dream—a production T100 fitted with Triumph's racing kit at the factory. This example, restored by Jerry Romano, wears its standard street-legal exhaust—Grand Prix–type open megaphones were available for track use. *Brooke photo*

painted ones, the handlebars on most of the road models were now painted. Machine colors changed too—blue for the Thunderbird and red for the Speed Twin. And West Coast bikes arrived with high-rise handlebars—another nod to American rider tastes—although some high bars found their way to the East as well. The Tiger and Trophy models retained their chrome-plated bars.

When the 1952 model line was announced in the fall of 1951, the 3T De Luxe was absent. The factory decided to discontinue the 350, partly due to its unpopularity but primarily because it stole valuable production resources away from the vastly more popular 500 and 650 twins. Demand was so great that Triumph simply could not build them fast enough. The expansion of the Meriden factory, begun a year earlier, was not yet complete, so there was only room enough to make the larger, more profitable models.

Price increases above the previous year were tremendous, as postwar inflation pushed most models up more than $100 in a single year. A Thunderbird that retailed for $712 in February 1951 now listed at $837. Even with these staggering increases, though, appetite for Triumph motorcycles could not be satisfied.

Many changes and improvements were introduced on the 1952 line. The nacelled models got a bigger 7-inch headlamp and, for the first time, the wiring harness was color coded. The electrical system polarity was also changed from a negative to a positive ground. The Thunderbirds were fitted with a new constant-vacuum SU carburetor, similar to those on many British cars, and the frames were modified to accommodate a connecting tube to the air filter—an uncommon fitment in the wet UK but a necessity for US operation.

For 1953, American dealers pushed Triumph to offer the Thunderbird in classy black paint, highlighted in gold lining on the fenders and wheel rims. These "Black Birds" far outsold the standard metallic blue 6T. This restoration by Mike Benolken wears a TriCor leather tank bag, a popular period accessory designed for Triumph's parcel grid and originally supplied by Warren Leather Goods. *Jeff Hackett/ Brooke archive*

The 1950 economy scheme directed at chrome plating was now expanded to include wheel rims. Some of Triumph's touring models arrived in the US with wheels completely painted in the machine's color, but this proved unpopular and the program was short lived. The painted handlebars were disliked as well, especially in California. By 1952, both distributors offered the HO787 American-style high-rise bars in chrome as an option. Many of JoMo's handlebars were designed and supplied by Earl Flanders's accessories house. A folding kick-start lever was also a popular extra (it took Meriden until 1954 to fit these as standard on the road models).

Ninety dealers attended the Triumph Corporation's first service school held at the Baltimore warehouse on January 22, 1952. The school was a learning process for both student and teacher, and it was a huge success. Forty of the visiting dealers actually stayed an extra day after the school ended for a special racing/tuning seminar given by Coates and Jones.

A NEW LIGHTWEIGHT SURPRISE

By the following year, Triumph was riding tall in the saddle. The marque stunned Harley-Davidson by taking the first four places in the 100-mile AMA National dirt track race in Langhorne, Pennsylvania, in 1952, and swept all three classes at the 1953 Laconia, New Hampshire, road race National. Triumph dealers

across the US promoted their products with these important race victories and with high-profile displays at the motorcycle shows in Daytona and Laconia. Johnson Motors even used the Los Angeles County Fair in Pomona as a venue for lavish motorcycle exhibitions.

Triumph seemed to be everywhere at once. You couldn't open a motorcycle magazine or race program without seeing a Triumph road test or advertisement.

The 1952 model range was highlighted by the surprise introduction of the 150cc T15 Terrier. This lightweight single was a complete reversal of Triumph's postwar big-displacement, twins-only policy. At the 1951 dealers' banquet in Florida, Turner had been asked if Triumph ever expected to make an engine smaller than 350cc.

At that time, Triumph was still producing the 3T, and Turner's response, reported in the May 1951 *Buzzzz*, was "Why should we? That market is being excellently catered to by several manufacturers. We never want all of the market and will be quite satisfied with our fair share." The Terrier seemed to contradict this philosophy, and Turner would have to chew a bit of shoe leather during his next American meal!

The T15 was a departure from features that were long identified with the Triumph name. The engine and gearbox were unitized, while the H-section connecting rod had a roller-bearing big end. A sprung hub was nowhere to be found, having

Continued on page 56

1955 T100/R.

As a frequent spectator at Daytona and at California desert races during the 1950s, Edward Turner witnessed how US race success correlated to new bike sales. Following the Grand Prix model's demise in 1951, it became clear that dealer-fitted Speed Kits and a handful of T100Cs were not enough. So, acquiescing to his American distributor requests, Turner approved small batches of factory-built race machines for export to the US and Canada from 1955 to 1957 (all images taken at Meriden).

T100/R—A genuine over-the-counter dirt tracker priced at $829 and developed exclusively for American privateers to compete with the popular BSA Gold Star and Harley KR. The T100/R used a rigid TR5 frame, forks, and gas tank; BTH magneto; Vokes air cleaner; reverse-cone megaphones; Dunlop rubber solo saddle and pillion; right-side folding footpeg; alloy rear fender; and 20-inch front wheel. A 1955 TriCor brochure announced that lights, horn, brakes, and front fender could be purchased separately—in case the T100/R owner wanted to put this 307-pound bullet on the street! Factory records show 130 bikes and 10 spare engines built in late 1954. All machines carried matching engine/frame numbers.

TR5/R—In 1956 Meriden added a production road racer for American customers. The TR5/R was the T100/R's stablemate, but featured a T100 swinging arm frame, oil tank, and seat. Forks, 3¼-gallon fuel tank, and aluminum fenders came from the TR5, and the racer even included TR6 quick-detach lighting to satisfy AMA Class C rules stipulating production-based machines. Reverse-cone megaphones were fitted. Factory records show that 112 TR5/Rs were produced.

T100/RS—The redesignated TR5/R for 1957, upgraded with 5-gallon fuel tank, new twin-carb Delta cylinder head, and Amal GP carburetors fitted on a downdraft angle on flexible mounts. Open GP-type 4-inch megaphones

1956 TR5/R.

were used. The finish was two-tone Ivory and Blue for the tank, Ivory on the fenders.

T100/RR—The rigid-framed dirt tracker was also renamed for 1957 with the same engine specs as the RS road racer. The peanut-shaped 2½-gallon tank was now painted Blue and Ivory instead of Silver Sheen, and a special cylindrical oil tank was fitted.

All of the race bikes, including the dirt-trackers, were built at the Meriden factory to AMA spec. They were not merely assembled at TriCor and JoMo (as some contend), according to Cliff Guild in a 1992 interview with David Gaylin. A memo to all dealers from Denis McCormack, dated January 21, 1957, confirmed Guild's assertion: "There is but a moderate quantity of these available and the effort that the factory has made to meet this special requirement is appreciated," the TriCor boss wrote. "Production on these machines is now in progress at the factory. They are expected here shortly and in good time for the general racing season."

1957 T100/RS.

1957 T100/RR.

Triumph's US sales potential grew exponentially after Baltimore-based TriCor was established. The company wasted no time advertising its new transcontinental muscle. *Gaylin archive*

The heart of the T100/R features matched Amal DS and TS racing carbs, rubber-mounted remote float bowl, and hard-to-find Vokes twin-carb air filter housing. The big-bearing T100 engine was certified to deliver 42 horsepower at 7,000 rpm, good for 115 miles per hour on a smooth half-mile in this 307pound bullet. *Brooke photo*

Continued from page 53

been replaced on the Terrier by a plunger arrangement. In fact, this model, as well as the early Tiger Cubs, were the only plunger Triumphs.

As much as it differed from Triumph's other offerings, the Terrier really did resemble a miniature Speed Twin. It was even finished in Amaranth Red, with a smaller version of the headlight nacelle and a tank featuring an abbreviated version of Triumph's famous four-bar emblem. Although the Terrier was really developed as a commuter bike for other markets, it did attract a following in the US before being overshadowed by the overwhelmingly popular Tiger Cub.

Motorcyclist tested a T15 with a nacelle-mounted gear indicator and found everything "rosy"—so rosy, in fact, that the bike was stated as being capable of 70 miles per hour! But as ground-breaking as it was, Triumph's little thumper still had to wait for assembly-line time as well as further refinement. As a result, Terriers didn't arrive in the US until late summer, making them 1954 models.

The Terrier employed an alternating-current, coil-ignition system that was also introduced on the Speed Twin. The 5T's alternator hung on the end of the crankshaft's drive side, and the chain case was given the appropriate bulge. Voltage intensity was determined by the position of the lighting switch—a dead battery could bring the full wrath of the alternator to bear on the starting coil by positioning the key. This Lucas system worked well enough to be installed on the 1954 Thunderbird.

The other big news was the Tiger 100C, built only for the 1953 model year. This was basically a T100 with a factory-fitted Speed Kit, improved float-chamber mounting, and mufflers (megaphones were extra). The model's 8.0:1 compression ratio met AMA Class C rules. The machine was designed in the same spirit as BSA's Gold Star—a high-performance, street-legal 500 that was easily converted for competition "with a few hours' work," proclaimed Triumph's magazine ad.

Meriden records show that 560 T100Cs were produced between November 1952 and August 1953. Most went to the US. The kitted Tiger was a harbinger of the small batches of special, US-only production dirt-track and road racers that arrived from Meriden in 1956 and 1957 (see sidebar). Turner may have complained about the expense of factory racing and regularly criticized Norton for it, but he knew how Triumph's competition successes sold motorcycles.

The rest of the 1953 range remained generally unchanged, except for the Thunderbird, which at US dealers' request was now available in black, in addition to metallic blue. The pinstriping on the fenders and wheel centers remained gold for both finishes. The availability of "Black Birds," as they were called, had been announced to American dealers the previous December. Demand eventually grew so strong that dealers scorned the blue machines and wanted only the black versions. By April 1953, Denis McCormack had to issue a bulletin, directing dealers to take some blue Thunderbirds.

TIGERS 110 AND CUB UNVEILED

The 1954 program was Triumph's most ambitious yet, introducing two completely new models and a multitude of detail changes. In addition, there were two carryover models from 1953 that would be phased out during the season as stocks were depleted. These leftovers boosted the total number of machines offered that year to ten.

The most significant newborn was the Tiger 110—a go-fast version of the popular Thunderbird, aimed again at the American market. The T110 engine had a more robust bottom end, with a bigger crank, beefier big-end journals, and ball bearings on the timing side as well as on the primary. All this strengthening was necessary to bear the additional stress created by the T110's larger carb, inlet tract, and higher compression. A replica of Triumph's racing "Q" camshaft (the famed E3134) was installed on the intake side.

The T110 was the fastest Triumph yet, easily capable (in box-stock form) of speeds in excess of 100 miles per hour. Just as important as the hot 650 engine was Triumph's new swinging-arm frame. This replaced the piecemeal, rigid frame-cum-sprung hub so disliked by Americans. The new frame finally brought Triumph into the twin-shock age, years behind AJS Matchless, Norton, Royal Enfield, and even Harley's K model. Remarkably, Triumph finished out 153 more rigid-framed T110s that year, with 115 going to JoMo, 15 to

TriCor, and the rest to other markets. None of the US bikes had sprung hubs.

By squeezing the gearbox and engine closer together to fit the new swingarm frame, the overall wheelbase grew no more than one inch, a remarkable accomplishment by Meriden's engineers. And a new, wide touring twinseat was designed for the rear subframe, which, combined with the new suspension, transformed the Triumph into a truly modern-looking and -handling machine.

The smaller Tiger 100 model inherited these design improvements as well, including the all-ball-bearing bottom end. With its close-pitched-fin engine and new Shell Blue color, the 1954 Tiger 100 was nothing short of art. For American riders, though, the Tiger 110 was one prayer closer to the speed god and so it overshadowed its little brother.

Johnson Motors supplied a T110 to *Cycle* for testing in the April 1954 issue. The bike was fitted with American-style H0787 handlebars and the smaller F3360 3-gallon fuel tank, popular in the western states. Editor Bob Shanz found the "Tiger-Bird" to be scarcely more comfortable than a rigid model but a heck of a lot faster, achieving 104 miles per hour.

Pete Colman also was on hand to aid in the speed runs. Simply by changing plugs and carburetor jets and removing the mufflers, Colman coaxed 109.9 miles per hour out of the new

The new-for-1953 T15 Terrier was styled like a miniature Speed Twin with Amaranth Red paint, headlamp nacelle, and similar tank emblem. The 150cc OHV single introduced Triumph's new AC coil ignition system. Original 1953 photo by *Motorcyclist* editor Bill Bagnall. *Brooke archive*

650, running against a headwind. Shanz commented that he believed 115 miles per hour was quite possible when the T110 had more miles on it. At the time, only Vincent's 1,000cc Rapide and Black Shadow were faster.

The T110 was also fitted with a new 8-inch front brake. Its racy air scoop caused Shanz some concern about moisture, but otherwise he found it adequate to handle the additional horses. The new front brake design was not found on all 1954 Tiger 100s, however; some early machines still carried the previous year's nonscooped unit.

The season's other big news was the introduction of the Tiger Cub. As the Terrier appeared to be a miniature Speed Twin, so the Cub looked like a downsized Tiger model. Its tank and fenders were finished in Shell Blue, while the rest of the machine wore black enamel. Adding to the effect was a twinseat fitted instead of the Terrier's solo saddle. This "Tigerized" Terrier had an enlarged bore-and-stroke, yielding 199cc to the Terrier's 149cc, or 3 more cubic inches. And, whereas Americans embraced the smaller T15 as an ideal lightweight, off-road tool, the T20 Cub was even more so.

This sporting focus eventually led to the Cub's rather unfair reputation of fragility, particularly in the engine's bottom end. When not severely over-revved, Tiger Cubs were basically reliable. Still, the Cub (and Terrier) were higher-quality machines than virtually all their lightweight two-stroke competitors in the 1950s.

Changes to the remaining 1954 models were mainly in details. The Thunderbird (6T/AC) received the AC lighting and ignition adopted on the 1953 Speed Twin. Magneto- and generator-equipped T-birds (6T/M) continued to be available until their supply was depleted partway through the season. Both touring models received new switch gear to accompany the new electrics, and all models, including the TR5, now wore the restyled teardrop-shaped "sports" mufflers. Like the leftover T-birds and T110s, rigid-framed Tiger 100s continued in the lineup.

TriCor and JoMo both saw personnel changes in 1954. Wilbur Ceder appointed two new, experienced sales reps to service and recruit dealers in the southern regions of JoMo's nineteen western states and thus combat BSA's expansion there. On the East Coast, McCormack employed Catalina GP champ Walt Fulton to handle dealers in the western half of TriCor's realm. Dick McDougall, who had won the Southwestern TT Championship in 1953 and was a veteran of Daytona and Langhorne, took over TriCor's southern region. Jack Mercer handled the remaining eastern territories.

In Baltimore's Service Department, Englishman Davey Jones was now able to step down from his temporary US assignment because Rod Coates had found a suitable replacement. While traveling through Richmond, Virginia, Coates often stopped at the area's Indian franchise. Most Indian dealers were by then handling Matchless, Norton, and

The 200cc T20 Tiger Cub debuted a year after the smaller Terrier and shared its plunger-type rear springing at launch—the only Triumphs to use this suspension. Note rider-friendly 16-inch wheels and Shell Blue livery on this original unrestored 1956 Cub owned by Michigan Triumph restoration guru Bill Hoard. *Brooke photo*

Vincent, so naturally Coates was interested in checking out the competition. There he met Cliff Guild, part owner of the shop, as well as a racer and wrencher of some notoriety.

Coates was impressed by Guild's tuning and mechanical ability and offered him a spot in Baltimore on a trial basis. A year later, the position was made permanent, to the relief of Jones, whose relationship with Coates was sometimes strained. Guild went on to become TriCor's chief mechanic and race tuner; he grew to be one of the world's experts on making the unit-construction 500cc twins not only go fast, but consistently finish races.

SWINGING-ARM TROPHIES

Ongoing improvements to the motorcycles continued in 1955. Swinging-arm suspension became available on the touring models, the flimsy center stands were strengthened, and Lodge became Triumph's original equipment spark plug, replacing KLG. Amal's new Monobloc carburetors were also fitted, initially to the Speed Twin and ultimately to the entire range.

One of the biggest changes that year occurred on the competition models. The TR5 Trophy finally gained a swingarm frame, although this added nearly 40 pounds to the bike's overall weight. At the front end, the metal fork shrouds disappeared, replaced with rubber boots. The Trophy's fuel tank was changed to the type fitted to Tiger models, and a small "ironing board" seat was used. The paint finish was Shell Blue, replacing Silver Sheen and chrome as the main color.

The upgraded, fully suspended TR5 marked the birth of the modern dual-purpose motorcycle. *Cycle* editor Don Brown tested a Trophy in the July 1955 issue, passing it "with a top score in both handling and durability." Brown's test consisted of 1,000 tortuous miles, mostly off-road, including several speed runs in excess of 102 miles per hour at the Rosamond dry lake bed. All tests were accomplished with standard road tires fitted. After a quick sprocket change, the TR5 was entered in the two-day Greenhorn Enduro alongside 300 other entrants.

Unfortunately, Brown got lost during the first day, which put him out of contention, but he and the Trophy finished the event with no problems. Bud Ekins provided vindication for the new Trophy later that year, however, when he won the bruising Catalina Grand Prix.

The rest of the range continued as in 1954, including the availability of an all-black finish for the Thunderbird. Terriers were also offered in black as a last-ditch effort to make them more attractive to Americans, who generally preferred the larger Tiger Cub. The 150cc singles were phased out altogether in 1956.

Rigid-framed Triumphs continued to be offered alongside their swinging-arm successors until all had been bought up (early in 1955). Models with both frame choices included the 6T/AC Thunderbird, T100 Tiger, TR5 Trophy, and the 5T/AC

Speed Twin. As a result, many 1955 rigid-frame Triumphs survive in the US today.

In October 1955, Johnson Motors ceased all retail motorcycle sales. JoMo's focus going forward would now be supplying and servicing its dealers in the western US.

ENTER THE IMMORTAL TR6

The year 1956 was memorable for Triumph in America, due to Johnny Allen's 214-mile-per-hour speed record, the arrival of the new 650cc TR6, and changes that took place in both distributorships. The Triumph Corporation moved from its former leased building to a more spacious, purpose-built structure located in the Baltimore suburb of Timonium. The

Johnny Allen's 1956 motorcycle world speed record set in the Thunderbird-powered "Texas Cee-gar" was reported by all the motorcycle publications, including *Triumph World*, the company's in-house newspaper received by the US distributors. *Brooke archive*

Gib Hufstader's 1956 TR6 Trophy is a time capsule, still wearing its Buco exhaust system, Tiger 100 front fender, and TriCor heel/toe shift lever fitted by the dealer when Gib bought the bike new in early 1957. The former General Motors Corvette engineer has covered 10,000 miles on the 650 twin but has never pulled the cylinder head. "Outstanding in the dirt and for hill climbing," he reports. *Brooke photo*

Triumph submitted this photograph to the AMA in late 1955 as part of process to get the new TR6 Trophy 650cc engine approved for competition. It was the first production use of the aluminum "Delta" cylinder head, which went through four design changes (and four part numbers) between 1956 to 1958. *Gaylin archive*

new facility was expanded twice during the late 1950s. A second addition was required when TriCor briefly took over the US distribution of Daimler automobiles. Daimler was then a division of Triumph's parent company, BSA, and was run directly by Edward Turner. This scheme lasted only a couple of years and, when Daimler left, the resulting space was leased to other companies.

JoMo's 1956 changes came not in facilities but in personnel. Sales boss Ed Brady resigned and Bill Johnson replaced him with Don Brown, who was then cohosting a motorcycle radio show on station KHJ in Los Angeles.

Brown was a longtime motorcycle enthusiast and off-road racer, with a few competition successes on both Triumphs and Matchlesses, including the 1952 AMA Amateur cross-country championship. The first major event Brown qualified for was the 1951 Catalina Grand Prix. He started dead last on the grid, 200th out of 200 riders, but finished a remarkable 16th.

After writing a racing column for *Cycle*, Brown became the magazine's editor and, along with fellow staffer Evan Aiken, co-edited a popular book on motorcycle racing, *How to Ride and Win*. He then joined motorcycle accessory maker Bates Manufacturing as a traveling sales rep, where he gained valuable industry contacts and sales experience. A year later, Johnson tuned in to Brown's radio show and soon offered him the new sales general manager job at Colorado Boulevard.

Johnson Motors had only recently ended its retail business. Brown recalled that, by the time he was hired, "The Triumph Corporation was certainly flexing its muscles. Bill decided to expand western operations and get better organized. He realized that if he didn't, [TriCor's] next step might be the West Coast."

In 1992, Earl Miller, Denis McCormack's closest advisor, steadfastly denied that a JoMo takeover, or any assault on JoMo's business, was ever discussed in Baltimore. Edward Turner would never have done such a thing to his old friend Johnson, claimed Miller. Still, the Californians continued to suspect their British expatriate colleague on the East Coast.

Real or not, the perceived threat from Baltimore spurred Johnson and Wilbur Ceder into action. They set their new sales manager to work determining how many dealers JoMo actually had and how many it needed. As of 1956, there were roughly 105 Triumph dealers in the western states, while in the eastern region TriCor had over 200. Brown's work was cut out for him.

"In the west, 40 percent of all business done in new motorcycle sales occurred between Bakersfield, California, and the Mexican border," recalled Brown. "If you look at the nineteen western states, there aren't many population centers—you can count them on two hands. Everything else is jackrabbits and Indians! We were doing a piss-poor job, especially in places like Texas. We really had to work on improving our dealer network."

Brown worked swiftly to expand JoMo's number of western agents. In addition, he began enforcing the franchise terms. By the mid-1950s, many US Triumph dealers had become complacent. The motorcycles basically sold themselves to the traditional clientele. Many dealers really had the Triumph franchise more for selling parts and used bikes than for selling new motorcycles. They could make 35 to 40 percent profit on a used machine and a solid 50 percent profit on parts.

Brown insisted that even veteran dealers live up to their contractual agreements. He told them that they must become aggressive and concentrate on selling new motorcycles.

Considering Triumph's model range, it's hard to believe that there would have been a problem. The TR6—or "Trophy-Bird," as it was originally dubbed in the States—was directed squarely at the off-road rider in the western US. It was basically a larger version of the TR5 with a Tiger 110 engine. However, the TR6's 650cc engine featured a new die-cast-aluminum cylinder head, known as the "Delta" head because of its shape. The new head replaced the old iron casting, which tended to overheat when put to the whip, and it also eliminated the external oil lines by routing return oil down through the pushrod tubes. Other TR6 features included a smaller 3¼-gallon gas tank, short "ironing board" twinseat, 20-inch front wheel, and a waterproof Lucas K2FC magneto. It also came equipped with a quick-detach headlight.

Triumph launched its new sports 650 at the appropriate venue. Three box-stock Trophy-Birds were entered in 1956's tortuous Big Bear Run, and the trio finished first, second, and third! Bill Postel, Bud Ekins, and Arvin Cox lead the entire race, competing only among themselves for first place. This sweep kicked off a predominance of Triumph 650 victories in US desert events. Later, when the T120C and TT Specials entered the fray, Triumph held a virtual monopoly on desert competition until the 400 Husqvarna and other two-strokes arrived in the early 1970s.

Cycle put one of the new TR6s through a punishing weeklong test and chronicled the results in their July 1956 issue. Apart from an occasional carburetor cough, the Trophy-Bird performed without a squawk.

Three friends pick up their new charcoal gray 1956 Thunderbirds at Shep's Motors in Holt, Michigan. The trio have also purchased police-style "biker caps" and black leather jackets resembling the classic Schott Perfecto—common American rider attire in the 1950s. *Brooke archive*

Back east, where deserts were in short supply and enduros and scrambles were preferred, the TR5 was still the bike of choice. To make the new 650cc model attractive to eastern buyers, Triumph changed the wheels to a 19-inch profile and added an 8-inch, air-scooped front brake. The "street scrambler" was born! Other American market deviations included the new H1014 US-pattern handlebar and an auto-advance magneto. These differences in east/west model details were not a new phenomenon, but from this time forward they became more pronounced and accepted in America.

Changes to other 1956 models involved the new Delta head for the T110, Monobloc carburetors on all machines, and new 3¼-gallon fuel tanks on all sport models, to allow more steering lock. Most paint finishes were unchanged from 1955, except the Terrier's, which was listed as black only, and the Thunderbird's, which changed to a Charcoal Gray. Black was also optional on the 6T. Late in the season, the T-bird's finish was changed again, this time to Aztec Red for the tank and fenders, with a gold-lined black center stripe. All the cycle parts were now in black enamel. This change was limited to eastern models, but "Red Birds" also began showing up in the west. For all practical purposes, this was a 1957 model, since the switch came in late summer 1956.

Triumph widened its US range in 1957 to thirteen different models, but many of these were created through the rearrangement of model designations. Most updates from the previous year were in minor details. The most visible change

US dealers created dozens of clever ways to use the tiger motif to promote their businesses. This saucy and now-classic decal from Bob Boutwell's Maryland shop graces a Speed Twin. *Brooke photo*

Charlotte "Charley" Enfield was one of many Motor Maids who found Triumph's Thunderbird the perfect touring machine in the 1950s. Her bike is personalized with accessories typically seen on many US Triumph twins during the period. *Brooke archive*

was the new grille-styled "mouth organ" or "harmonica" tank badge that was used through the 1965 season.

The Thunderbird was now officially finished in Aztec Red, while the Speed Twin was finally changed from its Amaranth finish to a color called Gold Bronze on the tank and fenders. The rest of the 5T's running gear was now in black enamel, aligning it with the rest of the range. Both 500 and 650 touring models got the full-width, 7-inch brake hubs. Otherwise, the lineup continued visually unchanged.

The differences between Triumph's American-market road and scrambler model Trophies were now designated in letter suffixes. TR5/A was the low-piped, street-equipped bike, while the TR5/B was the high-piped scrambler version. This nomenclature also extended to the 650 twins, with the addition of an economy version TR6/C, for those who could live without a tachometer. Its fenders and tank were painted in a solid Shell Blue rather than the two-tone Ivory and Red of the others.

The Terrier was finally dropped from the catalog, and a scrambler version of the Tiger Cub was announced to fill the gap. The T20C model followed Triumph's now familiar off-road pattern of upswept pipe, Trials Universal rear tire, and crankcase skid plate.

SINGING THE BATHTUB BLUES

The International Longshoremen's Association struck the US East Coast in February 1957, delaying the arrival of three shiploads of new Triumph motorcycles. Even with this setback,

Denis McCormack boasted 303 dealers in the east and was able to report a sales increase of 33 percent over the previous year, making it Triumph's best year in the US so far. It was also a good year against the competition: led by Bud Ekins, the Big Bear Run was dominated by TR6-mounted riders.

At JoMo, however, Triumph's growth in the western states was being impeded, partly by longtime stablemate Ariel. One of Johnson's problems was that each year's new motorcycle order was based on a rather arbitrary 10 percent sales growth rate, instead of true product demand.

By late 1957, this had developed into an inventory nightmare. "The warehouse was bulging with Ariel Red Hunter singles—not a bad motorcycle, but one which by then nobody particularly wanted," noted Don Brown. While taking orders for the 1958 season, he reckoned that JoMo didn't need more Ariels—and it didn't need many Triumphs beyond what had been sold in 1957. Using the relatively unsophisticated market analysis of the day, Brown reckoned the upcoming sales year would be flat at best.

When he presented his sales projections at the executive committee meeting, both Johnson and Ceder were shocked and alarmed at their rookie sales manager's numbers. Brown told them that he hadn't invented either the JoMo warehouse or all the costly unsold machines packed inside it.

"Your job is to sell them!" steamed Johnson. Brown replied that he couldn't do it under the present setup. They'd have to devise a new way.

Brown's solution was a sales plan integrated with Triumph's model-by-model production schedule. The plan proposed that JoMo would have the right to cancel machines ordered from Meriden if present inventory wasn't selling. If that was done, sales and marketing could work to turn over the distributor's inventory quickly. This way, shiploads of motorcycles wouldn't end up in the warehouse costing the company interest.

Finally, all dealers would be asked to plan their sales year and to place orders for a reasonable number of new motorcycles in advance of the selling season. Johnson and Ceder approved the plan, pending agreement by Turner. Working with three or four of his salesmen, Brown's first step was to clear out the crated Ariels to JoMo's dealer network, who retailed them rapidly—the dealers didn't want a shop full of unsold motorcycles, either! Eventually, the plan worked smoothly; within three years, JoMo's dealer orders crested the $1 million mark for the first time. More importantly, dealers were receiving popular models.

Before that could happen, though, there was a major glitch. Triumph was running at a furious pace—far ahead of all other manufacturers, or so it seemed. But the sprinter was about to stumble.

US dealers had been informed of Triumph's new Twenty One model early in the 1957 season. However, these motorcycles did not reach American shores until the fall,

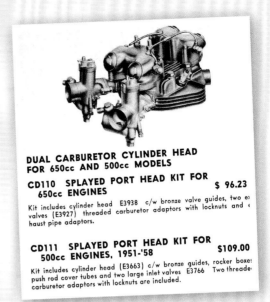

Before Meriden began fitting the new twin-carb Delta cylinder heads to production 500 and 650 twins, American dealers were snapping them up for retrofits through JoMo and TriCor. *Gaylin archive*

An Avon fairing and Geno helmet supplied by TriCor help shield the rider of this new 3TA while visiting his local Triumph shop— Shep's Motors in Holt, Michigan—in winter 1958. The "bathtub" 350 twin got a chilly reception in America. *Brooke archive*

Michigan graphic artist Ron Rae poses on his brand-new 1957 TR6B purchased from Sam Hawley at Saginaw Cycle. Note the Dunlop trials tires, siamesed exhaust, and accessory tank bag on the parcel grid. *Ron Rae*

making them 1958 models. The Twenty One's name derived from the Triumph Engineering Co.'s 21st anniversary, and the fact that its twin-cylinder overhead valve engine displaced 350cc—21 ci to Americans.

While the Twenty One's technical highlight was a unit-construction engine/gearbox, the short-stroke 350 also boasted Edward Turner's stamped-steel enclosures, which were the current trend in Britain's motorcycle industry. This bodywork enveloped the oil tank and upper portion of the rear wheel. Combined with deeply valanced front fenders, it greatly enhanced weather protection and made cleaning easier; to some eyes, it made the motorcycle look more modern.

The Americans called it "bathtub" bodywork. While that may have appealed to riders in perpetually wet Britain, where bikes were ridden daily in all conditions, it had the opposite effect on sports-minded US riders. The design added weight and hid critical fasteners, detracting from serviceability. Worst of all, it made the new Triumphs look like oversized scooters. In the US, motorcycle riding was a macho thing, and the Twenty One's styling was anything but macho.

With more than half of Triumph's product exported to the States, the "bathtubs" were the company's first major-league strikeout. And Meriden quickly compounded its mistake. As part of an overall styling theme initiated by Turner, the factory broadened the bathtub scheme to include the popular "hot rod" Tiger models. Some Triumphs retained partial rear enclosures, nicknamed "bikinis," well into the next decade. Turner's failure to accept America's love of the "naked" motorcycle cost Triumph incalculable lost sales in its biggest market.

Many US dealers had to remove the factory-fitted bathtubs from the 500s and 650s just to sell the motorcycles. This was especially true in sunny, dry California, where dealers often stripped the bathtubs as soon as they uncrated the motorcycles. At the larger Triumph dealerships, including Bud Ekins's shop in Sherman Oaks, it wasn't uncommon to find piles of bathtub enclosures stacked up behind the shop.

Almost immediately, the bathtub styling became an ongoing issue with Triumph's US distributors, who suffered with it through the mid-1960s. Among the dozens of official business communications between TriCor, JoMo, and the factory from this period collected by the authors, most contain negative comments about the bodywork. In his July 14, 1959, memo to Triumph export director A. J. "Mat" Mathieu regarding TriCor's reaction to the 1960 American model range, Denis McCormack wrote that the skirted rear of the 6T Thunderbird "will be a serious handicap rather than an assistance in this market." Similar bodywork on the T110 "will drive the sales further to the TR6 model"—which he expected to "now become outstandingly our most popular model." And, wrapped in its new steel skirt, the T100/A Tiger 500 "will have very little appeal in this market except where it steals orders from the [similarly skirted] 5TA," McCormack predicted.

Another unwanted 1958 feature was the Slick Shift gearbox fitted to non-unit twins. The Slick Shift was actually

ACCESSORY BIBLE: THE TRICOR CATALOG

One of the most popular items generated at Triumph Baltimore—and a useful tool for today's collectors and restorers—was a catalog of accessories for machine and rider. Launched in 1957, the twenty-eight-page booklet was conceived by Rod Coates, who was charged with developing and assigning the manufacture of items such as seat rails, windshields, crash bars, and saddlebags, in addition to various workshop tools. Many of these items were bought-in from various US and UK vendors, such as Bates, Buco, Webco, Wellworthy, as well as from the Meriden factory itself. Many of the catalog engine parts were designed and prototyped right at Towson.

"Rod was always in the process of trying to develop things made in America to improve on the British crap," TriCor sales manager Ed Nemec later explained. "Gaskets, seals, that sort of thing." There were also racing and high performance parts, Coates's ulterior motive for the catalog. Listed in the inaugural 1957 edition were such goodies as the CP162 tachometer kit then found on the TR6s.

Also listed was an item that bore no code number, only a price of $103.09. This was an aluminum twin-carb cylinder head for the 500cc twins. Offered for the first time, the head differed from the racing cylinder heads prepared at the factory through 1956 in that its inlet ports were splayed rather than straight. Some Triumph tuners thought that slightly spreading the inlet tracts created better flow and thus more efficiency and power. Others believed in parallel-port induction; these included

1958 TriCor catalog.
Brooke archive

Tim Witham, the famous independent tuner who worked with JoMo (and was the "W" in S&W springs) and Pete Colman. Every piece of literature connected with the new cylinder head carried a large-print disclaimer: "HEAD IS NOT AVAILABLE FOR 650cc ENGINES!"

These accessory books also detailed TriCor-distributed products such as Castrol Oil, Dunlop tires, Renold chain, and Bell helmets. For a time, the catalogs also listed dealer sales aids such as signs, display racks, and other advertising wares. Johnson Motors took a slightly different approach: rather than putting out a catalog, JoMo published individual accessory sheets offering items that were more useful to western riders and desert racers.

a clever design that brought the transmission one step closer to being automatic. Foot pressure on the shift lever in either direction disengaged the clutch before actuating the new gear, all without using the handlebar lever. The gearbox stayed between gears as long as pressure on the foot lever was maintained. A gradual release meant a gradual engagement of the drive again, just like a clutch.

To novice riders who had not experienced the traditional hand-clutch/foot-shift arrangement, the Slick Shift was easier to learn—in theory. But the design missed the mark because motorcyclists preferred to clutch and shift. Although Triumph's new gearbox could be shifted in the traditional manner—it still had a handlebar clutch lever—it had a poor reputation among experienced riders, and many gearboxes were retrofitted with the conventional mechanism.

Among the machines presented for 1958 were two new Tiger Cubs. The T20/J Junior Cub was designed to take advantage of restrictions in some US states that allowed a limited license for fourteen- to sixteen-year-old riders to operate machines with less than 5 horsepower. The Junior Cub was certified not to exceed 5 horsepower (it was actually rated at 4.95 horsepower at 5,700 rpm), thanks to a tiny 17mm Zenith carburetor with intake restrictor.

"Parents will be reassured in respect to the safety and reputation of this machine," said TriCor's sales literature. Of course, many young T20/J riders discovered that removing the restrictor would unbridle all the wild horses of the standard Cub.

Latter-day critics have charged that the British motorcycle industry's "total neglect" of the entry-level market allowed Honda

The Bonneville has landed—but it's wearing British clothes! A brand-new T120 Bonneville poses outside Triumph's Baltimore warehouse, early 1959. American motorcyclists wanted a twin-carb TR6. Note the US handlebar and UK market "pedestrian slicer" front license plate on the valanced front fender. *Brooke archive*

The new unit-construction, short-stroke 500cc twin came fully skirted at its 1959 debut—to the dismay of US dealers and American enthusiasts. Note the Lucas distributor unit driven off intake camshaft on this new UK market 1959 5T Speed Twin, photographed at Meriden. *Gaylin archive*

to gain its US beachhead. But Triumph's 1958 program, with its enclosed, utilitarian 350, semi-automatic transmission and beginner Tiger Cubs, proved that this wasn't the case. Meriden was clearly trying to attract new buyers into motorcycling.

Inspired by the growing number of motorcycle sales to students, Don Brown initiated a motorcycle instruction program through JoMo's dealer network. As detailed in the December 1958 issue of *Motorcyclist*, Brown used the beginner-friendly Triumph Twenty One to instruct then-associate editor Gray Baskerville, who had never before ridden a motorcycle. Within thirty minutes, the student was riding with confidence.

Not until the following summer did TriCor realize the value of this sales-through-instruction scheme and begin a program of their own. Long before Honda was credited with creating a new market for those who wouldn't be caught dead on a motorcycle, Triumph's US organizations already had their flags planted in this uncharted wilderness. This was revealed in a TriCor letter to eastern dealers, dated July 1, 1959:

> *Don't worry about the old hound; he'll be able to find you in the darkest alley. When we say "prospective" buyer, we refer to the non-riders; the young men and women in school, the professional man, the businessman, the bank president, the church minister, the commuter, the sportsman, the serviceman . . . just to name a few.*

This would be yet another page that newcomer Honda stole from Triumph's playbook.

Another significant though nearly forgotten model, the TR5AD, was launched in the US as a 1958/59 model. The last of the pre-unit, close-pitch-fin 500s, the TR5AD differed from the standard TR5A of the previous season with its twin-carburetor version of the "Delta" head that had been offered only as an option (hence the "D" in TR5AD). This super-sports machine was the ultimate pre-unit 500 twin, equipped with all the "good stuff"—one-piece crankshaft, E3134 cams and "R" followers, 9:1 pistons, tach-drive timing cover, and RC109 tachometer. Just 101 TR5ADs were made, along with twenty-five race engines set up for Daytona and Laconia. Premium priced at $18 more than a TR6/A, the TR5AD was a hint of what was to come. Both East and West Coast distributors had been flooded with dealer inquiries as to when a 650cc version of the twin-carb Delta head would be available. In that year's accessory catalog, such a cylinder head (part number CD110) was finally listed.

BUNGLING THE BONNEVILLE'S BIRTH

The circumstances under which JoMo and TriCor were founded made competition between them inevitable. While their rivalry was often unhealthy at the racetrack, cooperation between Johnson Motors and the Triumph Corporation on business matters was more the rule than the exception—especially when both faced economic threats.

Before Ed Nemec was appointed TriCor sales manager in 1959, Denis McCormack personally handled the task of requesting the new season's models from Meriden. This

In its final production year, the non-unit alloy 500 was available with the twin-carb Delta cylinder head, creating the TR5AD. Without excess sheet metal, it was exactly how Americans wanted their Triumph road bikes to look. This unrestored 1958 example was found in western Canada in 2017. *Ricky Pearson photo courtesy Keith Martin*

always entailed a coordinated effort from both coasts. McCormack would often write long, elaborate letters to Johnson Motors, and it was left to Don Brown to evaluate and answer these correspondences.

At the top of both distributors' shopping lists was a twin-carb 650 sports model. Dealers across the US were screaming for such a bike. Due to 1958's unprecedented requests for the splayed-port 650 head as an accessory, Brown and McCormack (who did the annual ordering for JoMo and TriCor) both knew how well such a factory-equipped model would sell. American dealers had been fitting twin-carb heads to both the Tiger 110 and Trophy 650 models since its availability in May. Naturally, this strongly influenced the US distributors when it came time to request new models from Meriden.

By all accounts, Edward Turner was hesitant about offering a twin-carb 650, and his reluctance then was not as difficult to understand as it may seem today. With each additional increase in horsepower (and the resulting internal stresses), Triumph's vertical twin moved further and further away from Turner's well-mannered, smooth-running original design. The downside of this development curve, Turner realized, was a hotter-running, rougher, more temperamental engine.

Another possible reason for Turner's opposition was his preoccupation with the enclosed models, or "streamliners" as they were officially advertised by the US distributors. Above all else, Edward Turner was an artist, and he yearned for success with these stylish models. The fact that they just didn't fly in America might have wounded the man's substantial ego. At the same time, the new unitized C-range 500cc twins were being introduced. Major resources went into publicizing them; another new model might steal some of their limelight.

Finally, Triumph was doing exceptionally well in 1958 America. The company not only outperformed all other imports, but all other motorcycle makers. Its products had won the toughest off-road endurance competitions in the US, plus major dirt-track and TT National races. A Triumph-powered streamliner was the world's fastest motorcycle. The factory's output was increasingly dedicated to the US market—and a new model might have appeared excessive in the showrooms and unwanted on the assembly line.

But after considerable pressure from JoMo and TriCor, Turner relented. This decision was made very late in the game—the new model wasn't even included in the US color catalog for 1959. Instead, it was announced by a separate leaflet later inserted into the brochure. It is ironic that Triumph's most famous motorcycle was introduced with such little fanfare. In stark contrast with the debuts of the Thunderbird, Terrier, and Twenty One, there was no elaborate promotion or stunt. In fact, Meriden's Publicity Department was uncharacteristically silent.

There has been some speculation that, because this bike was directed primarily at the US market, it was left to the American distributors to promote. But by launch time, no ad campaign or stunt could have inspired sales more than the simple appearance of the model itself. The rumors and anticipation that preceded it were merely stoked by the dealers.

This is not to suggest that Turner completely turned his back on the hot new 650. In fact, he afforded it the most significant birthday present of all—its name. Triumph had held motorcycling's absolute land speed record since 1956 (see Chapter 7), so what better name for an ultimate sports machine than the place where Triumph's speed legend was made: Bonneville.

For all intents and purposes, the new beast was basically a twin-carb Tiger 110, varying only in color. Of course, there were differences in detail. The T120 Bonneville wore a pair of "chopped" Amal Monoblocs, minus their internal float chambers.

The T20/J Junior Cub was aimed at learner motorcyclists whose speed ambitions were curbed by the engine's teeny 17mm Zenith carb, restricting output to 5 horsepower. Young Kenny White didn't seem to mind. *Gaylin archive*

Instead, a single remote mixing bowl was clamped to the seat post and insulated from road shocks via a rubber mounting block. This reservoir was then plumbed to feed both carburetors.

Late in the year, the rubber block was changed to a larger metal version that moved the bowl 3 inches further forward, between the carbs. The original layout had caused fuel load-up and starvation during abrupt starts and stops.

The rest of the T120 shared the 1959 T110's new parts, including a one-piece forged crankshaft, H1010 high-rise handlebars, and F3647 two-level twinseat. The spares catalog and sales literature for 1959 indicated that the smaller TR6 saddle was fitted, but most US Bonnies had the fuller touring seat as found on the Tiger. The paint finish was a Tangerine and Pearl Grey two-tone, though John Nelson, ex-factory service manager, suggested in his book, *Bonnie*, that some 1959 examples wore blue instead. It is likely that this was a premature 1960 finish, as even the leftover models the following year were painted in Tangerine.

As they arrived in showrooms across the country, the first Bonnies were a disappointment to the go-fast crowd. Everyone had expected a twin-carb TR6, which was then hotter than the Tiger 110. Indeed, most of the splayed-port heads sold during 1958 were used to convert Trophy models, not T110s, according to TriCor internal memos. Surely the factory knew this! Compared to the "bathtubbed" T-110, the "naked" TR6 was far sportier, with its smaller tank, fenders, seat, separate chromed headlamp, and a tachometer. Americans had expected the TR6 to get the dual-carb upgrade.

While everyone knew the 1959 T120 was the fastest non-racer that Triumph had ever made, it sure didn't look like it. Triumph's sporting flagship—wearing deeply valenced fenders, a headlamp nacelle, and a wide seat—simply didn't look the part. Many US dealers heard the same speech from their customer: "Boy, if only it looked like a Trophy, I'd buy it in a minute!"

Sales resistance was such that US dealers began converting new TR6s to Bonneville spec by ordering a splayed-port cylinder head and extra carburetor. TriCor, at least, accepted this and on February 27, 1959, issued a dealer bulletin on the matter:

> *If you feel that you will lose sale of a T120 because of its style with nacelled forks, and that there is a definite demand for the TR6/A-style T120 (sports headlight, tachometer, etc.), there is a simple method of conversion by fitting a splayed-port cylinder head and extra carburetor to a TR6/A to give the rider what he wants: a TR6 "Super Sports" Bonneville. It is recommended that this conversion be made in extreme cases only, where a sale might be lost. Otherwise, sell the T120 as is.*

TriCor's memo then directed dealers to charge an additional $100 conversion fee on top of the regular price for a T120. Amazingly, these converted Trophies didn't experience the early carburetor problems of the Bonneville, which were attributed to the remote float bowl.

Meriden, realizing their styling mistake, changed the 1960 Bonneville to TR6 specifications, but not before a glut of original nacelled T120s jammed American warehouses. These had to be sold off as 1960 models the following season. As if to emphasize this point, neither of the two major US motorcycle magazines road tested a Bonneville in its inaugural year.

UNIT 500 AND TRIUMPH'S FIRST SCOOTER

Magazines at the time were focused on the new unit-construction 5TA Speed Twin. This enlarged version of the 350cc 3TA had been disclosed during the previous season and was given much more attention by the factory than the Bonneville. Like many new Triumphs, though, its arrival in America came a year late. The spotlight given to the fresh 500 was not unwarranted: many believe that this was the best engine design the "old" Triumph company ever produced. But the oversquare (69 x 65.6mm bore-and-stroke) twin came wrapped in an Amaranth Red bathtub and headlamp nacelle, identical to the bodywork enveloping the Twenty One; this caused American enthusiasts to scratch their heads in bewilderment.

The racing camps on both coasts immediately saw the rpm potential of new short-stroke layout and began building racers based on the unit 500. In May 1959, a detailed bulletin was sent to all dealers, instructing them on how to convert a standard 5TA to Class C road or dirt track specs. A year later, JoMo and TriCor both offered complete "ready race"–unit 500 engines, built by both distributors under the T100S/RR designation. The Americans gained more race-tuning experience on this engine from 1959 to 1965 than Meriden itself had achieved. Their faith in the design was justified by countless track successes at all levels, including Don Burnett's 1962 Daytona 200 victory on a TriCor-built machine.

Also overshadowed by the Bonneville was Triumph's first motor scooter. Turner had finally produced a competitor to the stylish Italian Vespas and Lambrettas that were becoming popular in US college towns. Again, though, it was late to market, the prototype having been unveiled in 1955. Originally, the Tigress was intended in two engine capacities, a fan-cooled 250cc overhead-valve, four-stroke twin; and a 175cc two-stroke single. But the models that finally appeared in America during late summer 1959 were the 250s.

Manufactured by BSA, which marketed its own model in the UK, the TW2 and TW2S (electric start) Tigress was attractively finished in a light shade of blue. American models featured optional windshield and chrome covers on their 10-inch pressed steel wheels.

But US dealers weren't smitten with the big scooter. First, with all the new models coming from Meriden, many dealers (particularly those outside of urban areas and college towns) didn't want to bother with such a departure from the traditional product line. Second, the Tigress's serviceability was poor compared to the Italian scooters because the Triumph's bodywork was not easily removed. And it was not competitively priced.

"I question with an open mind, the need in this market for a $600-plus scooter," wrote Don Brown, in an August 1958 memo to Denis McCormack. The expensive Tigress had obvious problems, noted Brown, which the JoMo staff discussed with Turner during his annual visit.

"I think that we will all be disappointed in the initial sales of this item through purely motorcycle outlets," Brown predicted accurately. He added that a separate scooter franchise was probably needed, although this never happened. To Triumph's credit, though, the company never tried to pressure its US dealers into selling the Tigress, or the later Tina, by linking their scooter sales with their allotments of Trophies or Bonnevilles. By 1967, Triumph's unsuccessful US scooter foray had ended.

Including the Tigress, TriCor and JoMo listed sixteen different models for 1959, unquestionably their most ambitious lineup yet. Triumph's nationwide dealer network, and the organization behind it, were the envy of the US motorcycle industry. Even with the goofs in launching the Bonneville, the bathtub fiasco, and an unwanted scooter, Triumph was still the motorcycle preferred by those who wanted to ride and those who wanted to sell.

Being an American Triumph dealer in the late 1950s, as the saying goes, was a license to print money. The marque turned many "grease monkey" dealers into financially secure citizens. Some even became wealthy enough to take on lines of smaller machines just coming into the American market for the first time. But with funny-sounding names like Honda and Yamaha, others felt that these "sidelines" would be a temporary distraction.

More importantly, Triumph attracted a new postwar group of riders into the sport and led the way in greatly expanding the motorcycle business in sales, accessories, service, and competition. But as good as the 1950s were for Triumph in the US, the next decade would rise high above it.

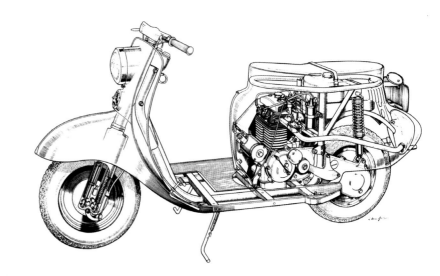

Factory "ghosted" illustration of Triumph's 250cc Tigress scooter shows the simple parallel-twin engine and chassis construction. *Gaylin archive*

06
TRIUMPH IN THE 1960s
THE ULTIMATE IN MOTORCYCLING

The new Bonneville and unit-construction 500s sent Triumph charging into 1960. Sales of large-displacement motorcycles were slumping as the decade began, but each of the company's US distributors was approaching $1 million in annual sales—the "big time" in an industry that had grown incrementally in the previous decade.

ABOVE: **The TR7 marketing used in 1960 only was aimed at separating the trim, restyled Bonnie from its unpopular nacelled predecessor. The engines and frames were still stamped T120.** *Brooke archive*

LEFT: **The multiple-award-winning Detroit custom Triumph "So Rare" in 1963. The bitchin' 650 wore various paint schemes during its reign as a perennial Autorama trophy winner.** *Bob Leppan photo*

Meanwhile, in England, motorcycle and scooter sales had already hit their all-time peak (in 1959) and were beginning to decline. The US market now proved crucial to the British motorcycle industry's future growth. Over half of Triumph's 1960 production was being exported, most of it destined for American customers.

Of Triumph's twelve 1960 US models, three were 200cc Tiger Cubs. Also cataloged were a trio of unit-construction twins, the 350cc 3TA, 500cc 5TA, and T100/A. The 650 "B-range" included the venerable 650cc Thunderbird and Tiger 110; high- and low-piped Trophy-Birds (TR6/A and /B), and, of course, the T120 Bonneville.

Meriden was still deeply into its streamlining phase—"Conservative and intelligent weather protection," said the year's sales brochure. But Americans continued to shun the bathtubs and deeply valanced fenders. The controversial styling trend was impeding sales, moving Johnson Motors' sales manager Don Brown to voice his own misgivings to export manager Mathieu, who had spoken out against enclosing the 1960 road-burners during high-level planning meetings at Meriden. Despite Turner's belief in the enclosures, Mathieu knew what the Yanks wanted. In August 1959, he and Brown exchanged revealing letters on the subject, key excerpts of which follow:

Mathieu: Even the T120 and TR6 were originally scheduled to appear in full skirts in the new [1960] season. It was a veritable tooth-and-nail battle before that was reversed.

Brown: Believe me, we endeavored here to ignore many bothersome aspects about Triumph's program,

TriCor sales manager Ed Nemec's daughter Kim gets a rider's-eye view of her dad's new 1960 TR6/A Trophy, kitted out with the popular B-1 dealer accessory kit: a Plexiglas windshield, leather saddle bags, molded tank bag for the parcel grid, and special mirrors, all for $90.50 when ordered with a new Triumph. *Gaylin archive*

in order to present to you only those requests which we felt were directly pertinent to the sale of Triumph products in our part of the country. This has been Mr. Johnson's specific direction.

It seems that with all the growing competition throughout the world, the factory would, where possible, bend to the desires of distributors who have proved to have expert knowledge of marketing within their own territories, and who face difficult dealer-distributor relations as the result of arbitrary decisions on specifications which are simply not applicable to the area.

It makes no sense to me to force "continental styling" on consumers who obviously, and of necessity, have not real use for it.

TriCor president Denis McCormack had sent Mathieu a similar memo five months earlier that included the following: "It is entirely frustrating and results in considerable increase of sales resistance and loss of actual sales to try to push the streamlining down the throats of those who want to buy sporting motorcycles."

The 1960 Bonneville reflected Triumph's change of strategy. TriCor's 1960 sales brochures showed three different Bonnevilles with two basic model designations. The big-fender nacelled bike was unchanged from 1959 and still listed as the "T120 Bonneville Super Sports." These were actually unsold leftovers that had to be cleared out. But the stars of the brochure were two "new" bikes—the TR7/A Bonneville Road Sports and TR7/B Bonneville Scrambler.

The low-piped TR7/A and street-scrambler TR7/B officially brought TR6 styling to the twin-carb 650. Gone were the nacelle and sheet-metal skirt. The revamped Bonnie now looked just like American (and British, truth be told) riders wanted their Triumphs to look—lean and sporting. Separate chromed headlamp, sports fenders, and rubber fork gaiters became the archetype for future Bonnevilles. While TR7 was the bike's market designation in the US, its crankcases were still stamped "T120." Toolbox transfers read the same.

Cycle's September 1960 cover was headlined "Triumph TR7/A" and the story inside did not mention the T120 at all. The TR7 nomenclature was used in no other market but the US until the single-carb 750 twin arrived in 1973. US Bonnevilles officially reverted to T120/R and T120/C codes in 1961. The high-pipe "C" Bonnies were slow sellers in the east. In 1962, TriCor created a kit to convert them to low-pipe roadsters, swapping the trials tires for street rubber.

If only the new Bonnie, and the rest of the popular 650cc range, had been as robust as they were handsome. New twin-downtube duplex frames, broken flywheel bolts, and AC-generator electrics for 1960 gave the US distributors and their customers headaches. The duplex frame transmitted more vibration to the rider than its single-downtube predecessor, causing fractures and catastrophic breaks at the steering head. Fuel tank straps broke by the score.

A rare view of two "bathtub" Triumphs—a 1961 duplex T110 and its 5TA little brother at the 2012 National Triumph Rally in Pennsylvania. The black-and-ivory 650 was TriCor's "Economy Streamliner" that year, costing $100 less than the non-skirted version. Triumph's unique tank bags were made by Warren Leather Goods, a long-time supplier of US Army pistol holsters. *Brooke photo*

TriCor and JoMo were caught between the factory's faulty engineering and their dealers' wrath, but they honored warranties and replaced the frames without question. Midyear, the factory added a lower tank rail to stiffen the frame, but it ended up increasing vibration levels. As a result, fuel tanks were splitting.

"Something has to be found to stand up to your 'cowboys,'" confided Meriden's design chief Jack Wickes, in a private 1960 letter to Don Brown. Wickes and Triumph's American distributors knew that the US was Triumph's toughest proving ground. Soon a new frame design was on the factory's drafting boards, but the duplex horrors remained in production through 1962.

Then came the notorious Prince of Darkness. "The 1960 electrics were beyond bad," remembered Detroit dealer Bob Leppan.

The Lucas AC generator system lacked proper voltage regulation; a fast ride would cause the battery to boil over. Some batteries were so badly damaged the plates would warp! The extra vibration from the duplex frame split battery cases, which then leaked acid on the frame and exhaust pipes. Needless to say, we dealt with a lot of angry 650 owners that year.

The backlash spilled over into TriCor's 1961 dealer meeting, where McCormack introduced the Lucas rep as "the man who's trying to put us out of business." His quip was meant to humor the audience, but they weren't amused. The dealers booed the poor Lucas man anyway!

Lucas was among various suppliers who were beginning to tarnish Triumph's reputation. In his correspondence with Brown, Wickes revealed problems with dipper switches, clutch material, wiring harnesses, and fuel petcocks. Wickes explained that Triumph was having so much trouble with suppliers that the factory needed tougher scrutiny of incoming components, particularly at the start of each model year. He admitted that "Rod [Coates] appealed to ET [Edward Turner] last April for a full-time quality overseer. The answer—as usual—was NO!"

Wickes also noted that Triumph was taking its complaints about deteriorating supplier quality directly to the offending companies' head offices. But at Meriden, cost was king. And engine vibration was the root cause of many electrical system issues. Besides, there were few (if any) alternatives to the British industry's traditional supply base.

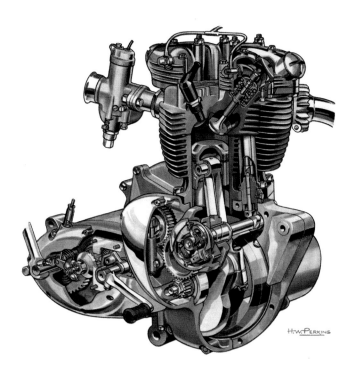

ONE-YEAR WONDERS: TR5A/R AND TR5A/C

As good as the new unit-construction 500 was proving to be, many potential American buyers were still put off by the bodywork surrounding it. That changed with the debut of two new models: the TR5A/R roadster and TR5A/C enduro/competition bike. These models attracted buyers who'd been waiting for a sporty "Triumph-looking" 500 to finally resurface amid the bulbous bathtubs and nacelles.

"For all-around sport riding, it would be rather hard to find a better motorcycle," reported *Road & Track* in its test of the 1961 TR5A/R. This street version differed from its brother by having a parcel grid, Dunlop K70s instead of Trials Universals, separate low exhausts instead of a siamesed two-into-one high pipe, large chromed headlamp, and a larger fuel tank. Both 38-horsepower twins shared single-carb cylinder heads and energy-transfer (ET) ignition, and had optional chronometric tachometers.

When Johnson Motors received its first TR5A/C in late 1960, they gave it to dealer/racer Bud Ekins for testing in cross-country racing conditions. Ekins liked the bike's steering and handling but complained that it wasn't as responsive as the old pre-unit TR5. Also, the gas tank mounting arrangement caused the tank to bounce around and leak after 20 miles of hard off-road use.

Three years in development, the unit-construction 650cc engine debuted in late 1962 and evolved into a 750 ten years later. *Factory illustration*

Triumph reprised the TR5 nameplate in 1961 with two new sporting 500s—the dual-purpose TR5AC with ET ignition and direct lighting and the TR5AR (shown here) roadster. Neither bike was fitted with a toolbox cover at the factory. *Factory photos/Brooke archive*

Everyone who saw the bike was attracted to its polychromatic Blue paintwork. Overall, it was an excellent effort—"very good commerce," as Bill Johnson liked to say. The TR5As were only offered in 1961, but they set the pattern for Triumph's 500cc "C" and "R" models into the next decade.

As the 1960s dawned, BSA Group began amalgamating the BSA and Triumph marques. This was the start of "groupthink" initiated by Chairman Eric Turner (no relation to Edward). In 1961, he hired international consultants McKinsey and Company to study BSA and Triumph with an eye to streamlining both organizations and their product lines, including distributing both brands under the same corporate banner in the US.

The report also studied the US market as it related to Triumph. Don Brown was given a sabbatical from JoMo in order to complete the US section of the report. The final 1962 document's sales projections for both brands were deemed too pessimistic by BSA's chairman. From that point forward, BSA and Triumph's future sales projections were handled by the Group's accountants instead of those much closer to the real market.

Triumph's two major rivals in the early 1960s were still Harley-Davidson and BSA. The contest with Harley for the "King of the Hill" crown played out across the American landscape. Bonneville versus Sportster was motorcycling's classic rivalry, pitting Milwaukee's hottest hog and its 883cc—54 cubic inches—against the "Trumpet's" 40 ci.

On the drag strip, the Sporty had a slight edge, able to turn high-13sec ETs depending on rider ability and tuning. A stock Bonnie was good for low-14sec in the quarter mile with trap speeds in the 90 to 95 miles-per-hour range, according to contemporary road tests. Not infrequently, however, Triumph versus Harley showdowns resulted in "smoked ham."

The more expensive Harleys presented a minor threat to Triumph sales compared to that posed by BSA. Triumph's internecine battle with Beeza was much closer. In 1959, Hap Alzina's BSA operation outsold Johnson Motors by nearly 100 motorcycles, and the eastern territory war was close as well. BSA was selling 650cc A10 twins everywhere, and dealers were clamoring for more Gold Stars too. Triumph's Sales Departments looked for ways to counterattack.

In the western US, the main difference between Alzina's BSA organization and JoMo's was the number and quality of dealers. BSA had about 250 outlets in the west to JoMo's 150. To narrow BSA's numerical advantage, Brown and JoMo salesman Elden Wright implemented a new plan: the Triumph "service depot." These were mini-shops, located in rural small towns. The typical service depot stocked high-demand parts that were purchased at a 24 percent discount, compared with the regular dealer's 60 percent discount. The depot kept one or two motorcycles on the floor (bought for the regular dealer discount) and displayed a Triumph sign.

"It was hard getting approval from Bill Johnson, and Wilbur Ceder was dead set against it," Brown told the authors. "He thought it was a stupid idea to extend credit to these people." But Brown eventually convinced his bosses that, if the depots sold lots of parts, the depot owners might then want to become full-fledged Triumph dealers.

The concept was a success. In January 1965, JoMo had 202 sales outlets in the nineteen western states—166 full-fledged dealers and fifty-six service depots. About half of the depots had converted to dealerships and many were not renewed as service depots. By the late 1960s, the western US territory included approximately 300 official dealers, nearly matching TriCor's 340 eastern stores.

YOU MEET THE NICEST PEOPLE ON A TRIUMPH

Years before the Japanese entered the market, Triumph's US distributors worked hard to promote motorcycling as a wholesome, clean-cut sport. For most American riders, it was. Triumphs, with their moderate size, easy handling, and innate beauty, opened up the sport to thousands of new buyers who never would have considered the more expensive alternatives—elephantine Harley-Davidsons, stodgy Earles-forked BMWs, or BSAs.

It was Honda's 1959 beachhead, however, that changed American motorcycling. The company entered the US motorcycle market just as the recreational market was about to skyrocket. Their inexpensive, reliable, easy-starting little bikes and the company's $5 million "You Meet the Nicest People" advertising campaign kicked off a phenomenal motorcycle sales boom.

It also helped the business gain a new respectability. "Little kids no longer said, 'Mom, there goes a motorcycle.' They said, 'Mom, there goes a *Honda*,' " recalled Pete Colman, then JoMo's parts manager. Colman said the first Hondas, with their pressed-steel frames, leading-link forks, and awkward styling, were regarded as "kind of a rinky-dink joke" by the motorcycle establishment. But attitudes soon changed after some of the Johnson Motors crew rode down to San Diego one day to check out an early Honda dealer named Saylor Main.

"He was selling Hondas by the truckload," Colman exclaimed, "running his store like a supermarket! He had fifty of one model lined up in a row! Nobody had ever sold motorcycles like that in the US. We were amazed."

It didn't take long for Triumph's US distributors to realize that Honda was going to be an entirely different competitor. Bill Johnson decided it was time to meet them in person. He contacted his former salesman, Jack McCormack (no relation to Denis), who had recently joined the new American Honda Motor Corporation, and asked him to invite Executive Vice President Kiyoshi Kawashima to a meeting at JoMo.

Kawashima was out of town, so sales manager Hirobumi Nakamura came in this place. Nakamura was anxious to visit Johnson Motors. Honda had long considered Triumph's two US distributors and their dealer networks to be the absolute best among motorcycle importers. In fact, Honda directly copied certain concepts used by JoMo and TriCor, including their dealer floor plan and new model warranty. Nakamura met Bill Johnson, Wilbur Ceder, Pete Colman, and Don Brown in Johnson's office.

"After some pleasantries, Bill asked Nakamura how many motorcycles he thought he could sell in the US," recalled Brown. "Nakamura responded, 'Five thousand.'" At the time, JoMo was selling about 2,500 new motorcycles annually in its nineteen-state western territory. Johnson replied that 5,000 bikes per year was "a lot of motorcycles."

But Nakamura raised up in his chair to clarify. "Five thousand per month!" he retorted.

Brown said his boss "turned crimson; he was flabbergasted by Nakamura's confidence." Honda had arrived to play hard ball. Indeed, by 1962 they were outselling the entire industry in the US. Initially, though, the JoMo brass perceived Honda not as a threat, but a boon to Triumph's business. The Japanese, they reckoned, would create future customers for Triumph's (and everyone else's) big bikes.

In retrospect, Triumph's American executives appeared to be naively cutting their own throats. But at the time their thinking was practical. Meriden was not offering them a new,

competitive lightweight. The 200cc Cub was six years old. Besides, they had been assured by Turner that it would be a long time before the Japanese could build larger-capacity machines to compete directly with Triumph.

Turner himself had toured the Honda, Suzuki, and Yamaha factories in 1960 and wrote a report about his trip. At the time, some Japanese plants were building 1,000 lightweight bikes a day, when no British motorcycle manufacturer had ever built 1,000 in a week. Turner noted the "somewhat frightening spectacle" of Japan's production capability. But he continued to believe that, when it came to building large, sporting machines for the true enthusiast, the Japanese would not eclipse the British.

Soon after the meeting with Nakamura, Johnson asked Brown to do a study of Honda's operation. He noticed in particular that they were setting up some top-notch dealerships, many of which had never sold motorcycles before.

At the time, JoMo's dealers were supposed to sell only Triumphs. Most did, with the exception of those who carried another line of scooters, or low-volume bikes like Jawa or Ducati. It was an unwritten, "handshake" policy, meant to avoid violating Federal Trade Commission fair trade laws (as Harley-Davidson had done trying to fight Triumph and the British years before). But two events sparked a drastic change in policy.

The first was when someone filed a complaint with the FTC charging that JoMo was forcing its dealers to handle Triumph exclusively. The feds quickly subpoenaed Johnson's records and sent an examiner to investigate his files. Fortunately, Johnson and Ceder were able to prove that many of their dealers already handled competing brands. The FTC eventually dropped the charge.

Then came another shock: Ed Kretz began selling Hondas.

Kretz, the famous racer, always seemed to be in the vanguard. He had raced Indians when they were the winning ride, then switched to racing and selling Triumphs with his son Ed Jr. Together, they ran one of Triumph's top US dealerships in Monterey Park, California. Now "Iron Man" Kretz was one of the first to add Honda, and it touched off a firestorm at JoMo.

"When we got word that Ed Kretz had taken on Honda," exclaimed Don Brown, "it was like getting a slap in the face!" Kretz's old pal Wilbur Ceder was the first to hear the news and he demanded that Brown "do something about it!"

Brown immediately called a meeting of the Los Angeles–area Triumph dealers, at which time he handed all of them an envelope. It contained a notice stating that, in thirty days, their contract with JoMo would be terminated. He then gave them another envelope that contained non-exclusive Triumph franchise contracts. Brown told them that JoMo needed to be in charge of how many dealers they appointed and where they were located.

They discussed the new sales environment and new challenges facing Triumph. The Japanese brands had entered the US and the overall market was expanding. JoMo needed a

Motorcyclist-actor Keenan Wynn was a Triumph rider long before the rest of Hollywood jumped on the bandwagon. Here Wynn and actress Martha Wyer stop their Thunderbird sidecar rig to chat with drag racer "TV" Tommy Ivo at Pomona Raceway, 1964. All three were there filming *Bikini Beach* with Frankie Avalon and Annette Funicello. *Tommy Ivo*

Folk music icon and 2016 Nobel Prize winner Bob Dylan shows his new scarlet-and-silver 1964 T100S/R Tiger Road Sports to his road manager Victor Maymudes (facing camera) and painter-musician Bob Neuwirth, in Bearsville, New York. Two years later, Dylan's infamous crash on the same machine would change his approach to music, and to life. *John Byrne Cooke*

broader hand in the placement of dealers, Brown explained, so that it didn't get outmaneuvered by other makes. By meeting's end, every dealer present signed the non-exclusive pact. It specified no territory, only stating the particular city that each could deal in.

In 1991, Ed Kretz recalled the incident to the authors. "Boy, they were mad at me up at Johnson's!" laughed the former racing star, then in his eighties. "I'll never forget it. But we kept selling Triumphs and continued making good money selling them." Kretz explained that "Triumphs were much more profitable than Hondas anyway, because we could make a lot more selling parts and service."

Honda's rapid success made it tougher and more expensive to get a Triumph franchise. In fact, it had gotten to where both JoMo and TriCor could pick and choose their prospective dealers. They targeted the larger, better capitalized Honda dealers who were thirsty for a line of larger motorcycles.

Bill Robertson, a former auto insurance adjuster, had started a Honda store in Hollywood and was soon selling

hundreds of the affordable little bikes. Like many dealers, though, he coveted Triumph. Robertson's location was very close to other established Triumph shops, causing them to protest the deal.

Over their objections, Robertson was eventually granted the Triumph franchise and placed his initial order for 125 motorcycles—$100,000 worth of new Triumphs! This was by far the largest single order Johnson Motors had ever received. He went on to become the West Coast's biggest Triumph dealer in sales volume and one of the top five Honda dealers; Triumph TT star Skip Van Leeuwen was Robertson's top salesman. But Robertson's example was atypical. In most places, existing Triumph shops were being approached by Honda's "road men" to take the Japanese franchise. And the Triumph dealers were taking them.

Remarkably, TriCor and JoMo road men encouraged some of their dealers to take on the Japanese machines. Honda signs soon appeared next to Triumph signs at dealerships

Michigan Triumph enthusiast Jeff Wing found this 1964 T120R survivor in dead-nuts original and unmolested condition—and he's keeping it that way. With their heavy flywheels, 8.5:1 compression and long "resonator" silencers, the 1964 Bonnies are great bikes to ride. *Brooke photo*

With a Triumph in the 1960s, it was always time for fun.

across the US, from Free State Cycle in Bladensburg, Maryland, to McLaughlin Motors in Duarte, California. For a few years, Honda's national ad campaign and the tremendous "floor traffic" it generated at the dealer level helped Triumph sell thousands of its larger and more expensive machines. It also sparked trade-ins and trade-ups; by 1965, Honda trades on new Triumph models accounted for 8 percent of JoMo's sales volume—a 75 percent increase over the previous year.

Because Triumph offered nothing in the lightweight class besides the aging Cub, the two companies' model ranges dovetailed nicely. Honda covered everything from 50cc to 305cc and Triumph served the 500cc to 650cc segment. At the time it seemed like a perfect fit. But not every dealer jumped on the Japanese bandwagon.

One day in 1964, TriCor road man Jack Mercer stopped in at Saginaw Cycle, the Triumph store in Saginaw, Michigan. Mercer made a pitch to shop owner Sam Hawley, an old-school businessman and Jack Pine Enduro rider. "Mercer wanted us to take a Honda franchise," Hawley told co-author Brooke. "He figured that Honda would help us expand our business for Triumphs."

Standing with Mercer amidst a row of gleaming Trophy 650s, Hawley imagined his modest showroom full of 50cc and 90cc step-throughs. Then he turned to his brother Don (the shop's mechanic) and said, "You know, Donny, sellin' Hondas would be just like sellin' lawnmowers."

Triumph expanded its own advertising beyond the motorcycle magazines. It followed Honda into other male-oriented, mainstream publications such as *Sports Illustrated*, *Esquire*, *Playboy*, and *Hot Rod*. The ads themselves, as well as Triumph sales literature, became more colorful and lavish.

They featured smiling young collegiates enjoying their Cubs, Trophies, and Bonnies. The company eagerly capitalized on Honda's success while keeping its traditionally loyal customer base. The plan seemed to work—as long as the Japanese built only smaller motorcycles.

THE UNIT 650s ARRIVE

"There is a lot of mental comfort, while passing cars, in knowing that hooking on a big handful of throttle will ram you ahead like something going into orbit," noted *Cycle World* in its inaugural January 1962 road test of that year's Bonneville. The new magazine found the T120R to be "comfortable and unshaken" from 60 to 70 miles per hour. The Bonnie's overall vibration was a "minor point." American motorcycle journalism was mostly uncritical in those days, especially regarding advertisers. But the 1962 Bonnie's vibes were really about par with other large, sporting motorcycles then on the market. Confident handling, powerful brakes, and a lustrous "inch-deep" finish were the test's other plaudits.

Later in 1962, the magazine tested Triumph's T100S/R sports roadster and concluded that the bike was "nice enough and fast enough that we would pay our hard-earned money for it." The short-stroke 500 was deemed "terrifically smooth" (a relative term), but *Cycle World* did muster a veiled criticism. The T100S/R's suspension was "rather spongy by sporting standards" and in need of stiffer springs or heavier fork oil for anything more than medium-fast touring.

For 1963, Triumph launched its unit-construction 650cc engine. Development had begun in 1960 "to meet the threat of a unit BSA," wrote Jack Wickes to Don Brown. Wickes had seen a prototype of the new BSA A50/A65 twin in late 1960—"a very clean, smooth-looking job but with poor porting." He was confident that the upcoming Triumph engine's valve gear "should give us the edge on performance."

The new 650's arrival meant all of Triumph's motorcycles now had an integral engine/gearbox assembly. "Completely New!" shouted the TriCor sales catalog, but the B-range engines were evolutionary, not revolutionary. New cylinder barrels added a ninth fixing bolt between the bores (thus their "nine-stud" nickname) and stiffer crankcases increased overall rigidity while creating a lighter, more compact powerplant. The crankshaft now spun on ball bearings on both main journals and was given a 2.7-pound-lighter flywheel and an 85 percent balance factor (from the previous 71 percent).

Primary drive was now by a $3/8$-inch duplex roller chain, and a new clutch featured a three-vane shock absorber and bonded friction material on the plates.

Both the splayed- and straight-port 650 cylinder heads were redesigned with increased fin area. Compression ratio on the Bonneville roadster and TR6 variants was 8.5:1, while the mild 6T Thunderbird stayed at 7.5:1. New finned rocker boxes employed knurled inspection caps, held tight with spring

JoMo sales manager Don Brown (at right) receives a $100,000 order, for 125 Triumphs, from Hollywood dealer Bill Robertson in 1965. *Brooke archive*

clips for the first time. Camshafts for the Bonnie and TR6 were Triumph's #3134 (the "Q" cam) racing intake and E3325 "sports" exhaust (the "N" cam). The docile T-bird utilized "soft" E4220 cams with the "Silent Ramp" profile.

Just as important as the 650's internal changes was it appearance. Like the C-range 500, the larger engine's various shapes blended organically with the overall lines of the motorcycles. Particularly nice were the stylishly modern primary cover and curvaceous gearbox outer cover, which flowed sensuously into Triumph's lovely timing chest.

A completely new frame carried the unit-construction engine. Triumph had realized the error of its 1960 duplex disaster, even with its 1962 upgrade that reduced the head angle to 65 degrees (from 67 degrees) to help improve high-speed handling. By comparison, the all-new 1963 frame reverted to a single front downtube and top tube, brazed to traditional iron lugs at the swingarm pivot and steering head. The rear twin-loop cradle was bolted on.

The new frame and rebalanced engine eliminated the "tuning fork" tendencies of the duplex item and so transmitted less vibration to the rider. But its high-speed handling did not inspire confidence. To cure the problem, Meriden development engineer Brian Jones first reduced fork spring preload by ¼ inch. New, stouter forks (identified by chromed slider extensions) were introduced in 1964. For the 1966 model year, Jones again

Continued on page 82

Triumph's success in two uniquely American forms of racing—TT Steeplechase and long-distance desert events—prompted Meriden to produce a pair of unique motorcycles aimed at the US market. The Bonneville TT Special (1963 to 1967) and the TR6SC Trophy Special (1961 to 1966) were requested by Johnson Motors. Many owners had stripped down their T120s for TT, scrambles, and Hare and Hound events, and modified TR6s were the desert racer's Holy Grail. So factory-built models were a logical move.

"We had been advocating and negotiating with Meriden for a factory-built TT machine, to be sold by our dealers, for some time," Pete Colman told the authors.

TT events, what they called TT Scrambles back east, had a big following on all levels, from local sportsmen through the AMA championship level. The basis of the bike would be the production Bonneville and Triumph was in agreement. It was a matter of finalizing specifications.

Colman noted that the duplex frame debacle caused the TT Special project to be delayed until the new frame and engine arrived for 1963. Still, there was "a lot of constant urging" from JoMo to keep the factory on track.

Coded T120C TT from 1963 to 1965—the "C" was dropped in 1966 to 1967—the 350-pound TT Special was as businesslike as a sawed-off shotgun. It lacked any semblance of civility, save for a tachometer. When leaned

against a paddock fence, the TT struck a cocky, desperado-like stance. This was Triumph's Billy the Kid, ready to shoot up the town, take no prisoners, then thunder out of sight.

The original machine was armed with 12:1 (E3613) pistons, dual 1³/₁₆-inch Amal Monoblocs, ET ignition, standard Bonneville 4.84:1 gearing, painted steel fenders, and 3.75-gallon fuel tank. Straight, high-level open exhaust pipes, one on each side, came on 1963 to 1964 models; in 1965 these were changed to the classic, downswept-and-tucked-in TT pipes that became the bike's visual signature. Triumph claimed 52–54 horsepower at 6,500 rpm—up to four more horses than a standard Bonneville roadster.

Early production changes included a drop in compression ratio to 11:1 and 5.41:1 gearing. In 1966 came the new slimline 2.5-gallon gas tank, detachable 46-tooth rear sprocket, heavy-duty fork springs, and modified fork dampening. The TT's fenders were painted steel, polished stainless steel, or aluminum, depending on the year. Most serious owner/racers removed the front fender. Retail prices started at $1,158 in 1963 and rose to about $1,300 in 1967.

The official record of Triumph's 1967 US Sales Conference, held at Meriden in November 1966, shows that JoMo ordered 500 TT Specials in the final batch, 400 having already been built earlier that season. TriCor asked for 400 but received half that many, according to UK TT special researcher Charles Rising. The Californians made a special request that 300 units be fitted with the steeper (65-degree) 1965-type

Rarest of the TT Specials are 1963 models, most of which were not fitted with air filters. *Brooke photo*

1964 TT shows black-painted air filter canister that arrived late in '63. *Brooke photo*

Thunder Road: TT Specials from all five years of production displayed by Kentucky collector HC Morris. *Brooke photo*

steering head, preferred by many top racers, including Eddie Mulder.

Evidence shows that at least some of these 1965-type frames arrived on 1967 TT Specials. The 1965-type frame also was specified for the 1968 TT Special before it was cancelled. According to TriCor memos, the '68 bike was slated to have a center-mount racing oil tank and aluminum wheel rims. The model was likely killed due to demand for the more profitable T120R roadster.

Like the TT Special, the TR6SC Trophy Special is also prized by collectors today. Few were built, most went to JoMo, and the majority were modified and ridden hard. Priced at around $1,200 in 1965, the single-carb SC was designed as a factory Desert Sled. JoMo wanted to cash in on the Sled phenomenon, so Meriden basically sent them a stripped TR6. Modifications were minimal: long, straight, open exhausts on each side (both pipes were moved to the left side in 1966), 5.41:1 gearing and Dunlop

Sports Knobby tires. There wasn't even a standard tachometer, but the SC came with a center stand and tank-top parcel grid.

Cycle World tested both Specials, an early TT in 1963 and an SC in 1965. Curiously, the magazine kept the TT on the pavement for speed tests only. At Riverside Raceway, technical editor Gordon Jennings achieved a best velocity of 123.5 miles per hour with little more than main jet changes and factory reverse-cone megaphones. Five other runs were over 120 miles per hour—stunning top-end velocities compared with a stock Bonnie. At the drag strip, the TT clicked off a 13.3-second blast at 100 miles per hour, on 5.68:1 gearing, before the test machine was handed over to the magazine for a full teardown. Jennings later modified the same bike for a successful record session at the Bonneville Salt Flats.

The test TR6SC was properly flogged for 600 miles in the desert. "It's such fantastic fun to ride," reported the editors, "with more hair on its chest than King Kong."

MOTOR CITY SCALLOPS

In early 1960s Detroit, if your custom motorcycle was good enough to be included in the prestigious Autorama car and bike show, chances were good it was painted by William "Wild Bill" Betz. A third-generation sign painter and pinstriper, Betz started doing custom paintwork for bikes after his navy discharge in 1959. He carried a painter's toolbox on the back of his new Tiger 110. At the 1962 Autorama, twenty-two show bikes wore his handiwork. Triumph-Detroit owner Bob Leppan then enlisted Betz to paint some customer tanks, fenders, and side covers.

"The Detroit area was full of talented automobile painters, but on the bike side there weren't many guys who could both paint and pinstripe," Betz recalled.

I was playing with different tank designs and one that became popular was the two-color scallop. Not just on Triumphs—I painted scallops on Harley tanks, too, along with flame jobs and panels. But Leppan and his customers really liked the scallops. He would give me five or six gas tanks at a time to paint.

By 1966, Triumph-Detroit's showroom typically included new bikes wearing tank scallops in bright, non-standard colors. At the TriCor service school meeting that year,

Leppan and other dealers complained about the '66 Bonneville's bland tank livery, which was entirely white when viewed in profile. "Bob told the Triumph people that he had a painter in Detroit whose work they should see," Betz recalled. Soon after, TriCor sales manager Ed Nemec visited Leppan's store and was intrigued by how natural the custom-scallop tanks looked.

Back in Baltimore, Nemec sent Leppan a batch of twenty new, primered gas tanks for Betz to paint and return. TriCor then shipped these eye-popping "experimental" tanks to Jack Wickes at Meriden for evaluation. Wickes was sold. He approved the first scallop paint scheme to enter Triumph production, on the Bonneville during early 1969 production. The design instantly became a Triumph hallmark. It was applied to many models and has been imitated on dozens of Japanese motorcycles through the years.

In 1972, Triumph's US management flew Betz and Craig Vetter to Britain for a week to help influence new design and styling directions for future models. "At Meriden we reviewed various tanks that I'd sent them recently, all with different paint schemes," Betz said. "But the Triumph guys kept coming back to the classic scallop jobs."

"Wild Bill" Betz with a Hinckley Bonneville tank he custom-painted with the iconic "scallops" in 2009. *Brooke photo*

Continued from page 79

relaxed the steering head angle to 62 degrees and cut the top tube by one inch, which dropped the engine down one-half inch. Triumph's forks gained two-way "shuttle valve" damping in 1968, the same year the 650 frame received a beefier swingarm. All combined, these improvements over five model years finally created a motorcycle with first-class handling.

The advent of the "unit" 650 carried on the street-scrambler version of the Bonneville begun with the 1960 TR7/B. This was the T120C Competition Sports—essentially the T120R fitted with high exhaust on each side, a small skid plate, and slightly lower gearing, while retaining the roadster's full street equipment. According to UK-based enthusiast Charles Rising, whose thorough research and analysis into Triumph's "American Competition Specials" and their production has brought new insights, only 198 examples of the T120C Competition Sports were built during 1963 to 1965. All but four of them (two each going to Canada and Mexico) were dispatched to TriCor. Models from 1963 are stamped "T120," the "C" being added in 1964.

The new 650cc engine finally eliminated the magneto from Triumph's model range. A new coil ignition used a dual-points set driven off the end of the exhaust camshaft. The 1963 500s, however, were sparked by three different ignition systems! The Tiger 100 S/R roadster adopted the 650-type battery/coil ignition. The T100S/C Competition had ET ignition with dual points and direct lighting (T20S/R and T20S/C Cubs also used the often-troublesome ET). And the 5TA Speed Twin kept its ignition distributor for another year.

THE 'AMERICAN' TRIUMPHS

As they watched the American motorcycle market grow in the early 1960s, some US Triumph personnel and dealers felt that the factory still hadn't responded to what buyers wanted and needed on the motorcycles. At the same time, Meriden was moving to simplify production and pressed TriCor and JoMo to narrow the differences between East and West Coast models.

"It was very hard to get Triumph to change even the smallest things," said Brown. Texas dealer/tuner Jack Wilson added that "the British wanted the sales over here, but they usually didn't want our input." Wilson said that, during his visit to Meriden in 1956 with the Johnny Allen streamliner, Turner had asserted, "Tell me how to sell more motorcycles—but don't tell me how to make them go faster."

The American distributors inquired about possible new features, such as five-speed gearboxes and electric starters, because these features were appearing on the smaller Japanese machines. Meriden's response was that such features weren't needed. Triumph revealed a prototype electric-starter-equipped Speed Twin at the 1960 Earls Court Show, but it was aimed at British police bikes only.

US input on simple things like new paint colors was often disregarded by Meriden supremo Turner, although Wickes, his design chief, was sympathetic to the American market's needs—particularly those of trendsetting California. For one of Brown's early 1960s visits to Meriden, Wickes had the factory's paint shop spray six or seven Triumphs in bright, two-tone color schemes—"California colors," Wickes called them. He said Brown could pick three.

Brown liked what he saw, sensing a "hit" for US dealers. Unfortunately, none of the paint jobs had been okayed by Turner, and the sharp new colors were declined. One of Triumph's most popular, distinctive styling cues was born in the USA, however (see sidebar).

Another "American" Triumph was the T20M Mountain Cub. It was the brainchild of two Triumph dealers and JoMo sales manager Don Brown, who hit upon the idea during a motorcycle camping trip in late 1963. After a day of trail riding on knobby-tired Tiger Cubs, the trio were sitting around the campfire talking about what they'd seen that day—a lot of riders on Honda Trail 90s. "But we noticed that once those Honda 90s got off the regular dirt roads, they couldn't climb the steep trails," Brown said.

A new type of customer was buying lightweight trail bikes for hunting, fishing, and camping. Brown and the dealers surmised that if Triumph's high-piped 15-horsepower Sports Cub was fitted with a wide-ratio gearbox, they'd have a nice trail bike. It would climb steeper hills and be faster

T20M Mountain Cubs were popular trail bikes from 1965 to 1967 and are prized by collectors today. *Brooke photo*

A BSA thumper by any other name . . . is a Triumph. The TR25W Trophy 250 was plagued with engine-quality issues that marred an otherwise robust motorcycle. *Cycle World* called it "slow but friendly." *Brooke photo*

By 1968, the great "desert sled" era had ended in the west and the handsome high-piped Trophy 650 was now the "king of the street scramblers." *Gaylin photo*

on the flats than the Hondas. Triumph/Honda dealers would immediately see the advantage over the Trail 90. Potentially, it could be a hot seller.

Triumph's TR20 Trials Cub gearbox seemed to fit the bill perfectly. It featured low-ratio and closely spaced first and second gears, then a wide jump to third and fourth, which also were closely spaced. Brown asked one of the dealers, Joe Sarkes, to build a prototype and send him photographs.

Shortly thereafter, during one of his regular visits to JoMo, Turner told Brown that he planned to discontinue the Cub range for the US. In fact, the production line was being moved to BSA's Small Heath plant, and the Cub engine was scheduled to be mongrelized with the BSA Bantam frame. To prevent losing his new trail bike in the shuffle, Brown sold Turner on the idea based on an initial order of 400 motorcycles.

Brown named them Mountain Cubs, mating the best parts of the Tiger Cub range, including the wide-ratio gearbox, a meaty 4.00x18-inch Dunlop Trials Universal rear tire, and 7.5 inches of ground clearance. The Mountain Cub resurrected Triumph's 200cc thumper in the US market. First cataloged by JoMo in 1964 as the T20SM (T20M in 1966 to 1967), it was an unqualified success.

"We sold every one we could get," said Brown, "and could've sold twice as many." To further popularize the Mountain Cub among outdoors people, JoMo offered many bolt-on goodies, including a fork-mounted rifle rack. There was even a ski conversion available (see Appendix). *Cycle World* tested a $650 Mountain Cub in July 1964 and declared it the trail bike they'd been asking for, "a real motorcycle, slightly undersized, properly equipped and geared." In 1966, the T20M engine added a square-barrel cylinder, roller-bearing connecting rod, and a larger-capacity oil pump. With Grenadier Red/Alaskan White paint colors shared by the 1966 Bonneville, the Cub remained in the lineup through 1967.

MANAGEMENT CHANGES AND THE BEEZA BUYOUT

Along with the revolution in the US motorcycle market came a changing of the guard at Triumph, both in the US and Britain. JoMo founder Bill Johnson died from a heart attack in March 1962, just hours before Don Burnett won Triumph's first Daytona 200. Wilbur Ceder assumed the western distributor's helm. In 1964, Denis McCormack retired from the Triumph Corporation after fourteen years as president and general manager.

Across the pond, Edward Turner—"Mr. Triumph" himself—retired as Triumph's boss and BSA Automotive Group managing director in 1964, but he stayed on as a BSA board director for another three years. Replacing him was the aggressive Harry Sturgeon, who also became absentee president of TriCor. Sturgeon and Turner toured the US in September 1964, personally meeting the employees of the eastern and western distributors. TriCor executive Earl Miller found Sturgeon to be "sales-oriented in a more vigorous way than Ed Turner."

On January 30, 1965, the BSA Group, which had slowly been consolidating BSA and Triumph operations in Britain, finally purchased controlling interest in Johnson Motors Inc. Now, both of Triumph's American distributors were factory owned, ultimately by BSA. For US Triumph dealers and many enthusiasts, it was an unpopular move, something that Don Brown and others had expected ever since the McKinsey Report was released three years earlier.

Soon after the consolidation, JoMo acquired the Western BSA distribution company of Hap Alzina and the directors agreed to change the name to BSA Motorcycles-Western Inc. Ceder was appointed president of the new BSA organization. Pete Colman, who had been JoMo's assistant general manager and parts manager, was made vice president and general manager of BSA Western, responsible for sales and marketing in the nineteen western states. For the first time since he'd joined JoMo in 1948, Triumph veteran Colman had to wear two hats.

"It was difficult for me," he recalled, "because motorcycles are a very personal thing. The British didn't understand it, because in England there was not outright hatred between the BSA and Triumph brands like there was here." Perhaps the British animosity wasn't as fierce as in the US, but a popular Meriden remark—"The only thing good coming out of Birmingham is the Coventry Road!"—indicates that, below the surface, rivals Triumph and BSA were not the friendliest of mates.

While all this was happening, Honda launched its first "large" motorcycle, the homely, but advanced, 450cc DOHC twin, in the US market. In March 1965, Brown submitted a confidential five-page report on the Honda to Harry Sturgeon. He had ridden an early 450 (which Honda almost named Condor), and he asked many Triumph-Honda dealers who had also ridden the bike for their impressions. One commented, "Here at last is a big bike that does not leak oil anywhere." Another dealer praised the Honda's electric starter. Rumor spread that Honda would enlarge the engine to 650cc.

"On the surface it would appear that we are now badly outclassed with the present 500 Triumph and BSA," summarized the report. "Now, really for the first time, we have serious competition for the big bike market."

The BSA-Triumph merger was consummated in 1966 when Johnson Motors completed its move from the old Pasadena headquarters to a new 60,000-square-foot BSA-Triumph Western Distribution Center in Duarte, California. JoMo was then doing about $10 million in annual sales volume. Triumph occupied one side of the modern facility and BSA the other. Inside the building the old rivalries continued, but many of the former Alzina and JoMo people grudgingly tried to get along as new partners.

Pat Owens, then JoMo's assistant service manager and Triumph stalwart, recalled one BSA fellow's credo: "Triumph's official color is blue, and BSA's is red. Blue and red make green—that's money!"

Ceder had occupied the new building only briefly before he died of a heart attack in May 1966. Sturgeon stepped in to succeed him and preside over BSA-Triumph's western US operations from Britain, as he did with TriCor. In the east, the Triumph Corporation remained in Towson (Baltimore) while BSA kept its Nutley, New Jersey, headquarters. To most of Triumph's US dealers, joining forces with BSA was unpalatable. A deeply proud lot, they saw Triumphs as a superior product with a stronger reputation among motorcyclists—both objectively true by 1966. So, it was understandable that they'd react mutinously when, in 1966, Sturgeon announced that US Triumph dealers would also have to sell BSA, and BSA dealers would likewise be expected to sell Triumphs. It caused a near-revolt within Triumph's US operations.

Triumph's new shuttle-valve fork dampeners introduced across the model range in 1968 further improved the ride quality and road holding of the agile, twin-carb T100R Daytona. *Brooke photo*

One Friday afternoon soon after the announcement, John Nelson was at the factory when he received a telephone call from Sturgeon. The boss ordered his popular service manager to fly to California immediately on a mission to solve a major problem that had erupted. "Do what you have to do," Sturgeon told him, giving him no other details.

When he arrived at Duarte on Sunday morning, Nelson faced a prickly scene. Dealers and some of the company staff were threatening to quit rather than sell BSAs, Nelson recalled in a *Classic Bike* interview. "Meriden was making 600 or 700 bikes a week, and 80 percent of the production was exported to the States," he noted. "This meant we had a lot of bikes in stock out there and nobody to sell them." Nelson and Colman then traversed the US for the next three weeks, promising Triumph dealers that they couldn't be force-fed BSAs. Most were persuaded to stay with their favorite marque.

When Big D Cycle's Jack Wilson remembered the infamous event, his usually jovial voice suddenly turned serious. "Pete Colman asked me what I thought about Triumph dealers selling BSAs, and BSA dealers selling Triumphs," recalled Wilson in 1991. "I told him it's a great deal for the BSA dealers . . . but it's like offering Triumph dealers 'the clap.'"

MODEL	TRIUMPH CORP	JOHNSON MOTORS
T120R	8,800	2,100
TR6R	3,900	1,600
TR6C	700	2,100
T120TT	400	500
T100R	2,000	1,300
T100C	1,400	1,200
T20M	1,000	1,700

By 1969, the Meriden factory was working flat-out to keep pace with booming demand for new Triumphs. On a factory tour, Detroit dealer and speed king Bob Leppan snapped this photo of US-spec '69 Bonnevilles on the final assembly track. The single-scallop paint schemes were the second of three tank graphics that season. *Bob Leppan*

THE BOOM YEARS

At the time of the BSA merger, the US motorcycle market was running at full throttle, kick-started by the Japanese and revved up by a healthy economy. Fewer than 60,000 new motorcycles of all makes had been sold in the US in 1960; by 1965, a total of 609,000 new motorcycles, scooters, and mopeds had been imported—an increase of over 900 percent in five years! Japan brought in 465,0000 bikes in 1965, followed by the Italians with 69,974. Most of the machines from both countries were 250cc or smaller.

The British imported 33,406 motorcycles to the US in 1965, mainly 500cc to 650cc Triumphs and BSAs. Their average value ($538) was over twice that of the Japanese bikes ($205) and about three times more than the Italians' ($182).

Triumph rode the crest of this tidal wave of motorcycle mania. In 1963, the company sold 6,300 new motorcycles nationwide; by 1967, the official order programmed for the US had quadrupled to 28,700—a total of 18,200 bikes for the eastern states and 10,500 for the west. The 1967 model order list, by distributor, was as follows:

Note the overwhelming demand for the T120R Bonneville in the eastern states, and the continued steady popularity of the high-piped TR6C in the west.

The Triumph Engineering Co. had kept its balance sheet solidly in the black since the beginning of the Turner era. Average annual profits after taxes were around £644,000 from 1950 to 1969—about $2.5 million per year, depending on exchange rates. Overall returns hit an all-time high in the late 1960s; the BSA-Triumph Group's record exports earned it the coveted Queen's Award. Thanks to the apparently insatiable American market, motorcycles had become the United Kingdom's third leading export in dollar terms behind Scotch whiskey and automobiles.

Despite the deepening Vietnam War, which pulled thousands of potential Triumph customers into the US military, TriCor and JoMo together planned a "conservative" 1968 order of 35,000 new bikes, although the actual number imported that year was considerably less. The Meriden factory was nearing its production limits and demand (particularly in the US) was far outstripping capacity. Of the 37,721 British machines imported into the States in 1969, the majority were Triumphs. But US dealers quickly sold out their allotments and shouted to their distributors for more.

Triumph was unprepared to meet the ever-steeper volume demands of the expanding, sophisticated US motorcycle market in the 1960s. By comparison, the 1950s' steady, predictable sales had been ideal for Meriden. During his tenure, Edward Turner preferred to set production at or below his "ideal" level of about 360 bikes per week, never exceeding 20,000 in a year. This kept quality high and appetites whetted.

By 1969, though, Meriden was working flat-out, building 900 machines per week; this caused quality to vary wildly. British bike and car manufacturers never mastered the high-volume/high-quality equation of the Japanese, which Turner had seen for himself during his extensive 1960 tour of Japan. Along with its BSA parent, Triumph also lacked a future product strategy to keep it competitive.

The British ceded the huge market below 500cc to the Japanese. When Mountain Cub production ended in summer 1967, a badge-engineered BSA 250 (the TR25W Trophy) became Triumph's sole "lightweight" offering. American dealers who were "dualed" with Japanese brands realized that Meriden was not changing with the times.

"[Edward] Turner would come over to our Baltimore dealer meetings and talk about 'our little factory in England,'" Ed Fisher, a Triumph-Honda-Yamaha dealer in Parkesburg, Pennsylvania, told the authors. "That was one of the problems. When you're making motorcycles for world-wide distribution, you've got to be able to keep up in every way. [Triumph] stopped doing that."

Still, in the 1960s a Triumph twin was, as writer Peter Egan keenly described it in a *Cycle World* feature, "just about the coolest, meanest, neatest thing a person could own." Egan noted that the Bonneville had become "a cultural icon . . . as much a part of the American scene as James Dean, '51 Mercs and Lucky Strikes." Triumph's classic attributes, which had won the marque so many friends, were as strong as ever. But the machines continued to be nagged by details that Triumph could have fixed.

The aura of owning "the world's best motorcycle" (as the dealer signs declared) was dulled, for example, when the bike left an embarrassing puddle of oil everywhere it was parked, piddled gasoline from its petcocks and carburetor, vibrated its bracketry to bits, and blew out its light bulbs. The Japanese were teaching the world that these headaches needn't be part of motorcycle ownership, though Honda and the others had technical issues of their own. British bike problems were becoming motorcycling's standard joke, and Triumph and its suppliers were delinquent in correcting them.

The Triumph Corporation's Earl Miller echoed this point to co-author Gaylin. He said his company's warranty costs rose steadily through the 1960s instead of declining, despite constant refinements to all three model ranges. Miller was especially frustrated by the lack of attention to the perennial oil leaks. TriCor Service Manager Rod Coates often requested visits to the assembly line during his trips to the factory in attempts to pinpoint the root cause of customer issues in the field. Coates's direct, straightforward style made few friends among the conservative British, as various memos obtained by the authors attest.

In the mid-1960s, Triumph's brief use of German-made Siba ignition coils also caused a rash of warranty claims. "The heat would melt them," said Big D Cycle's Jack Wilson. "But the British tried to tell us that we were the only ones having this problem."

AMERICA'S "UNREALISTIC DEMANDS"

Record sales lulled Meriden and its BSA overlord into false security while their manufacturing base remained dangerously nearsighted. The two brands had fallen into the dark hole, chasing the short-term profits that UK shareholders demanded. There were scattershot efforts to take a longer view in both new product development and plant expansion, but these—BSA's new computerized assembly line intended to increase productivity at Small Heath, and the Umberslade Hall R&D center—became white elephants.

The free-spending Peter Thornton at Daytona in March 1970, about a year after being hired as president of the BSA-Triumph combine in the US. *George Hack*

BSA's leaders also began to lose touch with their customers—a far graver mistake. "Lovers of a marque run on high percentages of passion and don't disguise it," wrote *Cycle*'s Phil Schilling in 1970. That passion, an intangible to BSA executives, was what kept Triumph's US dealer body and customers so loyal to the brand, year after year.

BSA Group Chairman Eric Turner, who took command in 1961, was neither a career motorcycle industry man nor a motorcyclist. Nor were Harry Sturgeon or Lionel Jofeh, who became managing director in 1967 after Sturgeon's untimely death. These men had come to BSA Group from outside the motorcycle world; Jofeh was from Sperry's Aerospace division. Their professional backgrounds, however, should not be blamed for dragging Triumph and BSA to doom, as some critics later charged. Proving the point, Harley-Davidson's remarkable turnaround in the 1980s was led by a former diesel engine company executive and a management team made up primarily of non-motorcycle people. But the difference between Harley in the early 1980s and BSA Group in the late 1960s was that Harley never forgot who bought their motorcycles and what those machines meant to them.

Eric Turner and Jofeh openly declared motorcycles to be "consumer durables" while Jofeh blatantly favored BSA. "He literally hated Triumph's success," noted Doug Hele in Steve Wilson's book, *British Motorcycles Since 1950, Volume 5*, "and seemed quite determined to make Triumph the underdog."

CALM BEFORE THE STORM

While its foundation was cracking, Triumph remained a coveted brand. The US dealer body had grown to over 600 stores in 1967, the same year a new roadster inspired by Buddy Elmore's Daytona winner arrived. The T100R Daytona Super Sports was Triumph's first twin-carburetor 500 since the pre-unit TR5AD. It looked like a smaller Bonneville and bristled with features developed in Meriden's race shop.

A new cylinder head with significantly greater airflow was the big news on the Daytona. The head feature dramatically re-angled valves—39-degree included angles, versus 45 degrees on the standard T100. Intake valve diameters were increased to $1^{17}/_{32}$ inches. Straight intake ports, an advantage the unit-construction 500 always enjoyed over the 650 Bonneville, mounted twin $1^{1}/_{8}$-inch Amal Monoblocs on short stubs. Q profile (E3134) cams were now fitted on both the exhaust and intake sides, along with Triumph's R-radius tappets. All of these "Buddy-proven" changes resulted in a claimed 41 horsepower at 7,200 rpm.

The Daytona's steering head angle was relaxed from 65 degrees to 62 degrees, following experience on Triumph's 650cc models and a stiffened swingarm pivoted on extra-rigid braces. The new frame was stronger and 2 pounds lighter, with a half-inch lower seat height.

In a February 1967 road test, *Cycle World* called the new T100R "a superb handling roadster" with a perfect gearbox. The engine's race-bred top end created a "Jekyll-and-Hyde" personality: it was pleasant burbling around town, but above 4,500 rpm the Q-cams really came alive. "It's difficult to muster enough discipline to make gear changes at anything less than 6,000 rpm," beamed the testers. The Daytona turned a 14.9-second quarter mile at 90 miles per hour; top speed was an indicated 105 miles per hour in stock trim.

Triumph was at its absolute peak in the US during 1967 to 1970, and everything the marque stood for—excitement, race victories, versatility, and downright coolness—was exemplified by the T120R Bonneville. Among all the lovely late-1960s Triumph twins, the Bonnie was by far the most coveted—a lean racehorse, equally adept at humbling Corvettes in stoplight drags or cantering along a country road. It looked athletic just resting on the sidestand, twin Amals jutting from each side.

"It provoked a bad case of 'XKE Syndrome'—impossible to park and walk away from without looking back over your shoulder," wrote *Cycle World*'s Egan in "Down the Road Again," his eloquent tribute to the Triumph twin published in 1980. He remarked that his 1967 T120R was "a simple, clean design, with all its elements in harmony. I never looked at it and thought,

Two of the quickest and most desirable means of personal transportation in the late 1960s. The restored 1969 T120R shows its late-season twin-scallop tank livery and dual "windtone" horns under the front of the tank. *Jay Asquini*

'Nice bike, except for the gas tank,' or 'I'd buy one if I could throw the seat and mufflers away.' "

As Egan observed, there wasn't an incongruent line anywhere on the bike: "It seemed, like the DC-3 or the Winchester saddle gun, to be the final product and distillation of everything learned about balance and proportion in the era that preceded it." Indeed, the Triumph twin had evolved smoothly and logically into the purest expression of Edward Turner's 1938 art.

The machines themselves were buoyed by a cooperative US market, which had begun to stabilize after such explosive growth during 1960 to 1965. Motorcycling had finally stopped being a fad. The US was so saturated with small Japanese bikes by spring 1966 that most of the 652,000 machines imported that season were actually sold through 1968.

From 1967 to 1969, only about 30 percent of new bikes in the US were sold to beginners; the brunt of sales were trade-ups to larger machines including 500s and 650s—Triumph's cup of tea.

Meanwhile, Triumph's old nemesis and new "partner" suffered chronic quality trouble. Faulty ignition dwell on 1966 BSA 650s caused widespread overheating and piston seizures. On some Beeza engines, valves were nicking pistons at high rpm. Word of these problems spread fast, despite BSA's fast corrective actions. Dealers were saddled with unsold 1966 bikes well into the next season. Two years later, a disaster: 4,000 BSA twins bound for the US were damaged by salt en route. It was also discovered that the factory had shipped them with parts missing and seats that didn't fit. All 4,000 bikes were shipped back to the BSA factory for "remanufacture" and, according to Don Brown, the full cost to return them was charged to BSA Inc.

Former dealers told the authors that the company was paying an average $800 in US warranty for every A65 sold. "Back then, a smart BSA dealer would fix the bikes before they sold them, in order to make it through warranty before the bike broke at about 2,000 miles," quipped Triumph of Wellesley's John Healy. But he admitted that rising warranty costs were taking a toll on his business too.

Triumph basked in the changing market and BSAs misfortunes . . . until the CB750 Honda debuted in early 1969.

PROTOTYPE TRIPLES TESTING IN THE US

Eight years before Honda's Four was introduced in the US, Triumph's general manager had already planned his company's three-cylinder superbike. Bert Hopwood conceived the 750cc triple in late 1961. By October 1962, chief development engineer Doug Hele completed drawings for the triple's 120-degree crankshaft. "Back-burner" development continued until 1964, when the rumor of a 750cc Honda was dropped like a bombshell during a BSA Group senior executive meeting. The Honda news did not mention how many cylinders, but the threat sparked Harry Sturgeon to immediately greenlight Hopwood's three-cylinder project. From that moment on, the still-secret triple became a priority. Within twelve months, the first running engine was on the factory dyno.

Triumph-Detroit owner Bob Leppan visited Meriden in 1969 and was given a 750cc Trident to tour England and visit the Isle of Man TT. The triple engines were manufactured at BSA's Birmingham works and trucked to Triumph. *Bob Leppan*

The overhead-valve three-cylinder powerplant was hardly wider than the 650 twin, but it weighed 40 pounds more; the prototype had cast-iron cylinder barrels, swapped for aluminum alloy in production. Installed in a slightly modified 1965 Bonneville chassis for testing, the original Three looked like a proper Triumph and performed even better. With a claimed 58 horsepower on tap, factory testers saw top speeds above 120 miles per hour on the P2 prototype. According to Hele, the bike could have entered production in this form by 1966. But many months went by and "the new regime," as he referred to the Sturgeon-Jofeh period, had other ideas for their new flagship.

Because the new 750 was intended for both the BSA and Triumph brands, its styling was handed to Ogle, a British industrial design firm whose broad portfolio included Reliant cars, kitchen toasters, and refuse trucks. Ogle was charged with delivering a bold new style, and Triumph's senior designer, Jack Wickes, was not asked to participate. The lithe, organic Bonneville "look" of the P2 prototype was deemed too traditional. Instead, a more "contemporary" theme was chosen—rectangular fuel tank, flat side panels, and boxy mufflers with three outlets that resembled "ray guns" from an old Flash Gordon sci-fi movie.

Ogle's design direction was an extreme departure for Triumph. Top management's approval of the final mockups proved to be the kiss of death when the bike was finally launched in the US. To many American riders, the new triples looked odd and in some ways as garish as a 1959 Buick.

Cycle World teased that those slab-sided "TriPak" mufflers "would look more at home peeking from beneath the skirts of a motor scooter." Appearance aside, the ray guns performed efficiently. Their shape was retained "because it had sufficient volume to accommodate the very successful reverse-flow

Another forty crates containing new Triumphs arrive by flatbed at Triumph-Detroit in early 1969. *Bob Leppan*

element that we had made sure was inside it," Doug Hele explained to co-author Brooke. "Furthermore, the sound at the time seemed very acceptable and the performance good."

Indeed, the ray guns proved effective on many successful production-racing Tridents, including those that Jack Wilson prepared for Big D's Rusty Bradley and Virgil Davenport. In Britain, Les Williams's famous Slippery Sam won five consecutive Isle of Man Production TTs from 1971 to 1975, using the spaceship exhaust in each race.

Hele shepherded the Trident through its various prototype stages, including secret testing in Southern California. In October 1967, he brought two unmarked Tridents, two BSA Rocket 3s, and a small team of factory mechanics to Pete Colman's home in Claremont. From this top-secret "base," the bikes were ridden by JoMo service technicians up into the region's fast, twisty mountain roads, across hot Mojave Desert highways, and even into Mexico. Hele and his men followed in a car, collecting data. TriCor's Rod Coates and Ed Nemec flew out from Baltimore to ride the bikes during the three-week testing.

"My neighbors were wondering what was going on," recalled Colman. "It was all done in the daytime! We put about 2,000 miles on the triples altogether and were impressed by their performance—smooth and fast."

While they were in the US, the prototypes were also shown to key Triumph and BSA sales personnel. According to Hele, everyone liked the triples' acceleration, handling, and turbine-like smoothness—but not their stodgy appearance. "Much of the early Ogle styling was removed before production in 1968," he said, "but the machines never quite got back to the simple motorcycle that the Americans asked for." Five years after development began, the production plan called for both the BSA

and Triumph engines to be manufactured at BSA's Armory Road factory in Birmingham, where the Rocket 3 was assembled. Trident engines were trucked into Meriden for final assembly.

"BEAUTY KITS" SAVE THE TRIDENT

The Trident's debut was rumored many times in the world's motorcycle press between 1966 and 1968. While Triumph saved the "World's First Test" for the Americans, *Cycle World*'s October 1968 cover story mustered little real praise, other than calling it, "a big, fast groundshaker of a motorcycle." In fact, much of the road test of motorcycling's first modern multicylinder roadster was negative.

Low-speed handling was deemed "cumbersome" compared with the much lighter 650 Bonneville, and the front 8-inch drum brake came under hard criticism. The twin-leading shoe binder, while excellent on the 500cc Daytona and sufficient on the 650cc twins, was found to be inadequate for the speedy, 499-pound Trident. Along with the lack of an electric starter, the drum front brake was the triple's greatest feature flaw when rated against the electric-start, disc-braked Honda Four that was introduced two months later. The T150 didn't get a front disc until 1973.

And that first test machine was smeared by oil leaks. Why, asked *Cycle World*, was the new engine designed with even more vertical case joints than Triumph's twins? The answer was because BSA managers didn't want to invest capital on engineering and new tooling to manufacture horizontally split crankcases, explained journalist Mick Duckworth in his deeply researched 1997 book, *Triumph and BSA Triples—The Complete Story of the Trident and Rocket 3*.

The Trident nonetheless proved itself to be a stable and roomy two-up machine. It was also exhilaratingly fast, as quick as anything on two wheels. Its howling exhaust note was exotic music to enthusiasts. But these attributes weren't enough to offset the weird styling, the unloved Aquamarine paint, and the steep price tag. At $1,750, the Trident was one of 1969's most expensive motorcycles, retailing for about $300 more than the more comprehensively equipped Honda. The BSA-made engines were complex to manufacture and time-consuming to assemble properly and service.

As long as the T150 wore its funny clothes, Triumph had a difficult time selling the bike. Bob Leppan, whose Detroit dealership was among the nation's largest in sales volume, accumulated over 100 early Tridents in his warehouse. He'd purchased many of them from frustrated California dealers who couldn't sell them. Big D Cycle in Dallas, Texas, "couldn't give those 1969 Tridents away, they were so ugly," recalled Jack Wilson.

Leppan, Wilson, and dozens of Triumph dealers found an easy cure for the "Ogle blues." They stripped the breadbox tank, ray-gun mufflers, and clunky fiberglass side covers off of showroom bikes and upgraded them with a custom-painted TR6 or Bonneville tank, chrome fenders, and Bonneville mufflers using brackets they fabricated themselves. When Leppan sold his "Detroit Tridents," he included the original sheet metal parts with the bike. Wilson, however, admitted to the authors that he pounded thirty brand-new 1969 Trident tanks flat with a sledgehammer.

Strong buyer resistance to the Ogle styling pushed Triumph to introduce the Trident "beauty kit" early in the 1970 season. It was available to American dealers who wanted to transform the gawky 1969 and early 1970 triples into "real Triumphs." The kit consisted of a 3½-gallon tank, simpler black side covers, and the long-barreled, resonator-type mufflers used on some earlier Triumph and BSA 650s. Also included were exposed-spring rear dampers, chromed front fender stays, fenders painted to match the tank, a new seat, and passenger grab rail. Meriden incorporated these parts into the remainder of its 1970 production run.

The kit's tank and fenders were painted in the year's TR6 color—the greenish Spring Gold—with black Bonneville-style tank scallops and fender stripes, pinstriped in gold.

"I loved the Trident. We sold about 25 a year," recalled John Healy, owner of Triumph of Wellesley, in the Boston area. "The first 1969 model we got, I immediately pulled the engine, took it all apart and laid it out on the bench. I hadn't yet been to a service school for the triple and wanted to see inside. My sales manager could have killed me for taking a new bike out of stock, but it was a good thing I did."

The crankcase was full of casting sand. Healy telephoned TriCor and was told that similar reports were flooding in on this and other issues. Tom Gunn, an engineering co-op student at TriCor, was keeping record of the growing list of

design, machining, and assembly faults on the early Tridents. Hundreds of engines were involved, he told the author. One of Gunn's jobs was to take bikes out of crates, disassemble the engines, and rebuild them.

"Besides the usual seized pistons from water collecting in the main jet when the bike was ridden in the rain, I had twenty or so motors which would wear the center pressed-steel spline out of the clutch plate in less than 700 miles," Healy noted. "The transmission mainshaft was 100 thousandths [0.100 inch] out of line from the primary chain and the clutch was acting like a universal joint. They were ripping themselves apart."

Feedback from the Baltimore and Duarte Service Departments led to over 100 engineering changes aimed at rectifying the early triples' teething problems. Given regular owner maintenance—one Duarte mechanic clocked up over 100,000 miles on his personal Trident—the triples began returning stellar service. By 1971, *Cycle's* editors had praised the updated Three as "bulletproof."

Certainly, the bikes were living up to their performance potential. In 1969, four out-of-the-crate stock BSA Rocket 3s set new AMA time and distance records at Daytona, the fastest at 131.723 miles per hour. This created a longstanding myth that the BSA triples were faster than the Triumphs. Later that year, BSA-Triumph set up a "Speed Challenge" for their new superbikes at the Bonneville Salt Flats. Stock and modified Tridents set fifteen new AMA 750cc records; the Rocket 3s set none.

Many US dealers offered their own restyling packages in order to sell the ugly-duckling Trident. This one from Triumph-Detroit is shown with its new owner. At right is Michigan speed legend Roosevelt Lackey, who set AMA records on Triumphs and MV Agustas. *Brooke archive*

TriCor service manager Rod Coates used his own Trident for touring with wife Marge. Coates fitted TriCor saddlebags and one of Craig Vetter's early S1600 Windjammer fairings. *Gaylin archive*

Yamaha's 650cc twin competed with the Bonneville on road and track and is a classic in its own right. *Yamaha XS-1 brochure image*

Triumph wasted no time in running two-page magazine advertisements under the banner headline, "Triumph Sweeps Bonneville." The Trident also acquitted itself well in motorcycle journalism's first-ever comparison test. *Cycle*'s March 1970 "Big 7 Superbike Shootout" pitted Triumph's new 750 against its BSA cousin and the Harley-Davidson XLCH, Honda CB750, Kawasaki Mach III, Norton Commando S, and Suzuki Titan in a contest of acceleration, handling, braking, and price.

When the smoke cleared, the Trident ranked among *Cycle*'s favorites. Staff testers Jess Thomas and Cook Neilson found it to be the second-easiest superbike to ride fast (tops was the Norton), even with its hard-pull clutch and aggravating vibration between 5,000 and 6,000 rpm.

On the drag strip, the triple "came out of the hole like a freight train," wrote editor Neilson, with a best quarter-mile ET of 12.78 seconds at 104 miles per hour. Its road-course manners were hindered only by the ill-spec'd front brake and obtrusive footpegs. But these and other accolades weren't enough to overcome the styling and high price. In 1969, fewer than 7,000 Tridents and Rocket 3s were sold in the US, while Honda sold over 30,000 CB750s.

"The Four," former BSA sales manager Don Brown lamented to the authors, "just knocked the pins out from under us."

BSACI TAKES OVER

In August 1969, Lionel Jofeh summoned the vice presidents of Triumph and BSA's American combine to a meeting at New York's Pierre Hotel. Jofeh, like his predecessor Harry Sturgeon, was also president of all American subsidiaries owned by the Group. At the meeting, he outlined plans to merge the four US distributors—the Triumph Corporation, Johnson Motors Inc., BSA-Western, and BSA Inc. (East), all separate corporations—into a new parent company.

The Birmingham Small Arms Company Inc. (the name was always spelled out, but will be abbreviated as BSACI here) was set up to direct the sales, marketing, distribution, and racing of BSA and Triumph motorcycles in the US. Jofeh then surprised everyone by introducing the new corporation's president: Peter Thornton. He had been working as a US consultant to BSA as president of Sales Communications, Inc.—then part of Interpublic, one of the world's largest ad agencies. Jofeh considered him to be a marketing genius.

At the New York meeting, Thornton outlined his vision for the new company. He promised that BSACI would offer better and more uniform service support, advertising, sales promotion, and district representation, while eliminating duplicate activities among the four distributors. A press release trumpeted that BSACI was established for "meeting the challenges of the 1970s."

The new company encompassed three subsidiaries: Triumph Motorcycles Inc., BSA Motorcycles Inc., and Top Gear

An early Trident fitted with US "beauty kit"—what the triple should have looked like originally! *Jim Davies*

Inc. (an accessory distributor), headquartered in Verona, New Jersey. The former TriCor headquarters in Baltimore would serve as the eastern distribution center for both marques, while Duarte would operate as western distribution center. BSA's eastern base in Nutley was slated to close.

BSACI and Thornton clearly put off many of the key people who had helped build Triumph's remarkable US reputation and success. Rod Coates saw the writing on the wall; within a year he was gone, after twenty years as "Mr. Triumph" in the east. Pete Colman, Earl Miller, and Don Brown all expected to be fired to clear the way for Thornton's cronies. Colman saved his job by suggesting the creation of a technical center at Duarte and a combined BSA-Triumph race team. The new boss agreed, appointing Colman vice president of engineering and accepting his proposal to run both operations.

Don Brown had no faith in Thornton or in the BSA Group's lack of a forward strategy. He resigned after serving a few months as vice president of sales for the BSA Division, a brief stint in which he conceived the Rocket 3 speed-record effort and the Vetter Hurricane project. Earl Miller also awaited the axe but was retained as vice president of operations.

The former TriCor finance chief was guardedly optimistic about BSACI's plan to slash costs and overhead through consolidation. But his opinion reversed when Thornton immediately began busting the new company's budget with new efforts, including a $3 million racing program.

"They were violating [the budget] at every turn," Miller told the authors. "There was no way it could have succeeded. And when I explained that to Thornton, he didn't give a damn. So, we agreed to part company on principal." Miller took early retirement.

Thornton did not immediately appoint a vice president of sales for Triumph Motorcycles Inc. He was quick to send out a damage control memo to dealers, "to clear the air about the BSA and Triumph lines" and to end raging speculation that the two would be merged. "We have made studies that reveal many compelling reasons why the two lines should be maintained as separate entities," the memo said, "and virtually no sound reason why they should be merged or one of the lines dropped." As if this issued needed to be studied at all.

Also merged were the formerly separate Triumph and BSA Service Departments and race shops. In doing this,

Thornton lost the respect of two of motorcycling's most gifted tuners and service experts, Cliff Guild and Pat Owens.

"Thornton had us all fly into Nutley, where he gave us a speech," recalled western service manager Owens. "He tried to convince us that it didn't matter who you worked for—Triumph or BSA." Owens disagreed, of course, but stayed on to tune Gene Romero's Trident racers through the 1970 championship season. He left the company in early 1971, after declining an offer to manage the race team. The beginning of BSACI marked the end for some of Triumph's most loyal and dedicated US personnel.

"If your brand loyalties are bristling at the sight of these two fiercely competitive marques lumped together, you'd better settle down and start getting used to it," commented *Motorcycle Sport Quarterly* in its winter 1970 issue.

Dealers, too, were bristling when Thornton announced Triumph's new six-month warranty during the 1969 eastern dealer meeting. "At the time, we were all eating the three-month

A restored T120RT shows how the 750cc Routt big-bore kit looks "stock." *Charlie Hall/Brooke archive*

warranty!" exclaimed John Healy. "Rod Coates came up to me and said, 'This is going to kill us.' "

During the Q&A session, Healy raised his hand and stood up. "Is there anybody here who is owed warranty money?' " he asked the crowd. Nearly everyone raised a hand. "I then told Thornton that I'd honor their new six-month warranty after they paid me what Triumph owed me for three-month warranty work over the past three years," he said. Payment finally came in 1972, a year after Thornton was fired.

YAMAHA SPRINGS A 650 TWIN

In early 1970, the first-ever comparison test involving a Triumph twin was published. *Motorcycle Sport Quarterly* pitted the 1970 T120R Bonneville against Yamaha's brand-new XS1. The twelve-page test ran under the provocative headline, "Did Yamaha Top Triumph's 650?"

The 650cc XS-1 was Yamaha's first four-stroke production motorcycle and its first foray into the big-bike market. Where Honda, the four-stroke veteran, chose to leap beyond the British parallel twins with its 750 Four, Yamaha opted to slug it out with the acknowledged 650-twin champ. The XS-1 directly targeted the Bonneville—a shot aimed at the heart of Triumph's business.

Launched as a 1970 model, the XS-1 offered many technical features that the Bonnie couldn't match, including a single overhead camshaft, four main bearings, constant-velocity carburetors, and a five-speed gearbox. Yamaha claimed 54 horsepower, 2 more than the Bonneville, and the bike weighed 433 pounds wet—just 6 pounds heavier than the Triumph. The XS-1's 360-degree firing interval and megaphone-shaped mufflers gave the proper deep growl.

The Yamaha's styling may have lacked Triumph's time-honed purity, but its basic silhouette mimicked the Bonnie closely enough to snag buyers who couldn't afford the extra $230 for the T120R—decent money in 1970.

Yamaha and its dealers wisely emphasized the XS-1's oil-tightness. Finally, here was a 650 twin that didn't leak oil, thanks to a horizontally split crankcase, precisely machined covers, and effective gasketing. Yamaha dealers didn't need to place drip pans beneath their new 650s in the showroom. In Triumph shops, drip pans were as common as Dunlop tires.

Did Yamaha top Triumph's 650 twin? *MSQ* testers Bob Greene and Tony Murphy dubbed the effort a "near miss." The XS-1 was slightly quicker than the Bonnie at the drag strip, a bit more powerful at high revs, and torquier at mid-range. But the Bonneville was lighter, had better handling and braking, and delivered better fuel economy. Both bikes had equal 115 mile-per-hour top speeds. Remarkably, the Triumph was smoother, even with its two-bearing crankshaft. Actually, the two bikes were so close in every category that the Yamaha's price advantage was a persuasive draw—a twin-carb, overhead-cam 650 for the price of a 500cc Triumph Daytona.

"The first round is over," the testers concluded. "The Titans have met, and Triumph has been forewarned."

T120RT: THE FIRST 750CC BONNEVILLE

On May 4, 1970, Triumph's Baltimore office mailed a special letter to each of its top 125 dealers—those who had achieved the best sales volume in 1969. A similar letter from the company's Duarte facility went out to the top seventy-five Western dealers: "We are conducting a nationwide market test of a limited number of 750cc Bonneville models," began the Baltimore correspondence. "Involved in this test will be a total number of 200 machines."

Each dealer was offered just one of these very special 750 Bonnies, built to homologate Triumph's B-range twins for the AMA's new 750cc racing formula. Dealer price was $1,199, and suggested retail was $1,599—about $150 more than the regular Bonneville. All of them bore the model code T120RT stamped on their crankcase serial number pads, but the capital "T" was added in either Baltimore or Duarte, not Meriden.

Rod Coates masterminded the T120RT project. As a member of the AMA's rules-making Competition Committee in the mid-1960s, TriCor's service manager was anticipating the coming 750cc overhead-valve rule change. Even before the Committee voted to allow the 750s to compete on dirt tracks in 1969, Coates planned Triumph's response. He knew the Trident was on the way, but reckoned that a 750cc twin was a far brighter prospect for mile and half-mile dirt tracks.

Triumph, however, had no 750 twin in the works. And the AMA required 200 "production" examples of any race engine be available for sale to the public.

The answer was just a local phone call away. Coates and TriCor had a strong relationship with Hubert "Sonny" Routt, who ran a successful Maryland business making accessory big-bore kits for Triumphs that he used on his record-setting Top Fuel drag bikes. Sold under the Webcor brand, Routt's kits featured cast-iron cylinder barrels, larger pistons and rings, and stronger wrist pins. All were proven to be good, quality pieces. They bolted onto 650 twins with minimal fuss and were available in four different bore sizes.

Routt's 3-inch bore kit yielded 750cc; it appeared to be the fastest way to get 200 of the 750cc twins approved by the AMA, into customer's hands, and onto the racetracks.

"Rod contacted me in 1969 for an order of 240 big-bore kits, which included forty spares," recalled Sonny Routt. "The job costed-out at $88 per kit, including a pair of 10.5:1 ForgedTrue pistons, rings and wrist pins. Triumph got a great deal because my stock kits sold for about $200, retail."

For the cylinder barrels, Routt contacted his regular supplier, Motor Castings in Milwaukee, which made Harley-Davidson's cylinders. Routt claimed they were the only US foundry capable of casting deep fins like Triumph's. Coates had specified that the T120RT cylinder barrels look like a standard Triumph part, in order to convince the AMA that they were made by Meriden. So Routt fly-cut the perimeters of the four outside base-nut holes, instead of straight-cutting them as on his standard kits.

According to Routt, the special barrels carried embossed part numbers on opposite sides of their base flanges, front and rear. Interestingly the Motor Castings logo that identified every regular Routt kit—an "MC" inside a tiny upside-down triangle—remained in the casting mold for the T120RT job. On the 200 RT barrels, the logo appeared where it usually was on the base flange, next to the tappet holes.

The 76mm pistons were actually 0.008 inch oversize, in order to fit the 3-inch Routt bores. These components were given Triumph part numbers and eventually listed in a June 30, 1970, Triumph service bulletin. From the outside, the T120RTs looked just like standard 1970 Bonnies—"sleepers" in every way.

To convert the 200 machines quickly, Triumph set up makeshift "assembly lines" in Baltimore and Duarte. According to Pat Owens, brand-new crated Bonnevilles were brought in from the Duarte warehouse at random. Baltimore did the same. The bikes were partially uncrated, their stock top ends removed and the 750cc kits installed. Then they were recrated and shipped to dealers, along with a special memo from Coates that cautioned against using "hotter" spark plugs with the high compression ratio. The memo recommended 376/100–200 main jets "as a safety measure."

A total of 204 T120RTs were built, stated Owens. Four were prototypes, including the original assembled by Coates and Cliff Guild at Baltimore. According to a June 1970 memo from Pete Colman to the AMA, 145 T120RTs were approved at Baltimore by AMA referee Robert Rudy and the remaining 55 units were checked by AMA office Earl Flanders at Duarte.

T120RT buyers had to sign a liability disclaimer, as Triumph officially considered the bikes to be "experimental" models that were "designed and intended for racing and other competitive speed events." Both US distributors issued Service Check Forms to dealers so they could evaluate the bikes' performance and durability at 1,500-mile, 3,000-mile, and 6,000-mile intervals. In other words, Triumph wasn't sure how long the engines would last!

One T120RT that endured beyond all others was Pat Owens's personal bike. He bought the first RT assembled at Duarte and proceeded to make it one of the world's highest mileage Triumphs. In forty years of ownership, Owens and his wife Donna covered over 500,000 miles on their amazing prototype. When co-author Brooke visited their home in 2007, the T120RT engine still had its original cases, crankshaft, cylinder head, valve seats, layshaft, and most of its transmission gears. Not bad for a rare "experimental" motorcycle originally intended only to satisfy the AMA and win Triumph another Grand National Championship.

WORLD'S FASTEST MOTORCYCLE
SPEED RECORD TRIUMPHS

"As you accelerate to over 200 miles per hour, it's treacherous—very, very intense," noted Bob Leppan about speed runs at the Bonneville Salt Flats.

You hear the two engines behind you, sounding like one huge, angry Triumph twin. But there's little wind noise in the cockpit. The bike's weaving; its following every little rut and tire track in the salt. It's an entirely new dimension. You're extended; you're peaked. There's nothing to get you out of trouble—it's just you, the bike, and the salt.

And, you remember one simple thing: keep the throttle open, or you won't go fast.

ABOVE: Allen's 1955 record run was approved only by the AMA, not the FIM, but that didn't stop Triumph's US distributors from (rightly) claiming a world speed record. *Brooke archive*

LEFT: Bobby Turner astride "Wonder Bird," the first Thunderbird to arrive in North America, at Daytona Beach 1951. Tuned by JoMo mechanic Cal Makela (center standing), the bike ran 129.24 miles per hour on nitro and set an AMA Class C record, 132.26 miles per hour, on gasoline later at Bonneville. Standing at left is Pete Colman. *Brooke archive*

Rollie Free's famous "bathing-suit" Vincent speed record runs convinced many Salt Flats competitors to copy his minimalist attire, as this unnamed Thunderbird rider is doing in 1951. The trend ended a year later when swimsuit-clad Tommy Smith crashed his T-bird at nearly 140 miles per hour, losing much skin. Full leathers were then mandated. *Brooke archive*

"Triumphs have been setting records on the Bonneville salt longer than most motorcycle companies have been in business," stated a 1978 magazine ad. It remained true in 2016, with Triumph-engined motorcycles holding seven world speed records and thirty-five national records in classes encompassing sleeved-down Tiger Cubs all the way to the 3,000cc double-Rocket III-powered streamliner, Hinckley's proud bid to recapture world's fastest motorcycle glory.

From 1955 through 1970—except for a brief thirty-three-day period—Triumph legitimately owned that title. Over forty years later, the Hinckley factory effort found out how tough it is to reclaim.

JOHNNY ALLEN: 193 MPH

The genesis of Triumph's long reign on the salt flats came in late 1953, in Pete Dalio's Triumph-Ariel dealership in Ft. Worth, Texas. Late on a Saturday, Dalio, along with his mechanic and race tuner Jack Wilson and their friend J. H. "Stormy" Mangham, began plotting how to build a machine capable of exceeding the terminal velocity of the exotic factory NSU on which Wilhelm Herz had raised the world motorcycle speed record to 180 miles per hour in 1951.

Mangham was an aero engineer and veteran airline pilot who built fast cars and boats as a hobby. He owned a small Ft. Worth airfield where a speed record bike could be constructed and tested. In early 1954, he built a unique projectile-shaped streamliner with a mildly tuned Triumph 650 engine running on gasoline. Shakedown tests showed the bike easily capable of 155 miles per hour. The following year, Mangham returned

to Bonneville with one of Wilson's methanol-fueled 650cc motors installed and twenty-seven-year old Texas Short Track Champion Johnny Allen at the controls.

With the top of his helmet just visible above the tiny cockpit, Allen blasted a one-way 191 mile-per-hour run before the tire treads chunked—Mangham had fitted shaved-down street Firestones from his K-model Harley! With proper tires, the Texans believed, this bike was clearly a record-breaker.

It was an innovative machine, endowed with American know-how and simplicity. Instead of enclosing the bike with a modified World War II surplus aircraft drop tank, as was becoming popular for streamliners, Mangham designed and molded his own slender fiberglass shell. Its cigar-like shape gave the bike its nicknames, "the Devil's Arrow" and "the Texas Cee-gar." He tested its aerodynamics by whittling a small balsa wood scale model and attaching it just outside the cockpit window of his DC-6 airliner.

Underneath the 15-foot, 8-inch-long skin was a stout chrome-moly tube frame, 22.5 inches at its widest point and fabricated from a light plane's airframe. The Thunderbird 650 engine sat behind a thin bulkhead behind the driver. The missing link was high-speed tires. The solution came from Johnson Motors, who were anxious for the kind of publicity a world speed record would bring.

"Wilbur Ceder got the right tires for us," Wilson recalled. "We told him what we needed, and he immediately contacted the right people at the Triumph factory," including Frank Baker, head of the factory's Experimental Department. Baker and others worked behind the back of their volatile boss Edward Turner to help the Texans.

Pete Colman told the authors that, when Turner finally found out about the speed attempt and its grass-roots funding by US Triumph dealers—as well as the modest contributions from Dunlop—Amal, Lucas, Renold, and Mobil Oil, he deemed any factory support unnecessary. "The whole feat was basically sponsored by American Triumph dealers, JoMo and our suppliers," Colman recalled.

Ceder's operatives contracted Dunlop for proper high-speed tires, which were produced and shipped to Texas within three weeks. With special new tires fitted and the Texans back on the salt, Johnny Allen immediately cracked off a two-way average of 193.72 miles per hour. This was 8 miles per hour faster than the 1,000cc Vincent of New Zealanders Bob Burns and Russell Wright, who had earlier grabbed the world speed record from NSU.

Unfortunately, Allen's triumph was not recognized as an official world record by the Federation Internationale Motorcycliste (FIM), Europe's sanctioning body, because the FIM claimed none of its observers were present with the AMA timekeepers. No matter—this was the world's fastest motorcycle in the eyes of the AMA, Triumph, the US press, and just about everyone else. Then came that thirty-three day hiatus.

ALLEN AGAIN: 214 MPH

The exhaust pipes on the "Devil's Arrow" had hardly cooled when, in summer 1956, NSU blitzed into the Utah salt flats. With an army of factory mechanics, engineers, support crew, and riders, the German team broke the 200-mile-per-hour barrier for motorcycles and set records in eight different engine classes. NSU's weapon for the ultimate record was a streamlined 500cc, DOHC-supercharged parallel twin, tucked inside a wind-tunnel-sculpted shell. Running on methanol, the NSU produced a claimed 100 horsepower—enough to rocket Wilhelm Herz to 210.77 miles per hour, a new motorcycle world speed record.

When Wilson and Mangham heard about NSU going 210 miles per hour, they made sure their Triumph "Cee-gar" packed sufficient poke before heading to Bonneville. Wilson opted for the 1950 cast-iron Thunderbird motor, used so successfully in 1955. Even though his friends at Meriden had cast a special aluminum splayed-port cylinder head just for the 1956 record attempt, Wilson stuck with his proven iron T-bird head, milled and re-ported to mount twin 1⅜-inch Amal GPs. Camshafts were standard Triumph "Q" type, with "R" radius tappets. The valves, cut-down Harley KR items, were topped by double S&W springs.

Down below, a 30-pound billet crankshaft, made of Natralloy and built by Rich Richards in California, ensured high-rev safety. Wilson fitted standard Triumph roller main bearings on both sides and used Cadillac V-8 bearings on the rods. A Lucas magneto replaced the BTH mag used on the 191-mile-per-hour run. The gearbox was a special close-ratio unit, with a wide low gear, built specially at Meriden.

Running a 60 percent nitro load, the combination worked as the Texans knew it would. Johnny Allen's best runs averaged

Tuner Jack Wilson pushes the "Texas Cee-gar" out of Stormy Mangham's Ft. Worth hangar for a shakedown run in 1956. *Gaylin archive*

Mangham and Wilson built three "Cee-gar" streamliners from 1956–1959. One of them, powered by a full-house 500cc twin, carried Jess Thomas to 212.288 miles per hour in 1958, a class record that still stood in 2016. *Brooke archive*

There is only
ONE FASTEST MOTORCYCLE!

Triumph's Streamliner set the present world's official* speed record for motorcycles—still standing—at Bonneville Salt Flats, Utah, on August 24, 1962. Rider Bill Johnson [shown above on a 1965 Triumph Bonneville] clocked 230.269 mph.

This world record was made on a standard production Triumph Bonneville engine and is just one of 26 official* records held by Triumph

motorcycles in all classes and competitions during the last 7 years. That in itself is a world's record of records!

WESTERN DISTRIBUTOR Johnson Motors, Inc., 267 W. Colorado, Pasadena, California 91102 • EASTERN DISTRIBUTOR The Triumph Corporation, Towson, Baltimore, Maryland 21204. *Officially confirmed by the American Motorcycle Association.

TRIUMPH

Bill Johnson's 230 miles per hour record in 1962 carried the FIM's stamp of approval. *Brooke archive*

214.17 miles per hour, beating the NSU record handily. Seven months later, though, the FIM bosses refused to ratify Allen's speed again, even though they had initially accepted it as the new record. They claimed the California Institute of Technology timing clocks used during Allen's runs were not properly certified. Years later in a magazine article, former FIM executive David Goode reasoned that the record attempt was supervised by the AMA, which was not then an FIM member or affiliate, and there was no FIM steward present.

The FIM's refusal to accept Allen's runs sparked a lawsuit by the Triumph Engineering Co. and, inevitably, a long political rift between Edward Turner and the Europe-based FIM. In fact, in 1960 the FIM suspended Triumph from holding an FIM license for a period of two years. As in 1955, though, the FIM rejection really didn't matter, especially to Americans and the AMA.

"I had to agree with ol' Wilbur Ceder," laughed Jack Wilson in 1991. "He said we'd get all the publicity we needed after that record, with or without the damned FIM. And we sure did!"

And to prove that a naturally aspirated, pushrod Triumph 500 could outrun a blown, DOHC NSU 500, the Texans sent the Mangham chassis back to Bonneville in 1958. This time, it had a full-house Tiger 100 motor inside the shell and eighteen-year-old Jess Thomas at the controls. Thomas rode it to 212.27 miles per hour—a new world record for unblown, streamlined 500cc motorcycles running on nitro. As of 2016, Thomas's Triumph S-PF class (streamlined, pushrods, fuel) records remained unbroken according to records listed on the Southern California Timing Association website.

Thomas made seventeen runs with the 500cc bike, all of them over 200 miles per hour. "Even ol' Don Vesco tried to beat it [the 212 miles per hour record]," noted Jack Wilson, "but he could only do 195!"

Wilson and Mangham built two additional streamliners and, in 1959, Johnny Allen came back to Bonneville to try to top his 214 miles per hour speed. It was not to be. First, the weather was uncooperative; then, while running at over 220 miles per hour, the bike crashed and tumbled for nearly a mile. Allen was pulled out of the wreckage with a few broken ribs. His 214-mile-per-hour record stood until August 24, 1962, when it was broken by another Triumph-powered machine.

BILL JOHNSON: 230 MPH

Streamliner technology was raised again by a machine owned and built by Joe Dudek of Redondo Beach, California. Dudek was chief mechanic at North American Aircraft and was involved with the X-15 rocket plane project—then the world's fastest (4,000 miles per hour) aircraft. With advice from North American's aerodynamicists, he designed his streamliner's 15.6-foot shell to resemble a miniature X-15.

Pete Colman built the machine's splayed-port T120 Bonneville engine at Johnson Motors. Bored to 667cc, it featured a new, unproven camshaft developed from a previous Tim Witham cam design. Witham, an independent California tuner worked with JoMo in developing certain catalogued high-performance parts.

On the initial qualifying run at the Salt Flats in 1962, rider Bill Johnson—no relation to JoMo's founder—clicked off a faultless 218 miles per hour run on gasoline. The required backup run produced a new 205-mile-per-hour speed record for gasoline-fueled motorcycles. Then Dudek and his crew merely drained the gas, changed jets, fueled it with nitromethane, and completed a run down the Flats at over 230 miles per hour.

A successful return run, after blowing a piston, gave the Johnson/Dudek team a two-way average of 224.57 miles per hour for a new world motorcycle speed record. And this time, the record (over the measured kilometer) was fully recognized by the FIM—it had been run under the auspices of the US Auto Club, an FIM affiliate. Just to be sure this time, it was also observed by FIM technical boss Helmut Bonsch. Americans and the AMA, though, recognized the record as the bike's 230.269-mile-per-hour average speed over the measured mile. In 2016, it remained unbroken in the S-AF class (streamlined, altered frame, fuel).

Colman and JoMo mechanics were so pleased with their new camshaft's performance that they had it produced and cataloged for sale as the JoMo #15 cam. It immediately became the hot setup for Triumph racers. The Dudek/Johnson streamliner remained complete and unrestored until 1974, when it was destroyed during a fire at Triumph's Duarte, California, warehouse.

Ralph Gaebel's home-built DOHC Triumph 500 special was a fixture at California drag strips and the salt flats in the 1950s and 1960s. *Bob Leppan*

LEPPAN AND GYRONAUT: 245 MPH

A few years after Johnson's outstanding success, two men visited Johnson Motors and were seen scrutinizing the Dudek/Johnson streamliner on display in the lobby. The older of the two, mustachioed and aristocratic, was overheard saying, "No wonder it went so fast."

This was Alex Tremulis, former head of advanced styling at Ford Motor Co. and one of the US auto industry's most famous designers. He had been a stylist at Auburn-Cord-Duesenberg in the 1920s, and had penned the radical 1948 Tucker. By the early 1960s, Tremulis was again thinking ahead, toward gyroscopically balanced, fully enclosed motorcycles. Always a strong believer in aerodynamics, he dreamed of proving his design principles in a Salt Flats record machine.

With Tremulis that day at JoMo was Bob Leppan, who already knew plenty about making Triumph motorcycles go fast. Leppan had been a Triumph dealer in Detroit, Michigan, since 1957 and, along with his business partner, Jim Bruflodt, had campaigned a succession of dominant single- and twin-engined drag bikes in the Midwest. The quickest of these, the double-650 Cannibal MkII, was a consistent top eliminator against bikes and cars.

By 1962, Leppan and Bruflodt had set their sights on Bonneville records. They bought a used streamliner, minus its

two 500cc Triumph engines, from Burbank, California, Triumph dealer Bill Martin. The Detroit duo extensively modified the streamliner, setting it up for one of the 650cc engines from the Cannibal MkII. Leppan took it to the Salt Flats in October 1963 to gain experience. During this Bonneville trip he met Tremulis, and the two shared their visions about how a record-breaking streamliner should be designed and built.

The pragmatic twenty-six-year-old Leppan didn't share Tremulis's zeal for on-board gyroscopes, though they eventually built a gyro-equipped Triumph street bike that could stand upright by itself. But Leppan listened when Tremulis talked aerodynamics. Later that year in Detroit, the two, along with Bruflodt, became the core of a project to capture the ultimate land speed record, then held by John Cobb at over 400 miles per hour. Their gyro-stabilized, two-wheeled streamliner was to use a Shelby-built 289 ci Ford V-8.

But even with Ford Motor Co. assistance, achieving such a lofty goal took huge amounts of development. So, Gyronaut X-1—a twin-engined Triumph streamliner—was born as a "stepping stone" to the larger, Ford-engined machine. According to Leppan, the name Gyronaut came from the original idea to fit a gyroscope, combined with the era's fascination with astronauts. The X-1 was Tremulis's

"Rapid Robert" Leppan and Gyronaut at Bonneville, prior to raising the ultimate motorcycle speed record to over 245 miles per hour in 1966. *Bob Leppan*

indication that the V-8–powered X-2 and X-3 would follow. They never did, as the LSR project with Ford eventually died.

Tremulis made a clay scale model from his drawings. The basic shape of the narrow body shell—24.5 in cross section, 4 square feet of frontal area—incorporated a nose that could be adjusted from trim and a long, swept-back dorsal stabilizer fin. This fin, like a jet airplane's tail, was one of the first of its kind on a Salt Flats motorcycle. *Cycle* editor Gordon Jennings dubbed it "unnecessarily Buck Rogers in appearance," but Leppan, Bruflodt, and Tremulis had the last laugh.

"Alex didn't design that fin just for looks," noted Leppan in 1992. "It was absolutely necessary for high-speed stability and was copied later by many people, including Don Vesco."

Gyronaut benefited from the enormous engineering and tooling resources available in Detroit. Tremulis passed his specifications to custom-car body man Vince Gardner and fiberglass ace Bob Mattson, who produced the hand-laid fiberglass shell in three sections—removable nose and tail, center cockpit. With the shell complete, Leppan and Bruflodt contacted Gene and Ron Logghe, whose Logghe Stamping Co. built America's best Funny Car and Top Fuel "rail" drag-racer chassis. Logghe's project manager, Maynard Rupp, delivered Gyronaut's 4130 chrome-moly tube frame to Triumph-Detroit within one week.

Leppan and Bruflodt added novel touches of their own. Gyronaut was the first streamliner to incorporate active landing struts, pneumatically actuated from within the cockpit via surplus aircraft landing gear cylinders. This allowed the bike to start its runs from a standing position, without being towed or pushed, and

to stop virtually unassisted—it was only towed to bump-start the twin engines. They designed in a true roll bar, extending well above Leppan's helmet and serving as a frame for the cockpit bulkhead. Remarkably, most streamliners then lacked this feature.

The bike's handlebars were beneath Leppan's knees; this gave maximum steering lock because they were positioned in the shell's widest, lowest spot. And the low bars made it feel more like a racing motorcycle, with a standard twist grip and clutch lever. A left-side pedal worked the rear brake, while the right-side pedal shifted the four-speed, 1962 Triumph gearbox. First gear ratio took the machine to 170 miles per hour.

For safety, the machine carried two freon fire-suppression bottles inside the engine compartment, a Diest safety parachute tucked into the tail, and a full Diest quick-release sports car harness for the rider. Originally, Leppan had Diest add race car–type arm restraints to hold the driver's arms inside the cockpit in the event of the bike flipping over at speed. During Gyronaut's 1966 tech inspection by long-time AMA Salt Flats referee Earl Flanders, Leppan was told that arm restraints "weren't in the rule book" and couldn't be used.

As on the Dudek/Johnson machine, Gyronaut's front suspension employed center-hub steering. It was built from a Triumph sprung hub, chosen for its overall strength and ability to accept a kingpin. The kingpin also controlled trail. Rough salt conditions prompted Leppan and Bruflodt to add two small Volkswagen shock absorbers for minimal front suspension.

In the rear, the original brake was an Al Gunter/Airheart hydraulic disc. This was later swapped for a special drum brake wheel assembly made by the Meriden race shop for Gyronaut.

Borrani WM3 19-inch aluminum rims on both ends were shod with very special and expensive Goodyear Land Speed Record tires, rig-tested to 300 miles per hour. Leppan and Bruflodt had interested Goodyear in the Gyronaut project, which would obviously pay big promotional dividends to the tire maker if a new motorcycle speed record was set. In 1965, Gyronaut's first time on the salt, Goodyear spent $1,700 per day for the Triumph-Detroit crew to test and run at Bonneville. It also set off major political fireworks with Triumph's old rival, Harley-Davidson.

Harley had taken a Sprint-engined streamliner to Bonneville that year to try for the world 250cc speed record. Harley boss Walter Davidson came to see the attempt, and he quickly noticed whose tires were mounted on the impressive new Gyronaut X-1.

"Walter became enraged when he saw our bike with those special Goodyears on it," said Leppan. "He claimed he had paid Goodyear to develop those tires for his streamliner!" Harley-Davidson was used to twisting the AMA's arm if the rules didn't suit, and now Davidson threatened to drop Goodyear as Harley-Davidson's production tire supplier unless Leppan removed the special 90psi high-speed tires. Caught in the middle, the Goodyear reps met privately with Leppan and Bruflodt.

"They didn't want to take the tires away from us, so I told them I'd fix the situation very quickly," Leppan said. "I just took my Dumo grinder and ground off the "Goodyear" raised letters from the tires' sidewalls. Now it no longer appeared that we were running those tires. Problem solved." Walter Davidson stopped complaining, particularly after George Roeder rode the Sprint to a new 250cc record.

In Gyronaut's engine bay, two pre-unit Tiger 110 twins mounted on their own subframe were coupled together by a single-row Renolds chain on the drive side. Leppan's drag racing experience had taught him to keep the engines as reliable as possible, which meant stock 641cc displacement and straight-port TR6 heads, mounting either four Amal 1⅛-inch 289 carburetors and 510GP float bowls or 1¼-inch Amal GP2s. The heads had unit-construction rocker boxes and Webco oil manifolds. For valve gear, Leppan chose S&W springs, 1⅞-diameter intake and 1½-inch exhaust valves, high-lift Harman & Collins camshafts, carefully lightened rockers, stock timing gears, and steel-tipped alloy pushrods made at Triumph-Detroit.

Down below, 12:1 Hepolite pistons made specially for Gyronaut rode on stock Triumph rods and Vandervell shell bearings. Main bearings were ball races on each side of the flywheels—the "heaviest standard Triumph units I could find," explained Leppan. Sparked by two fixed-ignition Lucas racing magnetos and running on 100 percent methanol, the engines produced about 70 horsepower each. Top gear redline was 8,200 rpm.

The result of the Gyronaut team's design, development, hard work, and expense—roughly $100,000, reckoned Leppan—was worth it. At the Salt Flats in 1965, Leppan rode the bike to 175 miles per hour on a warmup run, then to 229 miles per hour in standing water during the Goodyear testing. The wet salt (it had rained heavily that month), slick tires, and a loose kingpin bushing caused intense speed wobbles at 200 miles per hour—"worse than someone putting a gun in your face," recalled Leppan. "I got out of the bike and shook for an hour."

Gyronaut set a new AMA ultimate gas-powered speed record of 217.62 miles per hour, breaking the previous record by 5 miles per hour. But the bike aquaplaned and crashed at 80 miles per hour, sliding for 200 yards. Leppan was uninjured—and encouraged about Gyronaut's top speed potential.

The Triumph-Detroit crew and Alex Tremulis returned to Bonneville in 1966, with some support (motel fees and spare parts) from the Triumph Corporation and accessory maker Hap Jones. While preparing the machine, Leppan and his crew wore Triumph T-shirts emblazoned with "Bill Johnson 230 miles per hour," the shirts serving as a constant reminder of the week's target.

Conditions that year were perfect—"a beautiful nine-mile run over hard, dry, smooth salt was available," reported Cycle. As soon as Speed Week began, Triumph again shot into the record books, with Boris Murray's amazing 191.302-mile-per-hour two-way average on his unstreamlined, double-engined, nitro-burning drag bike. Murray, one of America's top motorcycle drag racers, broke the existing class record by 27 miles per hour. Making his new record even more impressive was the fact that he was halfway through his first run before he realized the fuel petcocks were closed! This was the fastest any open-framed motorcycle had ever gone at Bonneville.

Leppan and Bruflodt rolled Gyronaut to the starting line with the same pair of proven alcohol-fueled twins used in 1965, but now making about 75 horsepower each. Warming up, the

TriCor racing boss Rod Coates (at left) invited Leppan (in white jacket) and his Triumph-Detroit partner Jim Bruflodt (second from left) to Baltimore to promote their new world record. *Brooke archive*

two engines sounded like one huge, raucous 650cc twin. After making five qualifying passes, all faster than Bill Johnson's 1962 record, Leppan blasted off a 243.572-mile-per-hour run. The speed wobble experienced in 1965 had been cured by new Timken tapered-roller bearings installed on the front kingpin.

All Triumph-Detroit needed was a backup run in the same speed range—no problem, as Leppan and Gyronaut had been entering the measured mile at 235 miles per hour in third gear and were still accelerating out of it at nearly 260 miles per hour. Tremulis calculated that, because of its slick aerodynamics, Gyronaut was only using 4 horsepower at 100 miles per hour to overcome air drag. Indeed, reclined inside the cockpit, Leppan marveled at the relative lack of wind noise and how, after a run, he could coast for seven miles with the engines shut off.

Within the required hour, the record was theirs: 247.763 miles per hour, averaged with the earlier run, equaled a new ultimate motorcycle speed record of 245.667 miles per hour. Like Johnny Allen's record in 1956, however, only AMA officials witnessed Leppan's achievement. Lacking an FIM presence didn't matter, though: for the next four model years, Triumph T120R Bonnevilles left the factory wearing decals proclaiming "World's Fastest Motorcycle." And Gyronaut became the third American streamliner, after the Allen and Bill Johnson bikes, to be proudly displayed by Triumph at London's famed Earl's Court Motorcycle Show.

Triumph drag-race maestro Boris Murray became the fastest motorcyclist without a fairing after his 192.302-miles-per-hour record on this double-engined machine at Bonneville 1966. *Brooke archive*

TRIDENTS SWEEP BONNEVILLE

The superbike war that shook American motorcycling in 1969 was carried over into that year's Bonneville Speed Week. In the fall, sixteen 750cc-class AMA speed records were up for grabs, contested by the new 750s of Triumph, BSA, Honda, and Norton.

Both Johnson Motors and the Triumph Corporation targeted Speed Week as the perfect event for publicizing their new triples' capabilities. To lure competitors to the Salt Flats, the two distributors put up a combined total of $25,000 in prize money, coupled by a public relations and advertising blitz. Although the Trident's odd styling wasn't earning rave reviews or selling many motorcycles, the bike's performance appeal remained impressive.

All week, not a single 750cc record was set by the many Honda CB750s in attendance. BSA hired a movie company to film the event, expecting their rapid new Rocket 3s to dominate the Salt. But after no BSA triple set a record, the film soon became "lost." When the smoke finally cleared from Speed Week 1969, fifteen of the sixteen 750-class records were owned by Triumph Tridents.

Three Triumph-Detroit sponsored riders—David Early, Joe Baker, and Roosevelt Lackey—set seven of the records between them. Three records were claimed by Big D Cycle riders Rusty Bradley and Virgil Davenport; Art Houston's Tridents grabbed four more. Perennial Triumph man and Bonneville competitor Bud Hare brought along a partially streamlined triple that, running on fuel, took rider Jeff Gough to a 169.331-mile-per-hour class record. This was the meet's fastest record-setting Trident, although Rusty Bradley topped Gough's speed slightly with a one-way blast of 169.891 miles per hour.

Even with only a standard four-speed gearbox, the new triple was a fast machine. Joe Baker's stock Trident went 137.407 miles per hour without a fairing, bettering by 5 miles per hour the famous BSA Rocket 3 Daytona speeds clocked four months earlier.

With a fairing and minor modifications to Baker's Trident, he averaged 147 miles per hour for another class record. Bob Leppan, the bike's tuner, credited a careful 2,000-mile break-in, followed by a complete valve job, as the keys to the record.

As 1970 began, Triumph-powered motorcycles held thirty world speed records.

TRIUMPHS TOP 270 MPH

Triumph's annual success at Bonneville proved the classic advantages of the powerful, compact, highly tunable parallel twin. By Speed Week 1970, however, other fast guys were aiming seriously at the Leppan/Gyronaut 245-mile-per-hour record. During the high-stakes contest that emerged, the world record changed hands three times and nearly ended in tragedy.

Don Vesco had been aggressively pursuing the world's fastest motorcycle crown since the mid-1960s. And in fall 1970,

Boris Murray begins his 280-miles-per-hour run in Denis Manning's twin-engine Triumph streamliner at Bonneville, 1972. He crashed before the record attempt was official. *Denis Manning/Brooke archive*

he was first on the salt. His dual-350cc R5 Yamaha "Big Red" streamliner broke Gyronaut's record, but Vesco's 250-mile-per-hour mark only stuck for three weeks. Following him to Bonneville was the new Harley-Davidson–powered streamliner of Denis Manning and Warner Riley.

Powered by a monster 1,474cc nitro-burning Sportster engine, ridden by Cal Rayborn and backed by Milwaukee factory assistance, the Harley was the second machine to top Triumph's record. Rayborn, Manning, and company shattered Vesco's mark by 15 miles per hour, raising the world speed record to 265.492 miles per hour. It was a new ballgame.

By the time Leppan and Bruflodt's big diesel transporter reached Utah, the Triumph-Detroit team was staring at a whopping 20-mile-per-hour gap between their previous record and the new one.

"Vesco and Rayborn didn't catch us completely off guard, but Jim and I figured the serious challenge wouldn't come until 1971, when we'd have an all-new bike with twin Trident engines ready," Leppan recalled. As a stopgap, they'd upgraded Gyronaut's 650cc twin-cylinder units using special 820cc kits from Sonny Routt. The four Amal GPs previously set up for methanol were now jetted for nitromethane to give about 170 horsepower. To further cheat the wind, the bike's body panels (now sporting a blue-and-white paint job) were carefully finessed so that they fit precisely flush. The chassis was unchanged.

Leppan was confident. Right off the trailer, on a 40 percent nitro load, he and Gyronaut uncorked consistent qualifying runs above 260 miles per hour. One USAC-timed run was 264.437 miles per hour.

After a day of making final adjustments, Gyronaut was readied at dawn on October 21, 1970. Reclining inside the cockpit and warming up the engines, Leppan was intensely

focused on completing two record-breaking runs. The machine had handled superbly the day before. It was time to go.

Thundering down the 9-mile course, the bike was approaching a calculated 270 miles per hour when something happened. Unnoticed by the crew, a hairline fracture in the front suspension tubing caused the front end to collapse.

"The crash occurred at the 4.25-mile marker," he recalled. "Suddenly I felt a violent speed wobble. The bike was still accelerating—the tach read 8,300 rpm, which by our gearing calculations meant in excess of 270 miles per hour. I closed the throttle and pulled the parachute cord, but the bike was already airborne." Joe Petrali, the USAC timer, later told Leppan he watched Gyronaut fly 50 feet into the air.

While in the air, the canopy blew off. "Somewhere between going airborne and hitting the salt, my left arm was flung outside the shell and was caught underneath the bike," he continued. "And the arm restraints we'd designed into Gyronaut in 1965 still weren't allowed by the rules! I slid through the timing lights at 264 miles per hour and finally stopped at the 5½ mile marker."

His arm had been pinned underneath the 800-pound bike, plowing through the salt, for a full mile. Later, he admitted he should have been dead.

Amazingly, Leppan remained conscious through the sirens-blazing, 140-mile ambulance ride to a Salt Lake City hospital—the first 10 miles of it at over 100 miles per hour driving in the opposite lane on Interstate 80. The hospital was not equipped for such serious injuries, and Leppan steadfastly refused amputation. So, he was flown to a California hospital (taking up four seats on a commercial flight) where surgery was performed fourteen hours after the crash.

Although he'd lost a lot of blood, his entire bicep and much tissue, Leppan's left arm was miraculously saved. During

Steve Starrett prepares to launch Team Texas Triumph's twin-Trident missile at Bonneville 2005. The bike went 221.51 miles per hour for a class record in 1991, and went over 250 miles per hour one way. *Brooke photo*

his nine-week hospitalization, Leppan's friend Pat Owens outfitted his bed with a set of Triumph handlebars, complete with control levers, connected to a carburetor. Working this setup relentlessly helped Leppan recover partial use of his left hand. The handlebars proved so successful that the doctors asked Leppan for a few extra sets for other patients.

Despite his injuries, Leppan wanted to beat the Harley record and began planning an all-new Gyronaut for 1972 to 1973. But the project never blossomed. The original Gyronaut was run just once more, at a Michigan drag strip in the mid-1970s. In 2013, the machine was restored by Leppan and Steve Tremulis, Alex Tremulis's enthusiastic nephew (see sidebar).

If Leppan had returned to Bonneville with an all-new Gyronaut in 1972, the event might have been dubbed "The Battle of the World's Fastest Triumphs." Back on the salt that year was Denis Manning, who brought along his own new streamliner—this one fitted with a pair of nitro-burning Triumph 750cc twins.

Manning had admired the Gyronaut as a salt flats novice. He began working on the new machine after setting the 265-mile-per-hour record. It was a secret project, planned around another Harley engine, even though Manning was employed in sales at Triumph's Duarte operation! He designed a completely new chassis in 1018 steel tubing and hired Lyn Yakel, a Douglas Aircraft aerodynamicist who was legendary in the hot rod community. Yakel developed a new shell in

the Cal Tech wind tunnel. Harley-Davidson paid for the wind tunnel time, during which Yakel iterated scale models of the streamliner. The work paid off—the final shell showed a slippery 0.15 coefficient of drag (Cd).

Suddenly, Harley pulled the plug on the project's official support. Manning believed it was because Honda's Hawk Streamliner had recently crashed at Bonneville and Harley management was nervous about sponsoring a similar risky endeavor. So, Manning asked Pete Colman, then vice president of engineering at BSACI, for sponsorship. He also contracted Boris Murray, the Triumph drag racing maestro, to join the project as engine builder and rider.

Colman offered the team $2,000 in official Triumph backing and a special deal on parts. Manning recalled that Colman "really went the extra mile for me," allowing him time off to work on the streamliner and travel to Utah, providing other help when needed. While the shell design was already complete, the chassis was lengthened by 9 inches to accommodate Murray's 200 horsepower twin-Triumph powerpack.

Overall, the white, blue, and black Manning/Murray projectile was narrow and tiny—15 feet 9 inches long and 31 inches tall. With Murray aboard, it weighed 900 pounds wet. This was much smaller than either of its two main threats that year, Don Vesco's twin 350cc Yamaha or Bill Wirges's twin 750cc Kawasaki.

Behind the cockpit bulkhead, Murray's pre-unit engines used Chantland aluminum 750cc big-bore kits and Norris camshafts. Each TR6 cylinder head carried twin Amal TT carburetors that delivered an 80 percent nitromethane fuel mixture. An unusual feature was the bike's exhaust system, which exited inside the engine bay. The idea was that the exhaust gases would create a vacuum inside the shell, thus drawing in fresh intake and cooling air toward the engines.

Manning admitted later that Triumph pre-unit transmissions could not cope with 200 horsepower. A much stronger Harley four-speed transmission was fitted and gave no trouble after the team broke five Triumph 'boxes. But from the moment they arrived at Bonneville, Manning and Murray were dogged by problems. And the Salt Flats were so wet, they resembled a lake in some areas. Help from Jack Wilson, whose Big D Cycle Triumphs were also in attendance, briefly improved their outlook.

Murray's initial one-way runs were fantastic, nearly all faster than the 265-mile-per-hour record and one reaching 280 miles per hour, according to Manning. But when the salt dried, the surface became very rough. With $25,000 in contingency money being offered by Triumph to reclaim the world title, Murray opted for what he thought would be a smoother line to the measured mile. At speed, he hit a rough salt patch; a front wheel bearing failed and the streamliner fell on its side, sliding across the salt for over 2 miles. The bike tripped the timing lights at 277 miles per hour. Murray deployed his parachutes—which immediately tore off the entire rear shell of the machine! When it finally stopped, Murray was generally unhurt, but the shell was mangled.

Undeterred, the relentless Manning trucked the damaged streamliner to a local shop; within thirty-six hours it was ready to run again. The team's luck was all used up by then, though: both engines blew up the next morning. Boris repaired one of them using spare parts, but time and money had run out for the project.

"With Bonneville streamliners, you don't have the chance of a few laps to sort things out," reflected Manning. "You're more of a test pilot than a motorcycle rider."

THE TURBO ROCKET STREAMLINER

"It was really hard learning to go in a straight line on the salt," admitted Jason DiSalvo, the 2011 Daytona 200 winner, who in August 2013 was at Bonneville piloting Triumph's first factory-backed streamliner since the Manning-Murray machine.

Though DiSalvo had previously set a class record at 174 miles per hour on a modified, unfaired and street-legal Rocket III, the Castrol Rocket 'liner was a very different beast. This was Triumph management's shoutout that the company had finally gotten serious about recapturing the world's fastest motorcycle title. Its 25.5-foot Kevlar-carbon body is 2 feet wide and 3 feet tall. It covers a monocoque chassis that houses a pair

of destroked (to meet the 3,000cc class rules), turbocharged Rocket III engines.

Coincidentally, the new Triumph machine was exactly what Bob Leppan envisioned when the 2,300cc Rocket III was launched. "Now they have the perfect engine to take to Bonneville in a streamliner," he told co-author Brooke in 2004. "Plenty of headroom to make big power, liquid-cooled and an inline layout so it's narrow."

The boosted British triples were built by Bob Carpenter, a veteran Pro Stock motorcycle drag racer whose company specializes in go-fast packages for Triumph's biggest model. While he had not raced on the salt himself, Carpenter reckoned that two mildly tuned turbo engines, rather than a single

Eight speed records fell to Big D Cycle Triumphs in 1975, including Jack Wilson's 192.34-miles-per-hour blast on this 160-horsepower single-engine Trident, fitted with a turbocharger and Big D 1,000cc stroker kit. *Keith Martin/Big D Cycles archive*

The magnificent Triumph Infor (ex-Triumph Castrol) Rocket streamliner at Bonneville 2016. *Triumph photo*

Daytona winner Jason DiSalvo cut his "salt legs" on this unfaired Hot Rod Conspiracy/Carpenter Racing–built Rocket III Roadster, setting a class record of 174.276 miles per hour in August 2012. The record stood in 2016. *Brooke archive*

brutishly powerful one, would give the rider more traction on the unpredictable salt surface and a more manageable power delivery on the long 11-mile course. The bike runs in the S-BF (streamlined, blown fuel) 3,000cc class.

Each engine displaces 1,485cc by shortening the stroke from 3.75 inches to 2.4 inches. Along with the use of feather-light titanium connecting rods, this reduces mechanical stress on the bearings while enabling higher rpm. Together the pair of turbo motors produces a claimed 1,000 horsepower.

The streamliner in 2015 changed sponsorship from Castrol to enterprise-software company Infor, along with Belstaff apparel. It was designed and built by crew chief Matt Markstaller, a mechanical engineer and Salt Flats veteran whose day job is in Daimler Trucks' US development group. His company, the Hot Rod Conspiracy, is Markstaller's gearhead sideline.

During DiSalvo's brief time as Rocket pilot, the engineering team learned much through testing and their first year on the salt. Speed Week was shortened by rain and high winds, limiting DiSalvo to three runs that yielded a meager 104-mile-per-hour time slip. The machine also caught fire during a 95-mile-per-hour shakedown run, causing DiSalvo to bail out in 8 seconds flat.

Development at the Hot Rod Conspiracy and Carpenter Racing continued, and Triumph's change of sponsorship brought Isle of Man TT star Guy Martin in as driver. Still shooting for Ack-Attack-beating terminal velocities at Speed Week 2016, Martin and team raised the 'liner's best performance to 274.2 miles per hour, making it the fastest Triumph-engined motorcycle yet, the company claims.

"We are moving in the right direction, but it is just one step on the way to what me and team are here to do," observed Martin.

RESTORING GYRONAUT

The trailer door opened and the 18-foot-long missile was rolled carefully down the ramp, into the workshop at TT Motorcycles in suburban Detroit. Store owner Bob Leppan's eyes slowly cast over the signature dorsal stabilizer and across the freshly painted burgundy-and-silver shell, not yet wearing the lettering and stickers of its 1966 record run. Gyronaut had just emerged from a five-year restoration and Leppan had a lump in his throat.

"I have a love-hate relationship with Gyronaut, to be honest," the seventy-four-year-old speed king admitted. "It made my reputation as the world's fastest motorcyclist, and it also nearly killed me."

The restoration had been pending for thirty years. Since the bike was last run in 1975, Leppan had kept the chassis, the twin-engine powerpack, the surviving shell sections, and a small cache of unobtanium spares in storage. It wasn't until 2008 that he finally decided to restore the machine. First up was the chassis, which was outsourced to local experts Jim Lamb and Tony Kulka. They found it to be remarkably intact and true, despite the damage it suffered in 1970.

By the time the chassis was completed in 2010, Leppan had been contacted by Steve Tremulis, a San Francisco-area biomedical engineer whose uncle Alex had codesigned the 'liner nearly fifty years earlier.

The freshly restored Gyronaut emerges from final paint, 2013. *Brooke photo*

"In my many conversations with Bob, I recognized how he and Gyronaut were intertwined—but I also sensed that he might want to let it go eventually," Tremulis told co-author Brooke. Over time they struck a deal, and the fresh rolling chassis and unrestored elements were on their way to the Bay Area.

New owner Tremulis was not a motorcyclist nor a Triumph collector. Rather, he is the consummate historian of Alex Tremulis's amazing life's work, with insights into his uncle's Duesenberg design sketches, rare Ford concept cars, and the Gyronaut speed vision. Steve put the ambitious resto project on the front burner, aiming to get the fully restored 'liner to the 2013 Bonneville Speed Week. To tackle the bike's daunting shell, he enlisted Rob Ida, a New Jersey–based custom car fabricator, Tucker owner, and Alex Tremulis fan. Ida's team used period photos, original drawings, and computer design tools to recraft the iconic shell. After 200 hours of fiberglass work, fabrication, and paint, the 'liner went into the trailer for a ride back to metro Detroit.

Lettering and pinstriping were handed to the same custom painter who had done it in 1965. "I never could have dreamed that I'd again be working on this machine forty-seven years later," said "Wild Bill" Betz. He was chuffed to again have "the great piece of speed history" under his striping brushes.

Triumph specialist Jerry Liggett at Triple Tecs dug into the dormant powertrain and the bike's final assembly took place, appropriately, under Leppan's eye. His lead tech Butch Casaday and local vintage Triumph expert John Hubbard spent three weeks attending to the nitty-gritty details of finishing a motorcycle restoration. But when the van arrived to carry Gyronaut to Utah for the Speed Week celebration, the Detroiters were a couple days short of firing up the bike. While it went back to Bonneville as a non-runner, Gyronaut delighted those who saw it on display.

Triumph paint legend "Wild Bill" Betz applied his steady hand to Gyronaut's lettering and striping in 1965 and 2013. *Brooke photo*

08 TRIUMPH GOES HOLLYWOOD
STAR CYCLE OF THE SILVER SCREEN

Tom Cruise blasts through London's Trafalgar Square, flat on the tank of an 865cc Triumph Thruxton. He's trying to save humankind in the 2014 sci-fi blockbuster *Edge of Tomorrow*. Angelina Jolie is on the run from government killers aboard a matte-black Street Triple R in the 2010 thriller *Salt*. Clint Eastwood's detective "Dirty Harry" Callahan rides a Moto Guzzi cop bike—wait, it's really a Triumph TR6!—onto a docked aircraft carrier. He guns it up to the ship's flight deck before (cue the stunt double) Eddie Mulder jumps the Trumpet across to an adjacent flattop as *Magnum Force* hits its climax.

ABOVE: Promotional still from *The Wild One* showing Marlon Brando's character Johnny and his gang crashing a local motorcycle race. The rider in the "flat cap" seen behind the race official's raised arm is Bill Hickman, who played the villainous Dodge Charger driver in *Bullitt* fifteen years later. *Gaylin archive*

LEFT: Life doesn't get any better than a 1966 Trophy Sports 650, a new pair of Clark's desert boots, Persol 714 shades—and Jacqueline Bisset hanging on tight. Steve McQueen and his leading lady take time off from filming *Bullitt* to tour San Francisco on Steve's daily rider at the time. *Brooke archive*

McQueen practices with the Trophy-Bird on the set of *The Great Escape* in Bavaria. *Gaylin archive*

And was that a young Bruce Springsteen on a 1969 Trophy 500, cruising South Jersey between gigs at the Stone Pony? You bet it was—one of The Boss's first bikes.

Triumph motorcycles have been playing a lead role in Hollywood and entertainment ever since Bill Johnson uncrated his first Speed Twins in Los Angeles. They've been favorites of actors, musicians, and celebrities who loved to ride—and of those who simply wanted to be seen with the coolest bikes available. The bikes have costarred in box-office bombs (for example, 1996's *Barb Wire* with Pamela Anderson and a Thunderbird 900) and delivered iconic performances under the finest actors (Brando and his 6T Thunderbird in 1953's *The Wild One*, Steve McQueen and his TR6 in 1963's *The Great Escape*). Johnson Motors rarely missed an opportunity to glamorize its products through celebrity associations.

In 1942, the US was at war and everything was rationed, including vehicles and gasoline. One day, JoMo received a rare spares shipment from the Triumph factory, including a new leftover Speed Twin. According to Clyde Earl, a twenty-year JoMo employee and film historian,

Bill Johnson needed a pickup truck for the shop but no new vehicles were being built for the public. Robert Taylor, then Metro-Goldwyn-Mayer Studio's top actor, wanted a motorcycle. He fell in love with the gleaming maroon Speed Twin. So, Johnson and Taylor struck a deal: Taylor got the Triumph and Johnson got a Dodge pickup from Taylor.

TOP BILLING FOR THE T-BIRD

One of Triumph's most famous starring roles was in the original "biker" film, *The Wild One*. The 1953 movie was loosely based on incidents that occurred in Hollister, California, on July 4, 1947. That weekend, a few riders got drunk and disorderly during an AMA Gypsy Tour. The episode grabbed national attention when a *San Francisco Chronicle* reporter's story was picked up by the major papers. It went "viral" when *Life* magazine then published a full-page photo of a drunken Harley rider, awash in a sea of empty beer bottles.

Controversy erupted when motorcyclists realized that Stanley Kramer's film would portray them as a villainous bunch. Before the film was even completed, Bill Johnson—ever vigilant in promoting motorcycling's clean image—sent a letter of protest to the Motion Picture Association of America's president, excerpts of which follow:

It should be obvious that this film is calculated to do nothing but harm, particularly to a minor group of business people—motorcycle dealers throughout the USA. Certainly there is nothing educational about this picture, but on the contrary it raises a most unfavorable presumption against the sport of motorcycling generally, and is a stigma to anyone who owns or rides a motor bike. To say that the story is unfair is

Achtung, das Englisch Motorrad! TriCor and JoMo advised dealers to display a new TR6 in the lobby of their local movie theaters when *The Great Escape* was playing. *Gaylin archive*

putting it mildly and you cannot deny that the general impression will be left with those who see the film that a motorcyclist is a drunken, irresponsible individual, just not nice to know!

You must be aware that the great majority of motorcycle enthusiasts are reasonable and decent people. I urge that you give the foregoing comments your unbiased consideration, with a view of stopping production of this film.

Johnson's concerns were well placed, as a 1950 Thunderbird was featured front and center in this tale of antisocial mayhem. Until *The Wild One*, motorcycles had appeared in movies with their brand names painted over or tank badges removed. It is believed that this was the first major American film in which the motorcycles' nameplates were retained for the camera and audience to see.

Sharing the lens with the T-bird was the film's "other" star, Marlon Brando. The hot new leading man had owned a Matchless while a stage actor in New York, but he was unsatisfied with his riding ability and during filming practiced at night at Columbia Ranch.

To Triumph enthusiasts, it was fitting that the film's "bad guy," Lee Marvin, rode a Harley. At the time, Marvin's riding skill was reportedly not equal to Brando's, but his interest in motorcycles was stoked by the experience. Marvin became a devoted enthusiast and accomplished rider, competing in many western desert events. Although tame by today's standards (and now a cult classic), *The Wild One* was banned for a period in some countries, including Britain, because of its violence and "sinful" message.

A WYNN FOR STEVE MCQUEEN

Screen idol James Dean loved fast motorcycles as much as his beloved "Little Bastard" Porsche 550 Spyder. He purchased a new 1955 TR5 Trophy from Venice, California, dealer and former racer Ted Evans for use as his daily rider. When it came to bikes, this rebel had a cause. Dean was no poseur, but few of that era's Triumph-mounted actors were more dedicated motorcyclists than Keenan Wynn. Although he never achieved superstar status, Wynn is regarded as one of the top character actors of the 1950s through the 1980s. He appeared in more than seventy films and 220 TV shows,

Clint Eastwood on one of the two 1967 TR6R models prepared at Rick's Cycle Center in Bound Brook, New Jersey, for the 1968 film, *Coogan's Bluff*. Although the bike wears a '67 T120R gas tank, it's a TR6R—note the single throttle cable and single-carb head. *Brooke archive*

including *Dr. Strangelove* and *Nashville*. And he loved all motorsports, particularly motorcycling.

Wynn became a potent off-road rider, racing a modified Tiger Cub in the Catalina Grand Prix's 200cc class. He rarely missed an interview opportunity to promote motorcycling and fight its negative image. In 1959, Wynn was given his own short-lived TV show, *The Troubleshooters*, in which he and his sidekicks—Olympic track star Bob Mathias and two Triumphs—traveled the US looking for opportunities to perform good deeds. For most motorcyclists, portraying their sport positively was the best deed Wynn could have performed.

Steve McQueen credited Wynn for turning him on to off-road motorcycling. "I was riding along Sepulveda [in west Los Angeles] with Dennis Hopper when we saw these guys bopping and bumping along the weeds near there, off the road," recalled McQueen in an August 1971 *Sports Illustrated* interview. "It was Keenan Wynn and another guy on these strange machines—'dirt bikes' they called them. We asked Keenan if he could climb that cliff. 'Watch this,' he says.

"VAROOM! Right up to the top. Dennis and I were standing there with our eyes out to here. The very next day I went out and bought me a 500cc Triumph dirt bike." McQueen had already met Bud Ekins at his dealership in 1961, shortly after the actor purchased a used early T120 from Norm Powell, the son of actor Dick Powell, in whose studio McQueen was working at the time, Ekins told the authors in 2002. But for his off-road machine, he called Johnson Motors asking for a new 500 "at a great price." He also wanted the bike delivered personally.

Bill Johnson sent his sales chief to the Warner Bros. studio the next morning. "Steve and I met and talked briefly, then he went off to shoot a scene after inviting me for lunch later," Don Brown recalled.

I left him the keys to a new TR5, the owner's packet, and addresses to JoMo and Bud's [Ekins] dealership. Steve had told me during lunch that he already knew Bud. I left and we later rode the High Mountain Enduro together, with Bud. We stayed in touch over the years and he called me a few weeks before he died. And everything you've heard about him being an outstanding rider is true.

McQueen's 500 was supplanted by modified 650cc "sleds," at least one of them a T120-based job with TT Special high-compression pistons. Those bikes he raced in various District 37 Hare and Hound events, the High Mountain Enduro, and the 1963 Greenhorn Enduro. For the 1964 International Six Days Trials held in East Germany, McQueen rode a works-prepped TR6SC as part of the American Vase team.

McQueen and Triumph are best known, of course, for their roles in the World War II blockbuster, *The Great Escape*. Ekins also appears in the film, doubling McQueen—as his POW character Virgil "Cooler King" Hilts—in some of the stunts. McQueen lobbied director John Sturges to get a motorcycle chase scene inserted into the script that included a climactic 60-foot leap over a barbed-wire fence on the Swiss border. Since wartime BMW or Zundapp boxer twins were too ponderous for action-movie duty, McQueen and Ekins ensured that Triumph's punchy TR6 Trophy-Bird won the leading bike role.

McQueen's studio contract wouldn't permit him to perform the big jump, but his stunt double nailed it on the first take. Ekins said he earned $1,000 for his work in the film—a fat payout for a stunt man in 1962. He told the authors that two 1961 TR6/As with reinforced duplex frames were shipped to southern Germany for the filming after receiving a mostly cosmetic makeover by Ekins' custom painter/fabricator pal Kenny Howard, AKA Von Dutch. Ekins noted that the mechanical changes included fitting stock 5TA "bathtub" front fenders, Ariel pannier racks, 1956-type vented front brakes, and solo seats. Muffler tips were sawed off and the bikes' batteries were removed to save weight.

Despite the bike's olive drab paint and badgeless gas tank, the disguise couldn't fool Triumph-loving movie fans. During the action, McQueen stops right in front of the Panavision camera to kick-start his obviously British parallel twin. And because the production company ran short of qualified motorcyclists to pose as pursuing Nazis, the film editors inserted shots of McQueen in a Wehrmacht uniform, effectively chasing himself!

During the mid-1960s, many of Hollywood's blue chip stars were photographed on new Triumphs provided by JoMo's Brown, including Paul Newman, Dean Martin, and even Sonny and Cher. Elvis Presley rode a modified T120 in 1968's *Stay Away Joe*. Clint Eastwood was a Norton man off screen, but he piloted a TR6R fitted with a 1967 Bonneville gas tank during an intense Central Park chase scene in the 1968 thriller *Coogan's Bluff*.

A similar formula was used in 1973's *Magnum Force*, with Eastwood's TR6 dressed up to look like a CHP version of a Moto Guzzi. The ship-to-ship jump proved tricky for even "Steady Eddie" Mulder; he later noted that the tide had risen between the morning setup and the final shoot later in the day, which forced a different landing tactic. The late Dar Robinson actually rode the pursuing "bad guy" Triumph off the old carrier's deck and into San Francisco Bay.

THE GREAT KNIEVEL

Evel Knievel's brand of show business was equally spectacular. Before he switched to Harley XR750s, the motorcycle jump king used Triumph TT Specials for his low-altitude aviation. On January 1, 1968, Knievel attempted to jump over the fountains at Caesar's Palace Casino in Las Vegas. His landing was less than smooth: by the time he was done flipping and flopping, Knievel had broken several ribs, his pelvis and hip, and he'd sustained a concussion.

From 1969 to 1976, James Brolin played the motorcycle-riding Dr. Steve Kiley on the hit American TV drama, *Marcus Welby, M.D.* When the show debuted, he rode a JoMo-supplied 1968 TR6R (shown), then switched to a 1970 TR6C, before ending with a Yamaha 650 twin. *Brooke archive*

Candidate for the most recognizable TV Triumph is the 1952 TR5 ridden by Henry Winkler's character Fonzie in the long-running *Happy Days* sitcom. Two Trophies were used in the show, a 1949 square-barrel model used only in promo photos and the '52 shown here. It was sourced from Bud Ekins, who fitted it with Thunderbird engine 6T5160N. *John Lacko*

Richard Gere in dress whites poses one of two 1978 ½ T140E Bonnevilles he rode in the 1982 hit, *An Officer and a Gentleman*. Paramount Pictures acquired the bikes from Dewey's Cycle Shop in Seattle. *Brooke archive*

When he recovered, Knievel prepared a 1967 TT Special for an much-hyped Grand Canyon jump. The bike was equipped with a rocket-booster simulator, winglets. and even a parachute. Fortunately, the US Department of the Interior refused to cooperate.

One of Triumph's few 1980s movie appearances was in *An Officer and a Gentleman*, in which hero Richard Gere rides a 1978 ½ T140E Bonneville with extended fork. It was another case of perfect casting—a Harley was simply out of the question! In the final scenes, our star—and Mr. Gere too—motor into the distance with leading lady Debra Winger hanging on tight.

Since then, Triumphs have continued the brand's nearly seventy-year reputation as the premier bike of the silver screen, according to Christopher Wagner, president of motion picture and TV product placement company Royal Promotions and Placement. Pages of Triumph references in cinema can be found in the Internet Movie Cars Database (www.imcdb.org).

And Hollywood stargazers will continue to crane their necks to see George Clooney, Bobby Carradine, Hugh Laurie, Ewan McGregor, Matthew McConaghey, Orlando Bloom, Hugh Jackman, Keanu Reeves, Brad Pitt, and rocker Pink, to name a few, all riding Britain's "matinee idol" on the streets of L.A.

The great Evel Knievel warms up his nearly stock 1967 TT Special before a multicar jump at Ascot Park in early 1968. *Gaylin archive*

Angelina Jolie deftly balances her new Street Triple R without putting a toe down during filming of the 2010 thriller *Salt. Philip Ramey Photography/Columbia Pictures via Getty Images*

09
GRAND NATIONAL CHAMPIONS
TRIUMPH RACING IN THE UNITED STATES

Triumph's victory in the 2014 Daytona 200 is the latest milestone in the company's rich racing history. The results were decisive for the British brand: winner Danny Eslick also qualified his Riders Discount Racing 675cc triple on pole and led forty-four of the fifty-seven laps. Three other Triumph riders placed fourth (Bobby Fong), seventh (Luke Stapleford), and tenth (Steve Rapp).

ABOVE: Joe Gee and his trusty TR5 Trophy won the 500-mile Jack Pine Enduro in 1951. *Brooke archive*

LEFT: Danny Eslick and the Triumph 675R on a victory lap after winning the 2014 Daytona 200. *Brian J. Nelson*

Father and son Triumph racers "Iron Man" Ed Kretz Sr. (right) and Ed Jr. of Monterey Park, California, at Daytona 1954. Kretz Sr. won the 1938 Daytona 200 on an Indian but had bad luck on Tiger 100s. His son's best finish was thirteenth place in 1955, the same year he won the Peoria TT. *Brooke archive*

Still, if the trivia question "Who was the last Triumph rider to win Daytona?" was posted to the motorcycling public, there's a decent chance that "Nixon" rather than "Eslick" would be the popular answer.

Such collective memory is understandable, given Triumph's legacy of US competition through 1973. Three AMA Grand National Championships. Three Daytona 200 wins and four second places. Forty National wins in half-mile and mile dirt tracks, and road racing. Near-complete dominance of expert-level TT racing with stars such as Dick Dorresteyn, Sid Payne, Eddie Mulder, and Skip Van Leeuwen. Seven consecutive AMA Grand National Enduro Championships by Bill Baird. Dominance of long-distance desert racing. A claim to the world's quickest motorcycle (Boris Murray's double Top Fuel dragster). And a hammerlock on the world's fastest motorcycle title through 1970.

Add to that the scores of novices, amateurs, and club racers who won regional and local events—TTs, short tracks, half miles, hare scrambles, and road races. It's no stretch to say that the grassroots racing support of Triumph's enthusiastic dealer body was the strongest in motorcycling, encouraged by the two distributors and aided by a thriving speed-parts aftermarket that grew up around the Triumph twin.

"I always thought we had the right balance on racing," reflected Don Brown, who was Johnson Motors' sales manager from 1956 to 1965. "Those dealers who wanted to be up to their ears in racing could do it. JoMo provided parts and sometimes service assistance, and the rest could be had through independent tuners and specialists."

Triumph's US dealers knew the value of "win on Sunday, sell of Monday," and they understood that winning never came cheaply. Recalling the 500cc twin's racing successes in *Cycle*, Gordon Jennings noted that many American Triumph dealers were "motorcyclists first and businessmen second (if at all), and while that may have been bad for economics, it was terrific for the sport and a lot of riders."

"Triumph dealers," he continued, "wanted to be involved in racing, and wanted to race what they sold. The factory in Meriden couldn't be bothered."

Longtime *Cycle World* columnist Kevin Cameron devoted an entire chapter to the Triumph unit-500 twin in his essential 2013 book, *Classic Motorcycle Race Engines*. It was the only production engine he selected for analysis—a humble populist among the purpose-designed Grand Prix elite. He noted that, "in all its various modes, the Triumph engine 'system' was very adaptable and allowed a great many to build the bike they wanted," enabled by the tuner's booklets published by JoMo and TriCor and the vast offerings of the Webco catalog.

Triumph dealer/racer Ed Fisher picked up Triumph's first postwar road race win at the Laconia 100-miler in 1953. Here his Tiger 100 has its rocker boxes removed preparing for a post-race inspection. *Gaylin archive*

RELYING ON AMERICAN INGENUITY

Meriden's approach to US racing was, in hindsight, smart business. The factory provided small batches of 500cc race machines—the Grand Prix model in 1948 to 1951 and the Tiger-based production road and dirt-track racers in 1955 to 1957. These were interspersed with do-it-yourself Speed Kits and a few easily converted T100c models. In 1963, at JoMo's request came annual batches of 650cc TT Specials, assembled on the factory's Bonneville production track. But mainly it was stock machines taken from the showroom floor that provided dealers the feedstock to go racing. They and a cadre of independent tuners underpinned Triumph's success beyond 1966, when Meriden jumped in to meet the growing Japanese threat at Daytona.

In the 1950s, Triumphs were the bikes to beat in enduros, especially in the desert, but they posted relatively few wins on the important National Mile and half-mile dirt tracks. Their first Daytona victory, in 1950, was that of Rod Coates in the Amateur 100-miler. A year later came the first US National win by the hard-charging Jimmy Phillips at the 1951 Peoria TT.

Indeed, from 1954, when the points-based AMA Grand National Championship series began, through 1964, Triumphs won just fifteen of the 139 National events—a mere 11 percent. In the same period, BSA carried the Union Jack to

A cigarette for the winner! The immortal Bud Ekins gets ready for a post-race smoke after winning the 1957 Big Bear Run. Note the snow-encrusted wheels. *Don Emde archive*

For the Second Year

TRIUMPH

sweeps board
in classic U.S.

BIG BEAR RUN

America's most important cross-country event — 150 miles of rough and hilly desert.

Bud Ekins.

FIRST 12 PLACES

TAKEN BY TRIUMPH RIDERS!

Winner: Bud Ekins (Trophy TR6)

★ 720 STARTERS ★ 20 OUT OF FIRST 25 FINISHERS ON TRIUMPHS

★ 200 c.c. CLASS TRIUMPH T20C FIRST AND SECOND

TRIUMPH ENGINEERING CO. LTD · MERIDEN WORKS · ALLESLEY · COVENTRY

Brooke archive

Hard-charging Eddie Mulder made his reputation in California desert racing, sponsored by dealer Al Rogers and JoMo's Pat Owens. *Brooke archive*

twenty-four victories, a 17 percent win rate. Meanwhile, the Harley-Davidson team netted ninety-eight wins—70 percent of all Nationals.

During his frequent visits to the American distributors, Edward Turner got an earful regarding what was needed to win National races consistently. While visiting the Baltimore headquarters in early 1952, Turner called a meeting with service manager Coates and TriCor's top National racer, Ed Fisher.

"When Coatesie called me to come down and talk to Turner, I thought, 'How'd I rate this?'" recalled Fisher in a *Classic Bike* interview with co-author Brooke. He said he was awestruck when he arrived at Coates's office and saw Turner— "Mr. Triumph" himself.

After shaking hands, Turner immediately got down to business. "What do we have to do to make this Triumph win in Daytona?" he asked Fisher. The dealer/racer replied that the Tiger 100 badly needed a close-ratio gearbox, an advantage the Nortons were then using with great success. Turner listened closely and took the Americans' advice back to Britain. The next year, Fisher got his close-ratio gearbox and won the Laconia 100-mile National. Tiger 100s in the hands of Sherm Cooper and TriCor mechanic Davey Jones also swept Laconia's 50- and 25-mile events.

The brunt of American race bike development remained with the "colonists." JoMo's Don Brown and Pete Colman both acknowledged that Triumph's particular weakness against arch-rival Harley-Davidson was on the prestigious Mile flat tracks. "Frankly," Brown admitted, "we knew that was just a result of our unwillingness as a distributor to devote resources to it."

A racing program to beat Harley on the big tracks required more money than either US distributor cared to invest. Milwaukee's dedicated Race Department and their dealer allies fielded top-notch riders aboard potent WRs and KRs. They pursued dirt-track victories at the Springfield Mile like they were battles of national honor. The Motor Company was a tough competitor that committed the resources to get winning results.

Race boss Dick O'Brien, speaking to author Allan Girdler in the book *Harley Racers*, stated that, if Triumph, BSA, and Norton had worked as hard or spent as much, they would have run Harley-Davidson off the tracks.

US racing was dictated by AMA Class C rules, an engine displacement formula for road racing and flat-tracks that permitted 750cc for flathead engines and 500cc for overhead-valve units. TT events had their own formula: 80 ci flathead/61 ci OHV, changed in the late 1950s to 55 ci (900cc) for all engines. Class C was initiated during the Depression in the 1930s to help save what remained of the US motorcycle industry; this formula directed racing away from the exotic factory specials that were unrelated to anything available to the public. It was a formula that aimed to boost motorcycle sales by basing competition machines on production engines and frames.

Whether the Class C formula was a handicap to Triumph, BSA, and Norton has always been controversial. Some

The Parasite restored! One of the first Triumph gas "doubles" built by John Melniczuk Sr. in 1958, ridden by Tony Grazias (10.32 seconds at 150 miles per hour) and restored by Melniczuk's son, John Jr. *Brooke photo*

Triumph fans believed that the Harley flatheads' 50 percent displacement advantage always gave Milwaukee an edge. Others claimed it was more than offset by the higher rpm potential of the OHV 500 twin. Arguably, Class C rules made Harley-Davidson complacent and kept it from developing a competitive OHV engine in the middleweight class.

Privateer Triumph speed wizards Tim Witham, C. R. Axtell, Tom Sifton, Jack Wilson, Danny Macias, Jack Hateley, Bill and Richard Love, Bill Kennedy, and many others relied on their own ingenuity and various "AMA-approved" go-fast goodies. The TriCor- and JoMo-branded performance camshafts were supplied by Harman & Collins. Other "hot" cams included Sifton, T&M, and Norris. Race-quality valve springs made by Art Sparks' and Tim Witham's S&W company were eventually adopted for Triumph's production bikes, being superior to the British-made Terry's springs. US pistons favored by tuners included Robbins, ForgedTrue, and Jahn's.

Triumph tuners based in Southern California benefited from their proximity to America's aerospace and hot rod car industries. Their "connections" with the specialist machine shops, metallurgists, foundries, and fabricators meant that just about any trick part needed was only a phone call away.

In 1967, the AMA approved the Sonicweld rigid frame as the first aftermarket racing frame for Class C events. It was followed in 1969 by the twin-shock, oil-bearing Trackmaster frame (later followed by others) to make dirt-track, TT, and

Cycle World founder Joe Parkhurst shot California TT star Clark White fighting to stay ahead of Dick Dorresteyn at the Saugus TT, 1961. The image graced the cover of the magazine's first issue. *Brooke archive*

Don Burnett's Daytona-winning T100S/R contained every tuning trick developed by Cliff Guild and Dick Bender at TriCor. Their experience was shared with Doug Hele's development team in England and used to advantage in the 1966 and later works efforts. *Brooke archive*

even desert racing bikes faster and more nimble. And high-quality big-bore kits from Sonny Routt and Bob Chantland helped put 750cc Triumph twins on US drag strips (and streets) years before the factory's T140 appeared.

EAST VS. WEST RACING

Triumph's US racing, as in sales, was divided by geography. JoMo-sponsored riders generally contested events west of the Mississippi, while TriCor's ran the eastern ones. Sometimes a JoMo rider would race at Laconia, or both companies would attend a central event like the Springfield Mile or Peoria TT. Both organizations' race teams always attended Daytona.

Each camp had its own racing agenda, often carrying their sales feud with them to the track. "At Daytona, the Johnson Motors and Baltimore people were always fighting," recalled Texan dealer Jack Wilson. "[They] never even shared a Daytona garage," he said.

There were even different tuning philosophies according to Pat Owens, Triumph's western service manager from 1967 to 1969 and Gene Romero's road race tuner in 1970. "Where we got 65 horsepower one day, we wanted 70 horsepower the next," Owens said. "But the Baltimore guys always made sure they had reliability first." Owens held high respect for Cliff Guild

and Rod Coates, often working with them behind his boss Colman's back.

TriCor star Gary Nixon agreed that the Californians "just wanted horsepower, horsepower, horsepower," favoring the "big carbs and big cams" setup beloved by West Coast hot rodders.

In conversations with the authors, Nixon recounted the depth of the east-versus-west rivalry. In February 1966, when the five factory T100 race bikes arrived in Baltimore from England, TriCor mechanics Dick Bender and Ted Rivard hauled them by trailer to the nearby Marlboro, Maryland, 1.7-mile road circuit where TriCor did its pre-race testing. There the mechanics met Nixon, Coates, and Triumph's chief development engineer, Doug Hele, who had flown in from Meriden. Nixon tested each machine and selected the fastest for himself, leaving Coates to apportion the others for TriCor and JoMo riders. The same went on in subsequent years.

"The factory wasn't involved in US racing; it was involved in *Baltimore* racing," JoMo's Pete Colman groaned. "Baltimore did their racing and we did ours, even at Daytona."

TRIUMPH RULES OFF-ROAD

Privateers counted on Triumph's hallmarks—agility, power, and versatility—to win everything from local hare scrambles and TTs to desert epics. In terms of doing it all in American motorcycle sport, the Triumph twin had no peer. In fact, by 1966 Triumphs had won more cross-country and TT championships than all other motorcycle makes combined and was on its way to seven consecutive Grand National Enduro championships under Bill Baird.

Meriden machinery really began to shine in 1951, when TR5 Trophies won the Sandy Lane and Tomahawk Enduros and the prestigious 500-mile Jack Pine Enduro, as well as the inaugural Catalina Grand Prix.

Beautiful Catalina Island, 26 miles off California's southern coast, hosted the ten-lap cross-country race that started on the streets of Avalon. Over 200 riders lined up in rows of five; each row was flagged off at 30-second intervals. They headed west, over a narrow, partially paved road that led to the island's summit. Then the riders turned south on a slippery dirt road and down a hiking trail to the golf course. They blitzed across the fairway—hard to imagine this today—to the pit area, then around the clubhouse and back to the start–finish line. Each lap covered 10.3 miles.

Catalina was an AMA-sanctioned race, one of the era's rare events in which the best West Coast amateur riders competed against top AMA National experts. The Grand Prix was run for eight years, becoming an important, high-profile event. Triumph riders won Catalina's Open class five of the eight years, including the 1951 inaugural by Walt Fulton. They also earned seven Lightweight class victories along the way.

Similar success was earned at the tortuous Greenhorn Enduro and the Big Bear Run. During the 1950s, the number of

Burnett on his way to victory at Daytona, March 1962. *Brooke archive*

Big Bear entries exploded from 400 riders early in the decade to over 800 in 1958. The herd stampeded off the starting line at once, traversing a desert-and-mountain course so punishing that some years less than eighty riders finished. Both the Greenhorn and Big Bear were extreme tests of machine and rider, and Triumphs—particularly the 650cc TR6—were the choice of winners.

From its 1956 introduction until the advent of reliable two-strokes in the late 1960s, the high-piped TR6/B (later renamed TR6C) was motorcycling's best on-/off-road package. Relatively light for the era (about 380 pounds), the 40 ci, single-carb twin was easier to start than a big single and delivered more torque than its "30-inch" TR5 little brother. The high-pipe "Six" was an immediate hit, particularly in the western states.

"For Club competition and off-road enthusiasts," read TriCor's 1960 sales brochure on the TR6/B Trophy-Bird Scrambler. The "B" model" featured all the good stuff—quick-detachable lights, wide-ratio gearbox, Dunlop Trials Universal and Knobby tires front and rear, a skid plate, and raised exhausts with short "sports" mufflers. Like all Triumph twins, the TR6 was easily modified by the owner, making it the ideal tool for cross-country races.

The big Trophy's reign included four straight Big Bear Open–class wins between 1956 and 1959, three Catalina GPs,

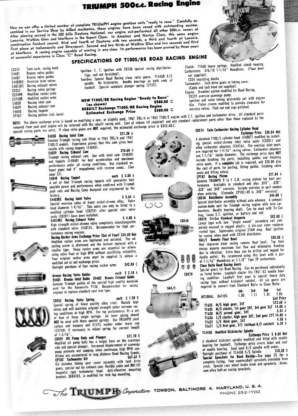

With TriCor's speed goodies available in 1962, you could build yourself a full-race engine, or buy one ready to install. *Brooke archive*

Portrait of exasperation: In 1962, JoMo lured three-time AMA national champ Joe Leonard out of retirement to race the new unit-T100. While leading at the Sacramento mile, his rear tire went flat. *Walt Mahony*

Gary Nixon's half-miler in the Cumberland, Maryland, paddock, 1964. Note the large automotive air filter unit typical of TriCor dirt trackers. *Brooke archive*

Master at work: Cliff Guild ports a 500-cylinder head at TriCor, 1964. Guild's right-hand man Dick Bender was an equal if not more talented tuning genius. *Brooke archive*

and two Greenhorns. In 1957, the TR6 ruled Triumph's most impressive Big Bear year: 177 of the entries were Triumph-mounted, as were twenty of the top twenty-five finishers—TR6s filled the top nine places! US sales of high-piped Trophies boomed, giving birth to a new Anglo-American hybrid with a great nickname: the Desert Sled.

TRIUMPH WINS DAYTONA!

Important events in the early 1960s set the stage for Triumph to become a victor in AMA National racing. In late 1961, the Triumph Corporation, along with BSA Inc. and Indian (now the AJS/Matchless distributor) finally obtained membership on the AMA's corporate board. This began a rebalancing of voting power within the organization. At the same time, TriCor's service manager, Rod Coates, became a member of the AMA's rule-making Competition Committee.

The introduction of the unit-construction, oversquare 5TA in 1959 gave American tuners an opportunity to find greater power through higher rpm. But first they had to overcome a few design deficiencies, including weak gearboxes, bushed crankshafts, and inferior British valve springs. By 1962, both US distributors had so many "trick" parts available for the unit-500 that they decided to offer complete race engines to dealers and privateers. The T100S/RR "customer" engines built up at TriCor and JoMo featured many items used by the East and

West Coast race teams, including twin-carb heads, flywheel magnetos, big-bore oil pumps, full-race valve gear, and close-ratio gearsets. The engines were sold to dealers in "ready to race" ($580) or "rebuilt exchange" ($380) versions.

In 1961, the Daytona races moved from the beach to the enormous, newly constructed Daytona International Speedway. TriCor's top rider Don Burnett finished second in the inaugural 200-miler on a Guild-tuned Tiger. Burnett's finish equaled Hugh McAfee's 1953 second place as Triumph's best yet in the 200-miler.

Then Triumph and Burnett struck gold. Again mounted on a Guild-prepared T100, the Massachusetts pavement specialist beat ninety-four other starters, including fast qualifiers Carroll Resweber and Joe Leonard, to win the 1962 Daytona 200. Both Harley stars had opened up a wide lead on the field and kept it through the 20-second lap, when Matchless G50-mounted Dick Mann and Burnett pulled up into third and fourth. Resweber's KR fried a piston and Leonard took over, only to retire with chain trouble soon after.

Mann and his overhead-cam Grand Prix single were now in the lead, but Burnett passed on lap thirty-five. Mann grabbed the lead a lap later, then Burnett picked it up again on lap forty-five, in what had become a fantastic seesaw battle for first place.

"In terms of top speed our bikes were pretty evenly matched," Burnett told co-author Brooke. "But the G50 had far

Classic Walt Mahony photo of Gary Nixon grooving the Sacramento Mile in 1965, while Dick Mann challenges on a BSA Gold Star and Triumph-mounted Dick Hammer has slipped the groove on the outside. *Dan Mahony*

Brooke archive

better brakes than my Triumph, which gave Dick an advantage in the infield."

On the fifty-fourth lap, Burnett pitted for a perfect, 20-second gas stop. He re-entered in second place as Mann now held a 34-second lead. His G50 was the only machine that hadn't stopped for fuel. He finally pitted for 19 seconds on lap sixty-one.

Burnett gained a 30-second lead during Mann's pit stop, but the hard-charging Matchless rider picked up 2 or 3 seconds on each of the next fifteen laps. By lap eighty-eight, Burnett was just 10 seconds ahead. In the TriCor pits, the mechanics were flashing boards that read "Burnett +9," then "+7," then "+5." On the final lap, the grandstand crowd was on its feet as both riders swept past, flat on their tanks. This was going to be the closest Daytona finish yet.

Megaphones blaring, the Triumph twin and Matchless thumper were side by side as they flew toward the finish line. But Burnett and his Tiger held the G50 at bay, crossing the line a mere 12 feet ahead of Mann.

American Motorcycling reported that, during the trophy ceremony, Lin Kuchler, executive secretary of the AMA, "stepped down . . . so that Denis McCormack, president of the Triumph Corporation, would receive the long-awaited thrill of presenting the winning trophy to a rider of a Triumph motorcycle."

Bill Johnson and Wilbur Ceder also saw the new unit-500's potential and funded development of a winning motorcycle/rider combination. They hired longtime JoMo affiliate Tim Witham to work with Pete Colman on race engines that were both powerful and reliable. Their efforts were first proven at the 1961 Ascot 8-mile National. At the time, the Ascot half-mile track was then dominated by BSA Gold Stars and Harley KRs, but Sammy Tanner and the JoMo Triumph 500 smoked 'em all for the win, making headlines in all the bike magazines.

Colman then lured three-time AMA champ Joe Leonard out of a recent retirement to ride another Witham-built 500. In the bike's first race at the Springfield Mile, Leonard set fastest qualifier, then led the race ahead of Harley stars Resweber and Bart Markel, until an oil line came off. The bike's next outing was at the twenty-lap Sacramento Mile, which Leonard had won in 1961.

Again, he qualified the Triumph on pole and took the lead as soon as the race began. Six laps in and still leading, Leonard was stopped by a flat tire. Hard luck! But Johnson Motors, having dipped its toes in the cold water of racing, decided it didn't want to dive in after all.

"I think all along, Bill wasn't sure of the racing program," said Don Brown. "I think he still carried some concern from when Harley sued for tariff increases against British bikes. Bill ultimately felt it was a better strategy to have private dealers building race machines, rather than committing a big-money race program."

Burnett and Leonard had proved that, in the right hands and with proper development, the new short-stroke

ONE LEG OF THE "IRON TRIANGLE"

When Honda and the Japanese makers landed in the US in the early 1960s, Harley-Davidson, Triumph, and BSA were the dominant brands in AMA racing. US racing was then governed by the AMA's rulemaking Competition Committee, whose members represented the motorcycle manufacturers and their key suppliers. It should come as no surprise, then, that the three dominant brands wielded great influence over the direction of US motorcycle sport.

Within racing circles, Harley, Triumph and BSA became known as "the Iron Triangle," often manipulating technical changes to suit their collective agenda within the confines of Class C rules. Interlopers who threatened to upset the Triangle's fragile equilibrium faced the political and economic wrath of committee members Dick O'Brien (H-D), Walt Brown (BSA), and Triumph's Rod Coates.

TriCor's blunt and loyal-to-the-core service manager held additional AMA power as a tech inspector at National races. It was Coates who precipitated banning the standard Matchless G50 from every type of US racing except TTs during the 1963 season. The ban, which effectively separated the Grand Prix single's frame from its engine, came after Coates witnessed Dick Mann's G50 nearly win Daytona, then handily beat Burnett at Laconia 1962, lapping the field.

Outlawing the G50 frame was a reprise of the Committee's previous banning of the Norton Featherbed frame. Ironically, the Matchless ruling enraged Dick O'Brien, who was then contemplating a new Harley frame. At a Committee meeting, O'Brien even warned Coates that his Triumphs "had better be legal" for the next season's Daytona 200.

"Legal" in the language of the AMA rule book was not defined as based on a street motorcycle. Rather, the rules called for "production motorcycles available for sale" typically in quantities of 25 to 200, depending on the year. As flat-track historian Bill Milburn has noted, "Any concept of 'street-based' Class C race bikes was gone by 1941, when Harley rolled out its WR in response to Indian's 'big base' Scout. Both were built specifically for racing under Class C rules."

Of course, NASCAR legend Junior Johnson's famous racing quote—"If you ain't cheatin', you ain't tryin' "—applies to all forms of competitive rules bending. Coates, and later Pete Colman, were able to work the AMA's "catalogued parts" rules on special racing equipment so that Gary Nixon raced with a big Norton Manx front brake in 1964, a lightweight frame in 1967, and a five-speed gearset in 1969—none of which were available for sale by

Triumph. Ditto the Rob North frame, approved by the AMA in 1970 but "unobtainium" for privateers.

"When I was a partner in Arlington Motor Sports, we tried to order listed [racing] parts as we were Triumph dealers," recalled Kevin Cameron. "Whoever was on the line in Duarte laughed. The part numbers were just whatever Pete Colman had worked out with the AMA." Later, he encountered a similar situation at Kawasaki for the H1R. These were signals that AMA Expert racing had drifted away from the letter of the Class C rule book.

Without remorse, Dick Mann remembered Coates as "a tremendous team player." Speaking to his biographer, Ed Youngblood, Mann said of Coates: "If you cut him, he would probably bleed Triumph engine oil. I always said that if Rod Coates had not already been tied to Triumph, he is the first guy I would want on my team."

TriCor racing boss and AMA racing inspector Rod Coates has a private chat with TriCor's Cliff Guild at Daytona 1965. *Gaylin archive*

ABOVE: **Happy day in June 1966 for Buddy Elmore, here with TriCor's Rod Coates (left) and Ted Rivard, after his hard-fought Laconia 100-mile victory over Bart Markel.** *Boyd Reynolds photo, Brooke archive*

RIGHT: **TriCor mechanics unload four new factory T100Rs at Marlboro, Maryland in early 1966, to be tested and selected by No. 9 Gary Nixon who has brought along his development bike (center) for comparison. Triumph engineer Doug Hele is at far left, with TriCor's Rod Coates. Mechanics Ted Rivard and Dick Bender are at far right.** *Bill Milburn archive*

500 could match the fastest KR Harleys and Gold Stars. The engine was robust: at Watkins Glen, Burnett saw 10,000 rpm on his Smiths tachometer as he reeled in Carroll Resweber. From 1959 through 1965, the US distributors and a few key American dealers were in the vanguard of 500cc twin racing development, identifying design flaws, finding solutions, and making the engine more reliable and powerful. Not so Meriden, who were mainly focused on the 650 during this period.

Sadly, Bill Johnson did not live to see Triumph's racing ascension in the 1960s. The fifty-seven-year-old Johnson Motors founder died of a heart attack on March 4, 1962, hours before Burnett's historic Daytona victory.

Colman joined Coates in 1964 as JoMo's representative on the Competition Committee, which became the Competition Congress in 1967. Democracy was coming to the rulemaking group as its membership expanded to include representatives from other motorcycle importers as well as Expert-class riders. In October 1965, the Committee voted 22–2 to limit all Expert and Amateur dirt-track and road race engines to 350cc/ five-speed gearbox, with 200 units required for approval, according to AMA records. This was to be implemented for the 1969 season and remain in effect through the 1971 season. Triumph and BSA voted against this radical change, as neither had a competitive 350cc engine. Two years later, the Congress agreed to delay implementation of the 350cc rule until 1971.

It's hard to imagine 350cc as the top displacement class in US motorcycle racing. Counterproposals from Coates and Harley's Walter Davidson during the October 1968 Congress meeting finally established the 750cc overhead-valve formula that came into effect for the 1970 season. The new rule sparked Milwaukee's development of the immortal XR750. Triumph now needed a 750cc solution of its own.

MERIDEN JOINS THE FIGHT

Top management changes at BSA Group brought a greater focus on marketing of the BSA and Triumph brands. Edward Turner finally stepped down as BSA Group Director in 1964, a year that saw T100-mounted Gary Nixon win the Sacramento Mile (smashing the track record by 25 seconds) and finish second on Daytona's full 3.81-mile banked course. Turner's successor, Harry Sturgeon, saw racing as a vital part of marketing. He announced a serious factory racing commitment, which for Triumph meant works-prepared motorcycles for Daytona and support of the distributors' road race programs for the remainder of the season. Dirt racing would be supported by the distributors and their dealers.

At Meriden, the program was led by the brilliant Doug Hele and his small staff of skilled mechanics and fabricators. These men would create not only the 1966 and 1967 Daytona-winning 500s, but also the fabulous factory Tridents and BSA Rocket 3s of the early 1970s.

Impetus for the heightened effort came from the Americans. Rumor had it that Honda would enter its new DOHC 450cc twin at

Seven-time US National Enduro Champ Bill Baird with his Trophy 500 in 2007 at the AMA Hall of Fame in Pickerington, Ohio. *Brooke photo*

Daytona. TriCor and JoMo already realized that their T100 needed much development, as it was 30 pounds heavier than the Harley-Davidson that won in 1965. It also needed much more powerful brakes and more durable valve gear.

The Honda threat spurred Rod Coates and Cliff Guild to fly to the factory for a strategy meeting with Hele in September 1965. Given Honda's international Grand Prix prowess and the impact of a Honda Daytona victory, the Americans lobbied hard for superior race machines to be ready by March.

"We learned from each other on that [Coates and Guild] trip," Hele told *Cycle*, "not the least being the use of hard-faced camshafts which Cliff had been using. It pays to have the same size cams at the end of the race as the size you start with." Eutectic hardening had been used for many years by US automakers and speed equipment suppliers to increase camshaft durability.

The 1966 Daytona works bikes were highly modified T100s. Their frames were built with Accles & Pollock T45 carbon-molybdenum tubing but retained most of the production frame's lugs. Steering heads were lowered 1.5 inches and the frame was reinforced there and at the swingarm pivot. Center-mount aluminum oil tanks (a copy of the TriCor accessory tank) were used. The 1966 bikes were immediately recognized by their twin high-level, left-side exhausts and bulbous BSA/Lyta fuel tanks.

Pennsylvania dealer/racers Bill (No. 44) and Bob Sholly with their streamlined and sanitary Tigers in the Daytona paddock, 1967. *Bob Sholly archive*

Looking toward a future roadster version, Hele had designed a totally new T100 cylinder head, with narrow 39-degree included angles between the valves instead of the earlier 45-degree angle. Intake valve diameters were enlarged to 1.5 inches; the valves inhaled through twin $1^3/_{16}$-inch Amal 10GP2 carbs mounted on long rubber tubes. Compression ratio was 9.75:1.

To ensure precise ignition timing at high rpm, the engines had special Lucas racing ignition units mounted outboard of the magnesium timing covers and driven by an Oldham coupling from the exhaust camshaft.

Meriden shipped five 500cc factory road racers to Baltimore. The engines produced 46.5 horsepower at 8,200 rpm on the factory dyno, according to Hele—about 4 horses down on a good KR Harley. While the power deficit was offset by the Triumphs' lighter weight and lower frontal area, reliability quickly became an issue during 1966 practice week.

Connecting rod big-end failures resulted in three engines blowing up after the second day. Buddy Elmore's Meriden-built bike lost five engines during the week. Nixon's Meriden racer wouldn't top 127 miles per hour in practice. When he tried a max-speed run around the banking, the engine launched a con rod, destroying the lower end.

Cliff Guild had brought along some TriCor-built bikes for Nixon and Elmore, just in case. And, when Nixon coasted into the pits, he told Guild that he'd definitely be riding one of them, not one of the factory hand grenades, in the race. The Baltimore bikes weren't as fast as Hele's or Dick Hammer's Danny Macias-built T100 (the fastest Triumph in qualifying), but, like all of Guild's machinery, they would last.

The works bikes were fitted with prototype aluminum tappet blocks designed for the three-cylinder Trident then in development. This created a problem, as the aluminum blocks had a different coefficient of thermal expansion than the cast-iron cylinders. As the hot cylinder expanded, the tappet blocks loosened and twisted in their bores, damaging the camshafts.

Time was running out. To the Americans, it looked like the factory machines were headed toward one big DNF for Triumph.

"They were saying, 'Let's get back to standard specification—we know the bikes are reliable that way,' " Hele recalled in a *Classic Bike* interview. But he rejected appeals from Guild's crew and instead telephoned design engineer Brian Jones at Meriden. Overnight, Jones had a batch of cast-iron tappet blocks made and flown to Daytona. They arrived two days before the 200-miler—and one day before BSA chief Harry Sturgeon landed to watch the race.

Nixon bores through the infield en route to his 1967 Daytona 200 win. *Keith Martin archive*

By the night before the big race, the team had completely exhausted its supply of new engine spares. They'd also depleted the parts shelves of Lig Birch's local Triumph dealership, which was the usual go-to for Daytona race teams seeking parts. Rod Coates scoured the Florida dealer network for crankshafts. Still, Buddy Elmore was set on riding a factory bike. So, TriCor tuners Dick Bender and Ted Rivard worked all night to rebuild the Texan's engine for the sixth time.

When the green flag dropped the next day, Hammer and Nixon showed that both the Macias and Guild machines had the right stuff—until the seventh lap, when Hammer's engine packed up. Nixon, riding the reliable Guild bike, took the lead from the Harleys of Cal Rayborn and Roger Reiman. By lap twenty-one, he had teammate Elmore on his tail—remarkable, as Elmore and his rebuilt factory bike had qualified forty-sixth on the grid! He passed Nixon on the next lap.

By lap thirty, both Harleys were out with mechanical trouble, and the two little Triumph 500s played tag ahead of the field. Elmore pitted and Nixon regained first; three laps later, Buddy was back in the lead. They ran neck and neck until the forty-fifth lap, when Nixon's rear tire blew at 135 miles per hour on the high banking. He hauled the bike down safely, but at the checkered flag it was Elmore, over 60 seconds ahead

H52101, the ex-Dick Hammer works 500 with fairing lower removed, showing the Chevrolet Corvair oil cooler, magnesium timing cover, and Lucas ignition unit, at the AMA Hall of Fame Museum. *Brooke photo*

of second-place George Roeder. Buddy also set a new record speed: 96.38 miles per hour.

Triumphs won six of the fourteen Nationals in 1966, including a sweep of all three TT events by Eddie Mulder. Nixon won a thrilling Springfield Mile, America's premier flat-track event, beating Bart Markel's KR by a wheel length. He also won the Greenwood, Iowa, road race, while Buddy Elmore prevailed at Loudon (a non-National that year). In the points, Markel topped Nixon for number one, 434 to 361. Clearly, this had been Triumph's best season in American racing. The short-stroke T100 and the extra development behind it had caused big headaches in Milwaukee. It was now the equal of any KR.

Daytona 1967 was a milestone for AMA road racing: the beginning of a full-blown factory war between Triumph, Harley, Yamaha, BSA, and Honda (under the auspices of Team Hansen); Kawasaki was even there for the first time. Between them, TriCor and JoMo hired six riders for the 200-miler—first-stringers Elmore, Nixon, and Hammer, plus Eddie Mulder, Larry Palmgren, and Gene Romero.

A look at the 1967 Daytona bikes—designated "P11" in Triumph project code—showed that Doug Hele and his merry men had raised the T100R to yet another level. Combustion chambers now sported 0.030-inch squish bands that enabled compression ratio to be raised safely to 11:1. Lighter and stronger valve gear included titanium collars and retainers, stout barrel-shaped pushrods, hotter camshafts, and a more robust crankshaft. The mixture was fed by a pair of handed 1³/₁₆-inch Amal GPs.

On the factory dyno, the 1967 engines made 48.5 horsepower at 8,700 rpm. While this gain appears minor compared with the 1966 spec, 90 percent of peak power (more than 44 horsepower) was on tap at 6,500 rpm—6.5 horsepower more than the previous output there. This greatly boosted drive out of corners with the close-ratio four-speed gearbox.

In the off-season, riders and mechanics had requested downswept exhausts to replace 1966's obtrusive high-level pipes. According to Hele, there was no room for the left pipe to pass under the clutch housing and brake pedal, so it was kept high-level.

Chassis were similar to 1966's, with a 62-degree head angle, 2-inch shortened fork tubes, and new shuttle-valve damping that would be incorporated into Triumph's 1968 production models. Four-leading-shoe 210mm Fontana front brakes finally brought Grand Prix–quality stopping power to

Nixon tries his 1967 squish-head road race motor in his dirt-track chassis. *Ben H. Hall photo/Brooke archive*

TriCor race tuners Cliff Guild (with Nixon) and Dick Bender (with No. 79 Buddy Elmore) warm up the hardware for Daytona 1968 practice. Both bikes wear twin low-mounted aluminum oil tanks under their fairings. *Gaylin archive*

Triumph. The bikes weighed 310 pounds and all six machines were shipped from Britain with 18-inch front wheels and Dunlop tires. At Daytona, the tires and wheels were swapped for 19-inch Goodyears—a strategic change, since Triumph was the US distributor for Dunlop!

"Daytona has a very flat infield," explained Hele. "With the extra trail that we'd added for 1967, the riders were drifting the rear wheels out. We needed the 19-inch wheels to stop the bikes from dropping into the corners so acutely. The Goodyears gave an extra 3 seconds per lap in practice," he told co-author Brooke.

Slim rectangular 5.25-gallon fiberglass fuel tanks replaced the Beeza "beach balls." Aerodynamics were also improved by lower, more snugly fit fairings made by Britain's Screen and Plastic Company. Their Coventry Blue-and-white paint jobs established Triumph's team livery through 1973.

The superbly prepared Honda 450s showed up loaded with HRC racing bits. Team manager Bob Hansen aimed some psychological warfare at his old nemesis Coates during practice week when he warmed up the 11,000-rpm twins in the Daytona tunnel, their sharp wail getting everyone's attention in the paddock. While fast and reliable, none of the orange-and-white Honda twins were able to crack the top ten at the finish.

Fred Nix put his Harley KR on pole at 140.8 miles per hour, with Triumph's Dick Hammer second fastest at 135.7 miles per hour. Two more Harleys and two Triumphs (Nixon

Roger Beaumont was the man to beat in Canadian production racing during the late 1960s. *Brooke archive*

Roger Beaumont scored the T150 Trident's first worldwide competition victory in October 1968 at the Harewood, Ontario, production race. *Ed Cunningham photo*

TT phenom Eddie Mulder won the Peoria National in 1965 and 1966 and all three TT Nationals in 1966. *Brooke archive*

Elmore) qualified at 134 to 135 miles per hour. As soon as the green flag dropped, the big race became a 200-mile Triumph romp—and an outright duel between Hammer and Nixon. The pair shot away from the field, then thrilled the crowd by swapping the lead twenty-four times in twenty-six laps! The pace was so torrid that Nixon shattered Buddy Elmore's old lap record, boosting it to 98.22 miles per hour.

Hammer pitted for fuel on the twenty-sixth lap, the race half over. As he re-entered the track, a shop rag he had tucked underneath his crotch dropped into one of the carburetor stacks, causing the engine to bog. It took him almost an entire lap to find the problem, wasting 30 seconds. He crashed trying to catch Nixon a few laps later. With a broken collarbone and iron-man will, Hammer remounted his bent motorcycle—and managed to finish seventh!

Elmore then took up the chase. By the forty-sixth lap, he'd whittled Nixon's 16-second lead to 9 seconds. But the wiry Oklahoman could taste victory, going on to beat Buddy by 12 seconds. The winners' circle was a Triumph victory party. Nixon netted $4,000, and again Doug Hele was there smiling behind his two riders and their tenacious Tigers.

As *Cycle* put it, "It was a crushing defeat for Harley-Davidson," the first time the Motor Company had lost two consecutive Daytona 200s since 1952. Nixon and Elmore had lapped every rider in the field at least once and shattered their own lap record at 98.22 miles per hour. Triumph placed five riders in the top ten. All six factory bikes finished.

Doug Hele later praised the TriCor and JoMo Service Departments: "Much of the development feedback after each Daytona came via Rod Coates and Pete Colman," he explained, "all very helpful indeed."

NIXON'S THE ONE

Gary Nixon had been telling everyone who'd listen that 1967 was going to be his year to win the coveted AMA Number One plate. Since his professional racing debut in 1963, he had finished sixth in the AMA points standings twice (1963 and 1964), third in 1965, and second in 1966. After dominating Daytona, he predicted that he'd win 1967's other three pavement races, which earned the most points. The seven half-mile and two mile dirt tracks, he knew, would be much tougher game.

His prediction came partly true. In June, a sodden Loudon began like Daytona, with Nixon and Hammer rocketing away from the pack and riding so closely together that their gear changes sounded like one. Nixon's fear of racing on wet tracks had been cured after he and Cliff Guild rode new TR6Rs the entire 500 miles from Baltimore to New Hampshire, in the rain. The race ended as it had in Daytona—Hammer fell and Nixon rode to victory. That made it two for two for Gary on the road race circuits.

After Loudon came the Reading, Pennsylvania, half-mile where Nixon placed sixth. He then copped a second at the Columbus half-mile, was a no-start at Tulare, and finished twelfth at the Castle Rock TT. Then came a surprise win at Portland, the season's first Mile. Ascot's fifty-lap TT went to Triumph TT master Skip Van Leeuwen; Nixon finished seventh. At that point, Nixon led the championship chase with 312 points. Mert Lawwill trailed with 267 points and George Roeder with 231.

Indianapolis, 1967's third road race, saw TriCor roll out two T100Rs: a Daytona-spec machine with full fairing and clip-ons, and a Loudon-configured "naked" bike with roadster handlebar. After practice, Nixon opted for the Daytona setup. He led most of the 110 miles until a fried ignition coil forced him to limp home on one cylinder, giving Rayborn the win. Nixon watched 86 points slip away, while Lawwill picked up a 22-point lead over him in the standings.

As he predicted, Nixon won the Santa Fe short track on his ultra-trick, Dick Bender–built Tiger Cub. It was his third win there in five years. At Peoria, it looked like he would finally win his first National TT—until Dick Mann, aboard a BSA A65, beat him across the checkers on the last lap. Nixon could only manage a sixth at the San Jose half-mile. And, at the Sacramento Mile, he had third place nailed until a flat tire forced him out.

Dusty Coppage aviates his 650 at the Ascot TT, 1969.
Bill Delaney photo

TriCor mechanic Ted Rivard unveils Larry Palmgren's new Trident-powered, rigid-framed flat tracker in early 1969.
Gaylin archive

Awaiting its stickers, the restored 1967 Daytona winner outside Big D Cycle, February 2017. *Brooke photo*

After Daytona 1968, Texas Triumph tuning guru Jack Wilson purchased the ex-Nixon Daytona-winning T100 from TriCor. Wilson's Dallas-based Big D Cycle dealership needed a competitive race bike for his sponsored riders Virgil Davenport and rookie phenom Rusty Bradley. The factory 500, bearing engine and frame number H52104, fit the bill for two seasons, until the Trident arrived.

Wilson made minor upgrades, but for the next forty years, the famous Daytona twin remained track-worn but remarkably intact while it changed hands twice—first to New York's Team Obsolete, who raced it in early vintage events during the 1980s, then to British Only parts king Ken Grzesiak. He kept the bike in storage along with a cache of ex-factory racing bits that Wilson had included. In 2013, Grzesiak sold the racer to a Las Vegas–based collector of milestone ex-works roadracing motorcycles.

The collector wanted a full restoration and chose Keith Martin, Jack Wilson's protégé and current owner of Big D Cycle. Martin's obsession for correct detail, no-compromise workmanship, and deep knowledge of Triumph's US racing history meant the motorcycle was in ideal hands during its three-year restoration.

Martin compiled a thick dossier on the bike, including a copy of the Meriden race shop parts manifest, TriCor documents, and dozens of period photos, drawings, and schematics. Disassembly revealed the thorough work of Doug Hele's team in turning a Tiger into a Daytona winner. "These bikes were a strategic engineering program; this was evident to us as soon as we opened up the engine," Martin noted. "The amount of design, machining, and tuning work Triumph put into these is amazing. They didn't just pull six bikes off the assembly line."

Trick features abound, from the big tappets to the special crankshaft with its lightened flywheel, built-up bearing housings on the timing side crankcase, tiny sludge trap, and TriCor-supplied aluminum clutch basket. Caged needle bearings reside in the gearbox. The bike's steering head casting was machined at Meriden to reduce mass, and the swingarm was boxed near its pivot. Virtually every part was either specially made or highly finessed by Hele's experts.

The bike's Lucas ET coils are impossible to find today; Martin rebuilt and re-encapsulated them in his shop. The mandrel-bent exhaust pipes had to be recreated at a California tubing specialist. Megaphones were sourced from Ace Classics in the UK, the right-side (low-level) one cut and rewelded with a proper "flat" installed for cornering clearance.

New-old–stock racing tires—a 3.50x19 Goodyear rear and 3.00x18 Dunlop front tire—were discovered and fitted, as were lightweight spoke nipples and original Lodge waterproof spark plug caps. The blue piping on the seat was faithfully replicated. The Honda exhaust heat shields are as fitted before the 1967 race by Beaumont Triumph dealer Woody Leone. The fairing's panels are secured with bungee cords as in the race. And many small parts had to be sourced or fabricated.

"I scoured the flea markets at Davenport and the Barber Vintage Festival for years picking up the hard-to-find little stuff that's critical—correct Jubilee clips, clamps, fasteners," Martin explained. Even the Triumph transfers for the original Birmingham Fibreglass Moulding Co. gas tank, though not yet applied when the accompanying photo was taken in early 2017, had to be period-correct TriCor items with the circle-R copyright in the center of the Triumph "swoop."

Martin next turned his attention to the restoration of H52105, ridden by Gene Romero, who finished eighth in the 1967 race.

Gary Nixon tries out the first Trackmaster Trident miler, 1969. This "platform" would do well on the long Nazareth track and also serve as a road racer for Nixon protégé Gary Fisher. *Brooke archive*

With just two races remaining, Nixon trailed Roeder in the points, 394 to 406. Next up was the 75-mile Carlsbad, California, road race, which was heavily favored to go to 1966 winner Cal Rayborn. Nixon had placed second there in 1966—and this time he won.

The day was not all success for Nixon, however. Because rain threatened, the race organizers had moved the Expert race ahead of the Lightweight race. During the Lightweight event, Nixon's Yamaha two-stroke seized, causing him to crash and break his throttle-hand thumb.

The 1967 season then hinged on the last event: the Oklahoma City half-mile. It was Nixon's hometown and he stood 40 points ahead of Roeder. But the race was worth 53 points. A poor finish, or a Roeder win, would hand the Number One plate to the Harley rider. The Harley-Davidson team went gunning for Triumph's injured ace.

Roeder persuaded Rayborn and Nix to try to keep Nixon far back in the pack by blocking him. But ever-tough Nixon enlisted his own enforcers: teammate Dick Hammer and even BSA riders Neil Keen and Sammy Tanner; Keen had helped Nixon dial in his bike in practice, and Tanner was given a fresh Triumph for the main event. By race time, the two sides were like Wild West posses preparing for a gunfight.

Nixon could barely twist the throttle due to the pain in his broken thumb. Meanwhile, Roeder qualified fastest, setting a new track record. It was all or nothing for Triumph. Keen taped Nixon's injured hand into a claw shape and TriCor tuner Dick Bender wired a spring to hold the throttle wide open. Nixon would have to control engine speed with the ignition kill button.

The shootout was set. When the race started, Nixon did what he had to do: stay within the track's narrow groove and

Chuck (No. 38) and Larry (No. 5) Palmgren prepare their Trackmaster-framed 650s at the Cumberland, Maryland, half-mile, 1969. The brothers won four dirt-track Nationals between them that season. *Brooke archive*

Routt's Cycle Center in Hagerstown, Maryland, supplied Triumph with its proven 750cc kits for AMA Class C homologation in 1970. *Magazine ad*

BSA Group Managing Director Lionel Jofeh (left) and Triumph's US racing director E. W. "Pete" Colman tour the Triumph-BSA pits at Daytona, 1970. *George Hack photo*

Gene "Burritto" Romero's 165-mile-per-hour Trident has everyone happy in this 1970 Daytona gathering. Standing from left: Romero's road race tuner Pat Owens, TriCor service chief Rod Coates, and Meriden's top development engineer, Doug Hele. *Brooke archive*

keep ahead of Roeder. He finished second, behind Fred Nix; Roeder crossed the line in fourth, behind "hired gun" Tanner. That gave Nixon 508 final season points, to Roeder's 451. For the first time, a Triumph rider was AMA Grand National Champion! Nixon pocketed about $38,000 for the season's work and bought a new Shelby Mustang. National Number Nine was now Number One.

Much of TriCor's $30,000 race budget for 1968 was aimed at capturing a third consecutive Daytona victory. But since its defeat in 1967, Harley-Davidson had invested a reported $500,000 in developing new road race machinery. When Daytona practice week arrived, seven factory KRs rolled into the paddock sporting new frames, twin carburetors, and huge Ceriani brakes. Their low, slick Wixom fairings had been shaped in the Cal Tech wind tunnel. Gobs of newfound horsepower lurked underneath the orange, white, and black fiberglass.

On the first day of practice, Nixon was riding flat out on the banking, tucked in at 140 miles per hour, when Nix and Rayborn blew past him so fast he couldn't even get close enough to drop into their slipstreams.

"Fast sumbitches!" Nixon recalled to the authors. "Freddie even tapped me on the back once as he passed me, just to rub it in."

Harley's technical changes for the 1968 race "were much greater than we expected," admitted Doug Hele. While the works T100Rs had been upgraded, there had been no time for the further development he knew was needed. A Meriden-built, all-welded frame had been tested and was quickly nicknamed "the Wobbler" by the US riders. They reverted to the 1967-spec

The most original factory highboy Trident in the world resides, as of 2017, in a private road racer collection in Las Vegas. Originally Romero's 1970 ride, it went to Gary Nixon in 1971 and had the disc brake fork added. *Brooke photo*

frames, upgraded with US-made Sonicweld swingarms. Hele's limited resources were being stretched; further development of the 500cc twins for AMA racing was "diluted" by the intense UK 650cc Production Racing program, he said.

In the race, Nixon was 2 seconds quicker per lap than in 1967, keeping pace with Rayborn in the infield, but the Harleys were 10 to 15 miles per hour faster on the oval. Nixon was lapped by Rayborn, the eventual winner, but he hung on to fourth place—until his ignition quit. He finished nineteenth. The first two Triumphs home were Elmore (sixth) and Jim Odom (seventh). Triumph's only consolation was that every factory Harley, except Rayborn's, had blown up or crashed.

Nixon had won the 1968 season short-track opener at Houston, riding a Sonicweld-framed 250cc TR25W single. Harley riders took eighteen out of twenty-three AMA National races that year. But because no single rider dominated the points, Nixon was able to stay alive in the standings with consistent second- and third-place finishes. He battled with Rayborn and Nix for the points lead through the entire season; all three faced enormous pressure as the year wore on.

Besides Houston, Nixon's only other 1968 win was at the Columbus half-mile. His dirt-track bikes now featured lightweight Sonicweld frames; these had been fabricated in 4130 chrome-moly tubing by Californian Ray Hensley, who later created the famous Trackmasters. Rear suspension was finally

entering AMA dirt-track racing, and riders reveled in how it improved their control.

By the season's last race at the Ascot half-mile, it was down to Nixon versus Nix for the Number One plate. Nixon rode like a man possessed to finish fourth, while Nix could only muster a seventh. That gave Triumph's hero a second consecutive Grand National Championship, beating Nix by 9 points.

THE 750S TAKE OVER

Despite some upgrades to his T100R for 1969—including a five-speed Quaife gear set developed for Percy Tait's European Grand Prix T100 (but not available through US Triumph dealers), an aerodynamically cleaner UK-made Jakeman fairing, and Harley KR seat/tailpiece—Gary Nixon could only manage a ninth place at Daytona. It was Triumph's worst finish since 1960. The racing 500cc twin had reached the end of its competitive life just as Yamaha's new 350 was busting onto the AMA road race scene.

Light, fast, simple, and inexpensive, with superb brakes, the two-stroke twin was relatively cheap to rebuild. It had shocked the "old guard" at Daytona 1968 when Yvon Duhamel and Art Baumann finished second and third in the 200. In 1969, Duhamel qualified his new TR2 on pole with the first-ever qualifying lap above 150 miles per hour. Out of the crate, a stock 350cc TR2 made power equivalent to a factory Triumph 500—for a fraction of the cost.

Daytona 1966 winner Buddy Elmore didn't get a North Trident ride in 1970, but TriCor built him a super 650cc twin in a Yetman G.O. frame. It used a Harley XRTT seat/tailpiece and was reliable and fast enough for Buddy to finish eighth in the big race. *George Hack photo*

The 1970 inaugural motorcycle road race at the new Pocono Speedway was won by Gary Nixon on a triple built up from a spare North highboy frame that Doug Hele sent to TriCor. Nixon beat Yvon Duhamel for the non-National win. *Bill Milburn archive*

None of this was lost on Rod Coates. In March 1968, a confidential report from TriCor to Lionel Jofeh, the new head of BSA Group, proposed significant engineering changes to the T100R. The list of requested upgrades included stronger crankcase castings, larger bearings, aluminum cylinder barrels, the five-speed gearbox, and even titanium con rods. The report stressed the need to build 200 examples for AMA homologation.

The proposal never made it past early discussions. The focus was now on the AMA's upcoming Class C formula, which allowed any 750cc engines for flat track beginning in 1969 and for road-race Nationals in 1970. With no production 750 twin to homologate, Triumph's distributors campaigned the 650s while Coates secretly began the T120RT project described in Chapter 6.

What Triumph did have was its new 750cc Trident. Tuners had mixed feelings about the three-cylinder superbike. On the plus side, the long-stroke engine produced about 60 horsepower right out of the box and responded to tricks learned on the unit 500. It also had a stout, one-piece forged crankshaft with four main bearings. The triple was much heavier and wider than a 650 twin, though.

Triumph's first chance to flex the Trident's muscle was at the 1⅛-mile Nazareth, Pennsylvania, dirt track. Nazareth was the season's sixth National, and Triumph was winless thus far. The TriCor team came armed with 650 twins and Trackmaster-framed

750 triples; Nixon chose the latter and, in early practice, was turning 43-second, 94-mile-per-hour laps.

Confidence ran high—until the Harleys showed up. Right off the trailer, Bart Markel and Fred Nix cut forty-twos—on their prehistoric flathead V-twins! The race started out as a Nixon-versus-Nix, superbike-versus-dinosaur thriller, but, at the end of fifty laps, Nix had prevailed by half a straightaway. The Triumph boys were humbled. Their new triple was not a winning solution for the dirt, even with more development. The T150's best dirt finishes were Nixon's second place showings at Nazareth in 1969 and 1970, both with a twin-shock Trackmaster frame. This TriCor-built machine had been converted from a road racer (5-gallon aluminum tank, 210mm Fontana from the 500s) that AMA Junior Gary Fisher had ridden to second place at Daytona. Fitted alternatively with four- and five-speed gear sets, it was changed back into the dirt tracker that spit Nixon off when he dragged the primary case at the 1970 Sacramento Mile while running in second place. BSA's Rocket 3 fared slightly better in the dirt, winning two National Mile events in 1969.

In US and Canadian Production roadracing, the early Tridents racked up a number of wins, including Roger Beaumont's first-ever T150 victory at Harewood in fall 1968; the Willow Springs 12-Hour with Big D Cycle's Virgil Davenport and Rusty Bradley sharing the riding; and the inaugural 1970 Nelson Ledges 24-hour endurance race win by Jim Cotherman's C&D Garage team, which included *Cycle* managing editor Phil Shilling.

As the 1960s came to a close, Triumph's overall US racing fortunes were soured by Nixon's spectacular crash at the Santa Rosa Mile, where he broke his left leg. Harley's Mert Lawwill earned the Number One plate, but the year was bright for other Triumph racers.

Larry Palmgren and his younger brother, Chuck, collected wins at three National Mile tracks and one half-mile on their 650s. Young Donny Castro, an excellent all-around Amateur racer, had a great season and was hired for the 1970 Team Triumph as a first-year expert. And the highlight of 1969 was the rise of Gene Romero, who finished second in points.

THE MILLION-DOLLAR TEAM

When the separate US Triumph and BSA organizations were effectively merged into the Birmingham Small Arms Corporation Inc. (BSACI) in 1969, Pete Colman approached new company president Peter Thornton about forming Team Triumph and Team BSA. Colman made this pitch for two reasons: to save his job, and to consolidate the former TriCor, JoMo, and BSA racing shops at Duarte. Thornton approved and signed off on a $440,000 racing budget for 1970. Included with it was Colman's directive: "Dominate AMA Grand National Championship events."

Most bets were on either Triumph or BSA doing so anyway. Overall, the two brands had the best equipment and talent—Gary Nixon, Gene Romero, and rookie Don Castro on

Ex-Castro 250cc TR25W short-tracker used a rigid Sonicweld frame with tank by The Fiberglass Works. This little beauty is displayed at the Rouit Flat Track Museum in Clovis, California. *Brooke photo*

Don Castro No. 11y on a North-framed Trident dirt tracker conversion with Gary Nixon on the more successful Trackmaster-framed dirt triple. *Dan Mahony*

the Triumph team, and Jim Rice, David Aldana, and Dick Mann for BSA. (Mann rode Bob Hansen's semi-works Honda CR750 at Daytona only.) For them, the 1970 AMA season would be the toughest yet: twenty-seven National events (ten half-miles, five miles, five TTs, five road races, and two short tracks) spread across fifteen states. The circuit required nearly 70,000 miles of travel, crisscrossing the US in vans from February through October.

As 1970 arrived, the demarcation between the richly financed factory teams and the AMA privateers was wider than ever. Even the top-financed dealer teams couldn't hope to win against the powerhouse works outfits like Triumph-BSA, who could develop the most effective equipment (which was unavailable for sale) and buy the best riders. At Daytona in 1970 to 1971, for example, the Triumph-BSA juggernaut included three British road race stars with Grand Prix and Isle of Man TT experience: Percy Tait, Triumph's top factory test rider; Paul Smart (who replaced Tait in 1971); and the legendary Mike Hailwood.

To the dismay of Colman, all three Brits were paid out of his budget. Hailwood reportedly netted $5,000 in 1970 and more in 1971.

Everyone agreed that the new three-cylinder road racers were outstanding. Built by Doug Hele's Meriden race shop in just ninety days, the machines—blue and white fairings for Triumph, red and white for BSA—were based around special duplex frames contracted to independent British fabricator Rob North. He made four frames for Triumph and three for BSA for Daytona 1970, "about fifteen total" for 1970 to 1971, North told co-author Brooke. No two were exactly alike: all varied slightly in dimension and geometry.

For Daytona 1971, North built four new frames with steering heads lowered by 1.25 inches. Called "lowboys," these were given to Romero, Smart, Mann, and Hailwood. All the 1970 team machines wore massive four-shoe, 250mm Fontana drum brakes in front and 9-inch Lockheed discs (initially aluminum, changed to iron) in the rear. After Daytona, Pat Owens's crew replaced both teams' rear brakes with stock Honda CB750 12-inch rotors. Likewise, twin Lockheed front discs appeared on most of the triples in 1971—the world's first factory racers with triple disc brakes.

Engines on the "Beezumphs," as they were nicknamed, delivered 82 to 85 horsepower via cylinder head work, valve gear, camshaft profiles, and carburetion that were basically transferred over from the 500cc racing twins. Compression ratios varied from 11.1:1 to 12.7:1, depending on machine and year. The triples exhaled through a 3-into-1 collector exhaust with cannon-like 30x4-inch megaphone. Hele said his engineers had originally tested 3-into-3 exhaust systems before receiving a 3-into-1 "prototype" from Big D Cycle's Jack Wilson; with further dyno refinement, these helped raise output by up to 5 horsepower. Wilson had tested high-level 3-into-1 headers on the Big D Cycle Trident racers in 1969, and BSA West's Tom Cates had also used them successfully on his Rocket 3s.

For the 1970 race, the triples arrived at Daytona with five-speed gear sets made by British specialist Rod Quaife. However, since the standard Trident and Rocket 3 had four-speed 'boxes, the racing five-speeds were legal only if they were catalogued and available to customers. Colman and BSA Group boss Jofeh pressured Hele to change back to four-speeds. Meanwhile, BSACI scrambled to list the five-cog gear sets in its US parts books and on the shelves to meet AMA rules.

"Luckily, fifty complete five-speed 'boxes were flown to New York," explained Hele, "so homologation was legal on race day."

1970 AMA Grand National champ Gene Romero with his tuning team (from left): engine builder C. R. Axtell, Mike Libby, and Nick "the Greek" Deligianis. *Dan Mahony*

Team Triumph poses before the 1971 Daytona 200. From right: pole-sitter Paul Smart, Gary Nixon, Tom Rockwood, Don Castro, and Gene Romero. Smart is aboard a new lowboy Trident. *Mick Woollett image/Brooke archive*

Pat Owens recalled that some Yamaha and Honda team mechanics threatened to protest the five-speed triples prior to their approval. The canny Owens quietly reminded his competitors that some of their own bikes also flirted with illegality. "When Ralph Bryans' CR750 Honda crashed and burned, everyone saw its magnesium engine cases melt. No way those magnesium cases were available from any Honda dealer!" he said.

When qualifying began, the new triples showed their stuff. Romero was clocked at over 165 miles per hour through the Daytona traps. His 157.342-mile-per-hour qualifying average put him on pole, ahead of Hailwood and Nixon. Tait and Castro also qualified in the top ten, albeit with speeds under 150 miles per hour—slower than Yvon DuHamel's Yamaha TD2 had run in 1969.

A key to Romero's qualifying speed was Owens's use of ribbed 3.00x19-inch Goodyear tires front and rear, inflated to 40 psi. After Romero's three qualifying laps, the skinny Goodyears "had slivers of rubber hanging off, nearly shredded," Owens said. "But they reduced drag [rolling resistance], and we needed all the help we could get. Gene had gotten the slowest of the three Tridents sent from Britain." Romero's trap speed remained the fastest ever at Daytona as of 2017, as 1970 was the last year qualifying was done on the banked oval.

The triples incorporated several American-made upgrades that were shipped to Meriden before the bikes were assembled. S&W valve springs and titanium collars and keepers, along with aircraft-quality Bendix ignition points, were vital to season-long reliability, Owens asserted.

Streamlining helped too. The 1970 works fairings were designed at BSA's Umberslade Hall R&D center and refined

Motorcycle drag racing legend Boris Murray heats up the slick of his 305-pound Top Fuel double at Santa Ana in 1972. A year earlier, Murray set a drag bike record of 8.74 seconds at 175 miles per hour at Bowling Green, Kentucky. *Norman Mayersohn photo*

Not a significant Triumph racer, but one of the wildest: Don Castro's Red Line–framed 750 with its signature hippie-art "bodywork" made by Castro's sponsor Tracy Nelson at The Fiberglass Works. After its first race at the 1972 San Jose half-mile, the AMA banned the bike for violating an anti-slipstreaming rule. It was painstakingly restored by Metro Racing's Don Miller in 2008. *Brooke photo*

in the Hawker-Siddeley Aircraft subsonic wind tunnel. Tall tailpieces fitted for Daytona—and, later, Talladega—were worth an extra 200 rpm, the equivalent of 3 miles per hour, on the speed bowl.

The Triumph and BSA triples were the most powerful and fastest motorcycles at Daytona in 1970 and 1971. On the Triumph side, Nixon led the 200-miler in 1970, until his engine succumbed to the severe detonation that plagued Hailwood and others on the team. This was a result of running 38 degrees of fixed ignition lead combined with the high compression, marginal engine cooling, and, as Hele later admitted, insufficient pre-race testing in a warm climate.

Romero's Tridents ran flawlessly both years, giving him a pair of seconds, while Dick Mann's Rocket 3 won it in 1971. Racer-journalist Tony Murphy sampled Romero's pole-record Trident at Willow Springs, California, in a 1970 track test for *Motorcycle Sport Quarterly*. He was wowed by the factory triple.

"The engine is delightful," wrote Murphy, an ex-Honda factory rider. "The power range has to be the widest of any road racer around. The tach is red-lined at 8,500 but the engine will pull from under 5,000. And once it reaches 6,000 it's really singing." The howling exhaust reminded Murphy of

"a three-cylinder Offenhauser." The racing Trident performed like a muscle car, Murphy enthused: "just dial on more power when you need it."

The North-framed Trident's only AMA National win, by Nixon, came in June 1970 at Loudon, his favorite road circuit. He also won the inaugural motorcycle race (a non-National) at the new 1.8-mile Pocono, Pennsylvania, tri-oval in August. The Pocono bike was built up at TriCor for Gary Fisher using a spare North frame, Harley XRTT seat/tailpiece, and 250mm Fontana front brake. In 1971, this Trident was loaned to *Cycle* magazine technical editor Jess Thomas, an engineer and accomplished road racer. As Thomas chronicled in a feature article, the triple, while fast, was frustratingly unreliable.

PETE'S DIRT BOYS

"BSA-Triumph must have set a new track record for spending," noted *Cycle*'s report from Daytona 1970. Peter Thornton's big-bucks outlay included an air-conditioned BSA-Triumph press trailer for journalists, which was fitted with telephones, typewriters, a telex machine, and a refrigerator. BSACI also paid a film crew $17,000 to shoot a 16mm short documentary on the group's triples racing that was eventually produced in 1971. It can be seen on YouTube today.

Privateers in 1970 had no chance of getting a North chassis, a five-speed gearbox, or wind-tunnel sculpted fairings. In fact, a pre-Daytona TriCor memo to dealers recommended running 650cc twins! You could, however, purchase a lightweight Trackmaster or Yetman model G.O. frame, approved by the AMA and sold by TriCor. Buddy Elmore rode a very trick Yetman-framed 650 twin and finished eighth, beating factory guys whose bikes failed.

For flat-track and TT events, the equipment ridden by "Pete's Dirt Boys," as BSA engineering boss Bert Hopwood dubbed Colman's American race team, had become highly specialized. Only their engines and the stickers on their gas tanks signified the Triumph or BSA brands. A typical Expert-class dirt-track twin included a 650-based engine wrapped in a frame, fiberglass tank by Lipp Plastics, and a seat made by Tracy/The Fiberglass Works, Bates, or Maely. A typical chassis included a Trackmaster frame with Betor or Ceriani forks, Barnes quick-change hubs, and Barnes-Hurst rear disc brakes and Akront or Borrani aluminum wheel rims. Primary covers

Romero was the lone Triumph factory rider at Daytona 1972. Note brake calipers moved in front of the fork sliders, a Duarte modification. *Brooke archive*

Mechanic Sal Acosta wrenches Gene Romero's Wenco-framed triple at the 1973 Laguna Seca National. Teammate Gary Scott's Trident with side-mounted dry-break fuel filler is in the background. Both machines wear Morris cast wheels. *Dave Friedman photo/Don Emde archive*

The Duarte race shop's last gasp produced three 350cc Trackmaster-framed short trackers using BSA B40 singles built by Chuck "Feets" Minert for team members John Hateley, Mark Williams, and Rob Morrison. Triumph stickers didn't fool anyone. This is the ex-Morrison bike, at the Rouit Flat Track Racing Museum. *Brooke photo*

When Gary Scott returned to privateer status in 1976, he continued to use his trusty Trackmaster T140 for TT races. The beautiful steed was finally retired in 1983. *Brooke photo*

made by Carl's Sport Shop, Axtell, Kosman, and Barnes were popular. For TT events, front drum or disc brakes were added and footpegs were reconfigured.

Surprisingly, in early 1970 four North-framed road racers (two Triumphs and two BSAs) were converted at Duarte into Mile dirt-track machines under the direction of racing boss Pete Colman and team manager Danny Macias.

"It was an experiment," Romero told co-author Brooke in 2009. "Colman was under pressure for us to run the triples. The engine was too heavy and wide in a Trackmaster frame and worse in the road race [North] frame. I practiced on them but parked mine because my twin was superior in every way." Don Castro scored the North-framed Trident's best dirt-track finish, a third at Nazareth in 1970. The project was not continued in 1971.

At the track, the two proud rival brands had to work alongside each other. "All of a sudden we had to share paddock space with those 'watermelon' engines," quipped Pat Owens about the oval-case BSA A65s. Moving all technical and race bike development to California had deflated the morale of Baltimore stalwarts Coates, Guild, Bender, and Rivard. Their BSA East-based counterparts Walt Brown, Herb Neas, and Ralph Matysir weren't happy, either. The Triumph veterans believed the company was trying to orchestrate a BSA championship for the 1970 season. Owens agreed.

About halfway through the season, BSA team rider Jim Rice led the points and appeared headed for the Number One plate. But when Romero hooked up with tuner C. R. Axtell, who built his reliable 72-horsepower dirt-track motors (now displacing the legal 750cc), the Triumph rider started a serious run for the championship.

According to Owens, BSA's US management then cut off Romero's spare parts supply. "They didn't want Gene and the others to race twins because they were having trouble selling the triples. They wanted us to race the Threes at Mile events regardless of whether they worked well or not," Owens said. "At the same time, BSA was lagging badly; management was desperate for a BSA championship." Owens used his solid longtime relationship with TriCor to obtain vital parts for the eventual 1970 AMA Grand National Champion, without Colman's knowledge.

When Romero had showed up at a race with "Trackmaster Special" custom lettered on his Love Brothers–built bike's gas tank, Colman was "furious," Pete admitted to the authors in 1992. Gene's independent tack and success on the fast Axtell-tuned twin was not following the "team" playbook—but it proved to be the turbulent season's winning combination.

SOLDIERING THROUGH THE SEVENTIES

The 1971 racing season represented the pinnacle of Triumph's US racing success. Romero, the 1970 champ, finished as runner-up behind BSA's Mann for the Number One plate. Given the debacle occurring on the production bike side—and BSA Group's

THE WENCO FRAME

Wenco frame originally used on Mike Kidd's 1974 factory Trident.
Brooke photo

As excellent as the works Rob North frames were, Triumph race team manager Danny Macias believed they could be improved. Macias realized that additional horsepower for the triples would not be forthcoming, so lightweighting the existing machines was a priority.

In 1972, he contracted Wenco Industries, a Van Nuys, California, maker of race car driveshafts, to fabricate a small batch of new frames (twelve were ultimately delivered) reverse-engineered from the North design. Macias's aim was to reduce weight and have interchangeable oil tanks and sub-components. This was not possible on North's unique originals.

The Wenco frames were gas-welded in SAE 4130 chrome-moly tubing rather than brazed in T45 like North's originals. This reduced weight by 6 pounds. The Wencos' 28-degree steering-head angles mimicked the North lowboy; by comparison, the 1970 highboys used 26-degree head angles. Rear engine plates were 1/8-inch plate instead of boxed sheet, and the swingarms were reinforced. And their straight-tube reinforcements between the top and front downtubes, rather than the original J-shaped tubes, are one visual indicator of a Wenco frame versus a North. (Rob North believes the Wenco's straight-tubes are a structural compromise in that location.)

The Wencos entered service during the 1972 AMA season. "In addition to the set of frames for our factory bikes, I had Wenco make some extras so I could supply some of the Triumph dealers who had been asking for Rob North frames for their sponsored race bikes but couldn't get them," Macias told co-author Brooke in 2002. "I sold them at cost."

looming financial collapse—the millions spent on back-to-back winning race seasons was, in hindsight, beyond extravagant.

The development of competitive BSA/Triumph race machinery had also hit its zenith, and the doomed BSA empire had no capital for clean-sheet designs. Doug Hele realized this watching the 350cc TR2 Yamahas nearly beat his fastest 750s during 1970 and 1971. He knew Yamaha's 70-horsepower, six-speed TR3 was being readied for 1972. New 100-horsepower 750cc works triples from Suzuki and Kawasaki would follow.

"The two-stoke writing was on the wall, I told myself at the time, knowing that our engines were developed to the limit," Hele told *Cycle*. "All the money in the world couldn't have rescued the four-stroke triples from defeat by the two-strokes."

Overnight, the big money was gone. Triumph-BSA's powerhouse team was dramatically downsized. For 1972, Mann was the sole BSA team rider. Nixon and Castro were let go, to the dismay of Triumph fans. Young Gary Scott was hired by Colman and Macias halfway through the season to join Gene Romero on the 1972 to 1973 Triumph squad. The pair finished second and third, respectively, behind Harley's Mark Brelsford

in the 1972 season points, taking two half-miles and a TT race between them.

Romero and his old reliable Trident were superb at the 1972 Laguna Seca road race National, placing second behind Cal Rayborn's XRTT Harley. Since 1970, Macias had been modifying the US triples, attempting to improve their handling, aerodynamics, and reliability. He rented the Cal Tech wind tunnel for fairing tweaks and purchased a dynamometer and flow bench for the Duarte shop. Beyond the Honda 12-inch rear brake, Owens fitted stout fork braces at the request of some riders and experimented with a Victor Products single-points ignition unit tried by Tom Cates on some machines. Morris cast wheels and new fuel tanks with aircraft quick-fills made in California by Auto Research (a sprint car aluminum fabricator) were used in 1973. Macias also revamped the pioneering Rob North frame to lighten the triples and improve parts interchangeability.

Daytona 1973 saw Dick Mann on a new Wenco-framed BSA Rocket 3, painted blue and white and labeled Triumph. The veteran Mann's venerable triple started in the second wave of riders but rode a perfect, precise race—with lap time

In 1977, Ohio-based Triumph dealer and dirt-track sponsor Bill Kennedy enlisted former Meriden designer Jack Wickes to draw up a clean-sheet parallel twin capable of beating the XR Harleys. The result was the American Racer, raced by Ted Boody (who finished second at the Ascot half-mile), Ricky Campbell, and others. Kennedy's funds ran out before the 301-pound, 85-horsepower machine could show its full potential. *Dan Mahony photo*

Big D Cycle's Jack Wilson and his rider Jon Minonno with the Ducati-beating Formula 750/Battle of the Twins machine that served as Meriden's racing testbed for the new 8-valve TSS. The narrow Triumph engine enabled use of a Yamaha TZ250 fairing for improved aerodynamics. That's a 13-inch Kosman disc brake on the front Morris mag. *Keith Martin/Big D Cycle*

significantly faster than in 1971—to finish fourth, behind a trio of factory 350cc Yamahas.

Later that year, Gary Scott and his Trident were third at Loudon, while teammate Romero rode his 750 twin to Triumph's last Mile dirt victory, at San Jose, against increasingly powerful XR750s. During that period, California Triumph flat-track ace John Hateley briefly took to the pavement on the ex-David Aldana Rocket 3 highboy, in Triumph colors. Macias was running out of options to field competitive road racers. He even had two 750cc twin-cylinder road racers built at Duarte in early 1973, using Wenco frames and Morris mag wheels. Macias believed the twins' lighter weight would be an advantage on twisty "handling" circuits such as Loudon. One machine was tested, but none were raced, which was probably a good thing for Triumph.

The final year for a "factory" Triumph effort during the Meriden era was 1974. Mike Kidd entered the 200-miler on a Wenco-framed Trident with lightweight magnesium primary drive that saved over 9 pounds. With essentially the same 85 horsepower that the works triples delivered three years earlier, Kidd faced Yamaha's awesome new TZ700 fours. Tait arrived from England with another works Trident, but neither rider completed the 200 miles.

Kidd came back to win the Columbus half-mile a few months later, marking Triumph's last victory at an AMA half-mile.

The short but glorious "Beezumph Era" was finally over, until Vintage racing rejuvenated the triples in the early 1970s. Triumph 750cc twins continued to appear in AMA National

TT winners circles through the decade, culminating in Brad Hurst's 1979 surprise victory at Castle Rock. But the British brand's "factory" racing refused to die. In 1981, Big D Cycle's Jack Wilson began race-testing the new 8-valve Weslake cylinder head that was being prepared for the production TSS Bonneville. Big D's rider Jon Minonno (Wilson's son-in-law) was a five-time Western-Eastern Road Racing Association (WERRA) champion on modified T140s; he held speed records at the Bonneville Salt Flats.

Wilson built prototype 8-valve race engines and regularly supplied Triumph chief engineer Brian Jones at Meriden with data. A 750cc version ridden by Minonno at the 1981 Daytona Battle of the Twins race was clocked at 152 miles per hour on the speedway's banking. A long-stroke (860cc) version beat Jimmy Adamo's Reno Leoni-tuned Ducati 900SS at the Brainerd, Minnesota, superbike race.

"We were regularly protested by riders of Japanese four-cylinder race bikes," Wilson noted. "They couldn't believe they were gettin' beat by an ol' Triumph twin."

BACK IN THE DIRT, AGAIN!

Between the end of the "Meriden era" and the rise of Triumph Hinckley, Triumph twins, triples, and singles became the backbone of the Vintage racing boom in the US. They were particularly strong in Formula 750 and the 750 Sportsman road race classes. Then, in 2004, came Triumph's first AMA championship in decades: Chad Disbennet won the AMA Top Fuel Hill Climb Championship aboard his exotically modified twin.

In 2005, Triumph introduced the Thruxton Cup Challenge Championship, a "spec" class based around the new 865cc cafe racer–inspired model. Ted "Cannonball" Cobb won the inaugural series, winning seven of nine US events and banging elbows with Gary Nixon, whom Triumph hired along with Harley legend Jay Springsteen to add some star power to the popular series. Triumph awarded Cobb with a trip to England and $2,000 cash.

The same year, Bill Gately, the owner of Bonneville Performance, and his brother, Steve, decided to jump into Grand National Dirt Track, because racing does indeed improve the breed—in Gately's case, this meant high-performance components for the new-generation Bonnie as well as complete street-tracker machines. And, as Triumph history proves, racing is also an effective means to market and promote the brand.

The stock air-and-oil-cooled 865cc Bonneville engine, with its heavy twin balance shafts and hefty crank assembly, couldn't pretend to be a racing unit. It was engineered for durability and reliability, but the Gatelys were committed to steadily building a successful pro-level dirt program. Their high standard would have made Rod Coates proud: the race bikes were so well turned-out they could win concours. In 2010, they hired Shawn Baer and

Triumph TT and desert racing legend Eddie Mulder with "Triumphant," his C&J-framed, T140-powered custom racer. Mulder Triumphs have won the Vintage class at the Pikes Peak Hill Climb eight times, once beating factory BMW HP2s. *Brooke photo*

started to attract attention, but the machines still weren't in the running against the evergreen XR750s and Kawasaki 650 upstarts. AMA Pro Singles champ Mikey Martin joined the team in 2012, made six main events, and finished ninth at the Sacramento Mile.

Those results got the attention of both Triumph's Georgia headquarters and George Latus, an Oregon dealer and Triumph flat-track team sponsor. Very quickly, the Gatelys' were partnered with the official Castrol Triumph competition effort. The brand now had two teams: Bonneville Performance/Castrol Triumph, and Latus Motors/Castrol Triumph. As the 2013 Pro Dirt Track season closed, riders Martin and Johnny Lewis had placed 13th and 17th overall, respectively. They also brought on Shayna Texter, another

Pro Singles hot shoe. At the 2015 Sacramento Mile, Brandon Robinson gave Triumph its first factory-supported podium finish in an AMA Pro Flat Track Main since the Meriden era.

The Gatelys' team was building a new fan base for Triumph, just like in the old days. Jake Shoemaker, national number 55, took over the saddle in 2015 and, while an American Flat Track National win remained elusive, the bikes set some fastest-qualifier marks. Housed in a custom monoshock 4130 steel chassis built in-house at Bonneville Performance, the team has two engine configurations: the stock 865cc displacement for half-miles, and a monster 995cc Mile motor (97.6x66.5mm bore-and-stroke) that breathes through 42mm Mikunis.

The big engine lives on 112-octane Sunoco racing gas and is claimed to deliver over 95 horsepower at the rear wheel. Both units run sans balance shafts and use Triumph's 270-degree crankshaft.

No Cerianis or Betor forks on this machine: front suspension is a modified and fully adjustable Yamaha R6 fork. An Ohlins unit holds up the rear, and the lightweight dirt machine's forward momentum is curbed via a four-piston Performance Machine floating caliper biting the 10.5-inch cast-iron rear brake rotor. When rider Joe Kopp complained of quirky handling, Mike Owen of racing frame maker J&M supplied a better chassis.

As this book was being completed, the Gatelys, without Triumph R&D support, were preparing to unveil a new "BP Supertracker" race bike based on Triumph's new 900cc liquid-cooled twin. The 995cc racer will be a showcase of speed equipment aimed at giving the new XGR750 Harley, FTR750 Indian, and potent Kawasakis some "Limey" competition once again.

A Thruxton Cup racer in the Mid-Ohio paddock, 2008. *Brooke photo*

Jake Shoemaker No. 55 on the Bonneville Performance 995cc twin passes Dominic Colindres's Yamaha FZ-07 at the 2015 Springfield Mile. © 2015 Bonneville Performance/Randal Birkey

The air-cooled Bonneville Performance's dirt-tracker delivered 95 horsepower to the rear wheel. The 18.5-pound chrome-moly-steel monoshock frame was designed in-house. A new-generation liquid-cooled Bonneville engine using a 900cc lower end, 1,200cc top end, and stroker crankshaft entered service in 2017. © 2015 Bonneville Performance/Randal Birkey

10
OIL IN THE FRAME
TRIUMPH'S TEMPESTUOUS EARLY 1970s

In late summer 1970, Triumph's US dealer network buzzed with optimism. They had just ended their best-ever sales season. Demand had wildly exceeded supply. Sweeping changes were expected for 1971, including a new double-overhead-cam 350cc twin that was reportedly as quick as a stock 750cc Trident in early race-circuit testing. The 650s were getting a major makeover and Triumph was on the verge of clinching another AMA Grand National racing championship. However, few in the US motorcycle press—much less those Americans connected with Triumph—suspected the chaos brewing in Britain.

ABOVE: A new Umberslade-designed oil-bearing frame on an automated line-boring jig at Meriden, 1971. *Ivor Davies/Brooke archive*

LEFT: A stock 1971 T120R Bonneville on display at TriCor. Other than the rear Girling shocks and the engine, the machine is all new. *Brooke archive*

While Americans eagerly anticipated the new season, lack of management vision and misguided investment was hurling Triumph toward catastrophe. BSA Group's leadership under Lionel Jofeh and Eric Turner had squandered borrowed capital on a 50cc three-wheeled scooter, further consolidation of the BSA and Triumph brands, and a new R&D center that opened in 1968. Meanwhile, updates for the existing model range and the new DOHC 350 program fell dangerously behind schedule.

BSA BUMBLES, TRIUMPH STUMBLES

The pitiful Ariel 3 trike was an ill-conceived albatross. BSA factory manager Alistair Cave noted in a *Classic Bike* feature that BSA's UK dealers somehow convinced the company board that the firm could sell 60,000 trikes a year, worldwide! In reality, few were ever sold, despite the millions of pounds spent.

Massachusetts Triumph dealer John Healy recalled that the only Ariel 3 he ever saw in the US was one that Peter Thornton kept in his Verona, New Jersey, office: "Most dealers thought that was a good place for it," Healy said.

The concept behind the Umberslade Hall R&D facility certainly had merit. Creating a research arm separate from Meriden and Small Heath would bring fresh thinking to Triumph and BSA product development, the top brass believed. Nearly 300 new engineers, many of them hired from Britain's shrinking aerospace industry, weren't hampered by a hidebound mindset. Change was indeed necessary if Britain's largest motorcycle maker was to appear serious about challenging the Japanese juggernaut and the reinvigorated Europeans.

But BSA management never established clear priorities for the facility, Doug Hele told the authors. The result was polarization among the incumbent engineering groups, who considered Umberslade to be an unproductive money pit.

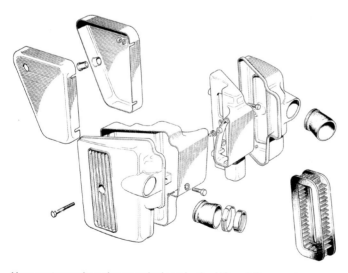

New motorcycle noise regulations in the US and Europe drove development of a proper airbox and filtration system for the new oil-bearing frames. The inner housings are cast aluminum. *Brooke archive*

Matt Guzzetta saw Umberslade through American eyes. The young industrial designer from California was given the opportunity to work there by JoMo's Don Brown. In an interview with co-author Brooke, Guzzetta recalled his time spent at "Slumberglades" (as it was nicknamed by Meriden staff) as being consumed by endless meetings.

From 1968 to 1971, millions of pounds were pumped into both the Ariel trike program and the R&D center. The facility reportedly cost BSA Group about £1.5 million per year, while the company's annual profits for 1969 to 1970 dropped from £588,000 to £352,000, according to Steve Wilson's *British Motorcycles Since 1950; Volume 5*.

To launch its 1971 models to the US motorcycle press in November 1970, BSACI rented the luxurious La Quinta Hotel in Palm Springs, California. It was the most lavish media preview yet held in the motorcycle business. Journalists were invited to the resort for four days of riding the new Triumphs and BSAs, chatting with the corporate honchos, and soaking up the hotel's hospitality.

With the press assembled on the first day, the wraps were dramatically pulled off each motorcycle in succession. Ten models for the new season! These included both street and dual-purpose versions of the 250 single and two variants (T35 roadster and T35SS street scrambler) of the twin-cam Bandit 350. The only Bandit at the La Quinta was the high-piper—and it was a nonrunner. This was a bad omen.

The Daytona and Trophy 500s were essentially 1970 carryovers with the addition of turn indicators, new electrical switch housings and control levers, and bobbed rear fenders. While they were paint-job revisions, at least Triumph didn't mess with the 500's "poetry" that had so absorbed *Cycle World* the year before.

The 650s, on the other hand, startled those who saw Triumph's 1970 models as the distillation of everything that was right about motorcycle styling and ergonomics. Gone were the classic mufflers, gaitered forks, bullet-shaped headlamps, and rounded side covers that had shouted "Triumph" to two generations of American motorcyclists.

The new 650s instead wore slimline "Ceriani-style" forks, developed at Umberslade, with shortened front fenders mounted with flimsy wires. Headlamps on the 650s and Trident were new, flat-backed Lucas units also suspended on wire brackets. The new front end's overall appearance was racy and modern. The conical hubs and brakes on the 650s and the triple were a new-generation drum design. This puzzled the American press: why did BSA-Triumph engineer a new *drum* front brake when Honda's benchmark front disc had already "trickled down" to the CB450 twin?

The centerpiece of the 650s was the new oil-bearing frame, Triumph's first duplex frame since the disastrous 1960 to 1962 item. Developed at Umberslade Hall using computer-aided engineering tools, the so-called P39 frame featured a husky, 4-inch tubular backbone that doubled as the main oil reservoir.

This was similar to the excellent American Trackmaster, British Cheney, and BSA works motocross frames. The new frame was Triumph's first 100 percent welded design. This eliminated the separate oil tank, which helped reduce weight and eliminated cracked oil-tank mounts, a perpetual service complaint.

Best of all, the new oil-bearing frame was significantly stiffer than its old furnace-brazed, iron-lugged predecessor. This helped sharpen the bikes' handling. Unfortunately, what looked ideal on chief designer Dr. Stephen Bauer's drafting table proved problematic in the real world. The frame's main failure was its height, which put the surface of the TR6 and Bonneville seat a towering 34.5 inches off the ground—3 inches taller than 1970 models.

A greater blunder was strategic. When production started in August 1970, Meriden had not yet received final blueprints for the new frames because Umberslade was still making design changes. Without these, tooling couldn't be built. Triumph's number one breadwinner was stalled. Meanwhile, the factory built out its entire 1971 run of 500cc models and produced hundreds of 650cc engines in anticipation.

When Umberslade finally released the 650s' frame drawings, Meriden's production team discovered that engines could not be installed with their rocker boxes in place. The assembly logjam that followed delayed production of new 650cc twins until January 1971 while the cylinder head and rocker boxes were modified to fit the frame. This time-consuming rework required altering the new airbox. According to former Triumph service manager John Nelson in his book *Bonnie*, three different 650cc frame configurations were ultimately produced during a chaotic 1971.

Five long months after the original start-of-production date, new 650cc Triumphs finally began arriving in American showrooms. But the prime US sales season was lost and with it some customers, who migrated to Honda 750s. In spring 1971, Triumph showrooms held only a mix of T25 singles, mildly refreshed 500s, and Tridents wearing the new slimline forks, conical brakes, and Dunstall-like mufflers.

The turn of events took US dealers by surprise. In autumn 1970, Triumph-Detroit's Bob Leppan was recuperating in a California hospital after his horrific Salt Flats crash when he was visited by Stephen Mettam, a BSA Group designer and former Ogle stylist employed at Umberslade Hall. Mettam had brought photographs of the 1971 models to show selected dealers like Leppan.

"As soon as I saw those photos, I knew we were in trouble," the speed ace recalled. "The one thing Triumph didn't have to change was the *appearance* of its motorcycles—*that's* why people bought Triumphs!" Instead, Triumph needed to improve the bikes it already had.

"We needed to reduce our warranty claims, so we could make our customers happy," he explained. "By doing that, we'd reduce our warranty costs."

Big D Cycle's Jack Wilson commented that 1971 was a

1970 AMA National Champion "Tiger" Gene Romero and a new TR6C at the 1971 Triumph-BSA press launch in Palm Springs. Note the tall seat and 8-inch conical front drum brake. *Brooke archive*

fiasco for one simple reason: "Nobody asked us dealers, or Triumph owners, if we *wanted* any of that stuff! If they'd just put a front disc brake on the old forks and kept the 1970 frame, and fixed the oil leaks and a few other things, we couldn't have sold enough of 'em."

When 650s finally straggled into the US, the new, taller frames attracted a lot of attention. "My sales manager was average height, but to sit on a '71 Bonneville he had to use his tip-toes to balance it," John Healy recalled. "Guys couldn't get them up on the centerstand. The seat height was a problem for us. Some customers who'd put down a deposit for the '71s wanted their money back when they finally sat on the bike."

Another discovery was made at Triumph's American

THE STILLBORN T35 BANDIT

After retiring from BSA Group management in 1963, Edward Turner opened his own independent design firm, ET Engineering Developments. There he created various forward-looking concepts, including a 1,000cc inline four-cylinder touring bike, aimed at the US market, and an enclosed cycle car. Turner also drew up a DOHC 350cc twin, which he prototyped for Triumph's consideration in 1968. But Doug Hele and Bert Hopwood determined the prototype to be so unsuitable for production that Triumph had to completely re-engineer the entire machine.

"It was crazy; they were doing the drawings, making hard tooling and building prototypes all at the same time," recalled Matt Guzzetta. "They had discounted everything Turner had done, and were rebuilding the entire bike from the bottom up. The engineers weren't even quite sure what the finished engine was going to look like. They were really strung-out."

Back in the States, a questionnaire form was sent to the executives of the Triumph and BSA distributors. It was a specifications sheet for the new 350; the Americans were asked to fill in what type of tires, gearbox, and other major features they thought the new machine should have. Don Brown, then vice president at BSA Inc., welcomed this solicitation.

"We needed a modern 350 badly in the US; Honda was selling a ton of theirs," he said. "I took Hopwood, Jofeh, and other British senior staff at their word—that they were going to compete with the Japanese with this bike."

Brown and his colleagues were finally shown the revamped prototype when it had been costed-out by BSA Group accountants. He was staggered by their presentation:

They said the least the 350 could have sold for in the US was about $1,500 and that a reasonable price would have been $1,600! At the time, Honda's 350 was going

Brief ride reviews published in *Cycle Guide* and *Motorcycle Sport Quarterly* in early 1971 were as close as Americans would ever get to Triumph's promising T35 Bandit DOHC 350cc twin.

for $800. If ours had come in at between $900 and $950, we could've sold every one they sent us. I became so depressed after that meeting.

As presented at La Quinta, the T35SS Bandit's 63x56mm engine was claimed to deliver 34 horsepower at 9,000 rpm. An electric starter was optional. The bike's beautifully simple, 23-pound frame resembled the works triples' racing frames made by Rob North.

In late 1970, *Motorcycle Sport Quarterly*'s Bob Greene became the first American writer to ride the 350 Bandit. The twin-cam engine performed impressively at high rpm, Greene wrote, but, off the boil, "the Fury lacked the lugging power of its popular Japanese contemporary." Handling of the 350-pound twin, he noted, "was quick and effortless."

Anxious American motorcyclists and Triumph dealers never found out for themselves. As chronic financial convulsions hit BSA's motorcycle operation in early 1971, the Group axed the 350 program. From that point on, Triumph had to stand and fight Japan's upmarket advance with three OHV engine families descended from Edward Turner's 1938 Speed Twin.

distributors: the bikes' frames had not been properly flushed clean after being welded. Once the engine oil in the frame tubes began circulating, it dislodged bits of weld spatter and other foreign particles still inside. Some engines were damaged as a result.

A quick cure was found by BSA service manager Tom Cates. He developed a pressurized flushing pump and a process for cleaning out each bike's oil reservoir while the motorcycle was still in its wooden crate. All oil-in-frame models in stock in Duarte and Baltimore were cleaned before shipment to dealers. The factory eventually had its own cleaning process on line.

The 1971 Blazer SS (street) and Trail Blazer 250 (dual-purpose) retained their underwhelming BSA-built engines but featured an excellent new oil-bearing chassis. The new 250s were lighter and more competitive than the old Trophy "twud."

According to Matt Guzzetta, Umberslade had purchased an early Yamaha DT-1 250 to benchmark the Group's revamped singles. The Triumph Blazers and their identical BSA Victor 250 cousins only remained in production for the 1971 model year. They were the company's final "lightweight" machines.

Ironically, Triumph had flirted with a thoroughly modern, three-cylinder 250 way back in 1965. Doug Hele's concept included two versions: a SOHC cylinder head and six-speed gearbox for road bikes, and a DOHC/eight-speed variant for roadracing. Prototype engines were authorized, and most of the castings were completed.

Hele told co-author Brooke that the 250cc triple project was shelved by BSA boss Harry Sturgeon when he authorized race development of the T100 twin in late 1965. Three years

later, Guzzetta stumbled upon the baby triple during his design stint at Umberslade Hall.

"I walked into a drafting room and one of the draftsmen was using this beautiful little double-overhead cam cylinder head for a foot stool!" Guzzetta recalled. "I asked him what it was and he told me it was from Hele's 250 Three. Then he took me to a large closet nearby—it was filled with castings for the engine."

Before the project was dropped altogether, plans arose briefly to build it as a 350-3. Triumph was in dire need of a bike to compete with Honda's hot-selling 305cc, then 350cc SOHC twins. But instead of finishing Hele's triple, management opted for a different 350 (see sidebar at left).

MCCORMACK RETURNS

Based on their sellout sales in 1970, Triumph Motorcycles Inc. predicted it could sell 50,000 machines in 1971. Given an on-schedule, uninterrupted supply, they probably could have done it. By year's end, the company had received roughly 30,000 machines—the highest volume in Triumph's history, according to Pete Colman. But its US market share had slipped badly. Together, Triumph and BSA clung to just 6.9 percent of the US motorcycle market—fifth place behind Honda (nearly 50 percent share), Yamaha (about 30 percent), Suzuki, and Kawasaki. In a rare interview, *Cycle Illustrated* asked Peter Thornton whether the parent company planned to offer a machine smaller than 250cc, or a two-stroke.

"We're not saying exactly what we are going to do," retorted the BSACI president. "But we will definitely cater more to the consumer! If they want a 500cc, we will build one; if they want a 1,200cc bike we'll build that too."

Closeup of a 1972 Bonneville fork-top components show the Ducati-style steel-wire headlamp mount used in 1971 to 1972, new instrument mounting scheme, and turn indicator. *Brooke photo*

Blazer SS "street scrambler" version of the 1971 250cc single used BSA MX-style oil-bearing frame. The huge steel muffler anticipated more stringent exhaust noise laws. The Trail Blazer model had a raised front fender, aluminum tank, cross-braced handlebar, and Trials Universal tires. *Brochure image*

The 1971 Triumphs were subjected to several magazine road tests. *Cycle World* was first to wring out the T120R Bonneville and deemed it "one of Triumph's best." The editors shared everyone's dislike for the towering seats and clumsy switch gear, but they loved the improved handling dynamics and steering precision of the new frame.

Cycle magazine, emerging as the most analytical US motorcycle publication, put one of the first five-speed Tridents to the whip in July 1971. The T150 had less than 200 miles on it when it came under the gun of editors Cook Neilson, Phil Schilling, and Jess Thomas. Its new conical drum brakes were the bike's biggest downer—"Pasting an airmail stamp on your duff and pre-addressing yourself to Saint Peter makes poor insurance," quipped Neilson.

But the triple's locomotion floored *Cycle*. It was the quickest standard production bike they tested that year, firing off a best quarter-mile run of 12.90 seconds at 102.7 miles per hour. The new Quaife-derived five-speed was subjected to twenty-one speed shifts under full power and didn't miss one.

Despite positive magazine reviews, warranty claims piled up alarmingly once 1971 models began selling. Valve seats fell out when some cylinder heads heated up. Clyde Earl, then Triumph's national warranty manager at Duarte, was told by his Meriden contact that this was due to dull tooling. A batch of Lucas batteries installed in the new bikes had been delivered to Triumph with plugged breather holes, causing the batteries to split, or even blow up.

"Lucas refused to pay for the damage done to the motorcycles corroded by battery acid," Earl said. "They sent a rep over from England to investigate the situation; our dealers wanted to burn him at the stake!"

Leppan grimaced as he recalled oil leaks on the new front forks and even leaks from various plugs and outlets on the oil-bearing frames. "I thought that at last, we'd done it," he said, shaking his head. "We'd developed a motorcycle that leaked oil where it never had for forty years!"

By summer 1971, BSA Group's Motorcycle Division was bleeding red ink and top management was drowning in the flood. Lionel Jofeh was replaced, a new board was formed, and orders went out to begin closing BSA as a motorcycle brand. The Small Heath works in Birmingham, once the colossus of the motorcycle industry, would continue to manufacture Trident engines and some Triumph parts along with a reduced 1972 BSA range.

The British bankers in control also wanted new American management. Peter Thornton's contract had to be bought out, reportedly for $400,000. A replacement was needed, and on June 10, 1971, Denis McCormack returned to take command of his old company.

The former TriCor pioneer was lured from retirement to restore American dealer confidence. And he was British—a prime consideration to those bailing the lifeboats in Birmingham.

"He wanted to come back," offered Earl Miller, his longtime TriCor financial man. "He was hurt by what had happened to Triumph." One former Triumph dealer who knew McCormack well reckoned he returned "because his life's work had been destroyed by overpaid buffoons." With help from Miller, McCormack reviewed Thornton's existing budget; they were appalled at the excessive spending. But it should be stressed that much of BSACI's frivolity was predicated on a promise of 50,000 motorcycles delivered and sold on time—the 1971 frame and 350 twin debacles saw to it that this would never happen.

No individual in the US could have greatly affected Triumph's turnaround at that time without a sound long-range product strategy in Britain to back him up. Colman believed that McCormack was brought back to destroy BSA, he told the authors. Yet for years it was realized on both sides of the Atlantic that, compared with BSA, Triumph had a stronger US dealer network, a higher-quality image, and, during the 1960s, greater annual sales.

Shutting down BSA cost the company millions in the US and Britain and created turmoil within the American sales network. Many BSA dealers had already lost faith due to the too-tall frames (painted light gray!) and boxy, Japanese-looking tanks. Small Heath's abrupt closure most severely affected those US Beeza dealers who didn't have a Japanese or other franchise to fall back on.

To avoid an onslaught of lawsuits, BSACI threw a juicy bone to the angry dogs: it offered BSA dealers the coveted Triumph franchise. This angered the Triumph dealers by carving up their sales boundaries. Competing dealers often found themselves right around the corner from each other. The old Triumph-versus-BSA rivalry threatened to erupt into a minor civil war. It was a miracle the company wasn't hit with a legal action as a result.

FIRE SALE FOR THE '71s

Triumph shuffled into 1972 amid continued losses by the parent company. Umberslade Hall was shuttered while the last motorcycles bearing the winged BSA badge (B50s and A65 Lightnings) were assembled early in the year at Small Heath. The B50MX motocrosser hobbled through 1973 as BSA's final model. It continued briefly, with slight changes, as the 1974 Triumph TR5MX.

Top management's exodus also continued. Eric Turner resigned after more than a decade as chairman of the board. He was replaced by Lord Shawcross, who brought in Brian Eustace from engineering giant GKN to be his chief executive officer.

"When BSA placed fresh faces at the top through managerial upheavals, they put old words and promises into new mouths. Only the costumes changed," Cycle's veteran British correspondent Jim Greening wrote in 1973. Greening noted that Shawcross "took the BSA bed of nails to save some factory floor jobs and to salvage something for the stunned shareholders. It was, if nothing else, a generous gesture."

McCormack also retired permanently, and the British bankers and BSA's embattled directors had to search for yet another Triumph US president. Colman claimed that he was formally recommended for the position by Triumph's Hopwood—"better the devil you know than the devil you don't," Hopwood was said to have reasoned to the board after mentioning the veteran Californian.

Despite the dedicated Colman's twenty-four years with Triumph, CEO Eustace eventually picked another outsider—Dr. Felix Kalinski—for the top American post. A West Point graduate and decorated World War II bomber pilot, Kalinski had held various executive positions after retiring from the US Air Force. But during his first 1972 meeting with Triumph's senior American managers, he admitted that he knew nothing about motorcycles. He then promised that he'd be an expert on the subject within six months!

"We are seeing executives, who may have been excellent sales and marketing people, taking charge of motorcycle firms while not having any knowledge of motorcycles or the people who rode them," wrote Cycle World founder Joe Parkhurst in his book A Hurricane Named Vetter.

Kalinski's initial challenge was to rapidly clear out 11,000 unsold 1971 Triumph and BSA models—millions in inventory—from US warehouses. Kalinski moved these unloved machines by using aggressive fire sale tactics, including a clever "Buy and Fly" program that earned dealers a vacation trip to Britain when they purchased a quantity of the leftover bikes.

" 'Buy and Fly' also was Kalinski's way to get us dealers back on his side," noted John Healy. "We were getting militant—we wanted good motorcycles to sell and we wanted the warranty money that was owed to us since the late '60s."

Kalinski's second priority was to press Meriden for more service parts, whose scarcity was crippling the US dealer network and causing some agents to abandon Triumph. Parts and service were "the franchise" for most Triumph dealers; the

A new 1972 Trident in Regal Purple displayed at TriCor during the annual eastern dealers' meeting. Triumph began offering two gas tank paint schemes that year: the "panel" style shown and traditional twin-scallop graphics. *Gaylin archive*

motorcycles were almost a behind-the-service business. But new consumer protection laws in some US states were forcing motorcycle dealers to turn warranty service jobs around rapidly or the dealer had to buy back the bike. Triumph dealers were thus double-punished by the shortage of spares and the new six-month warranty.

THE EARLY FIVE-SPEEDS

By April 1972, the final (series C) iteration of the Umberslade frames entered production with the lowered seat rails they should have had originally. *Cycle World* noted in its June 1972 650 Bonneville test that the Bonnie still possessed many of Triumph's finest qualities.

"For one thing, it doesn't feel like it weighs 410 pounds wet," the magazine reported. "It points easy and tracks well."

The test Bonneville was the new T120RV model—the "V" denoting the five-speed gearbox. Originally advertised as an option in 1971, the five-cog transmission didn't arrive on the 650s until spring 1972. It cost $200 more than the standard four-speed version, which made the V-model Bonnie a $1,725 proposition. "Perhaps, to a Triumph lover, price is no object," opined *Cycle World*.

This was the first Bonneville to record a sub-14 second (13.9 second) quarter mile in a *Cycle World* road test. It was even faster than the original T120TT Special tested in 1963!

As with many Triumph features during this uncertain period, there was a downside to the early five-speed gearboxes. Layshaft first and second gears and their drive dog were not carburized (cooled in an oil bath after heat treatment), and they broke under moderate-to-heavy use—often within the first few miles of operation.

"The gears were so brittle that the teeth flew off like popcorn," intoned Triumph's eastern service chief Cliff Guild.

In the field, the situation reached crisis levels. Some customers' five-speed gearboxes failed literally as they departed the dealership. The gear teeth and chips would break off, grinding shrapnel into the works and, in the worst instances, blowing a hole in the gear case. The standard four-speed gearboxes had no vices and performed faultlessly.

"You sell someone a new bike; the gearbox fails immediately, and then you tell them they won't have the bike back until the end of the summer. The customer's pissed and he wants his money back," groused Triumph-Detroit's Leppan. "But we couldn't afford to give them a new bike. Our warranty claims resulting from those early five-speeds were just enormous."

Pete Colman reckoned that at least 1,000 five-speed 650s—nearly $2 million worth of new motorcycles—in the Baltimore and Duarte warehouses would have to be repaired quickly. Replacement gears were taken to a Los Angeles metals specialist for heat treating and carburizing. Makeshift "assembly lines" were set up at both Triumph facilities and a repair procedure was established.

Once the root cause was identified, Meriden began carburizing the transmission gears. But the episode was another untimely blow for Triumph in the US.

The oil-bearing frame brought another consequence for Triumph dealers: it helped kill the accessory business that was a major profit center. Often there was more revenue in accessories than a dealer could make on a new bike. The pre-1971 frames with their bolt-on rear subframes had provided a popular "platform" for the custom aftermarket, including hard-tail rear sections that helped keep Triumph dealers alive during the "chopper" era.

11
THE TRIUMPH DEALER
FROM HUMBLE BIKE SHOPS TO BIG BUSINESS

America was built by entrepreneurs who believed they could make or sell anything. "Foreign-made" products simply presented a sales opportunity to those looking for something different—the lure of an exotic brand, perhaps. In the case of British motorcycles, it was machines offering riding qualities, technical specifications, visual aesthetics, and performance unlike those of the domestic competition.

ABOVE: **The workshop area at Reiber Motors in Washington, D.C., circa 1955 lacked the lighting and bike lifts we take for granted in 2017. Here mechanic Bill Armstrong services a plunger-frame Tiger Cub.** *Gaylin archive*

LEFT: **To motorcyclists returning from World War II, John Esler's storefront in Grand Rapids, Michigan, spelled excitement with a new Speed Twin.** *Brooke archive*

From an era that was decidedly non-PC, Ed Kretz's famous dealer sticker from the early 1950s. *Brooke archive*

Typical of many Triumph dealers in the 1950s, Bill Hazel's shop in Bowling Green, Kentucky, sold scooters, minibikes, and even lawn mowers. *Brooke archive*

Reggie Pink, Bill Johnson, Wilbur Ceder, Rod Coates, John Esler, the Nicholson brothers, and a handful of others in the US and Canada—the visionaries—saw a huge, wide-open market for Triumphs and other British machines before World War II. When the war was over in summer 1945, their numbers multiplied exponentially. Millions of returning veterans, many of whom had learned technical skills during their service, arrived home just as Britain was revving up a government-mandated export drive: 70 percent of the nation's production was aimed at earning hard foreign currency. A market and a future dealer base were born for those English vehicle factories making everything from three-speed lightweight bicycles to MG and Jaguar cars.

Triumph came out of the war with the world's newest motorcycle plant, its construction paid for by the government after the original Coventry works was destroyed by Luftwaffe bombs. Meriden's assembly lines were poised to get the postwar twins across the Atlantic to Johnson Motors and the dozen or so shops scattered across the US that handled Triumphs in 1946. As noted in Chapters 1 and 3, the efforts of JoMo and TriCor to set up the western and eastern dealer network yielded nearly 600 US Triumph outlets by the 1970s.

Ed Fisher's start as a dealer was typical. A World War II Army vet, and mechanically savvy, Fisher had the tough, compact build and quick reflexes that made him a natural motorcycle racer. Returning home to Parkesburg, Pennsylvania, he began dirt-track racing an Indian while operating a gas station.

"I met Rod Coates, who had just joined the Triumph Corporation in Baltimore. He told me the new distributorship was setting up dealers. He knew I was racing, had the gas station, and understood how machinery worked. That made me the type of person they were looking for," Fisher told co-author Brooke in 2012.

Coates soon set up Fisher with a race-prepped Tiger 100. "I was a 'factory' rider by 1952," he chuckled. "Rod said that he would supply me with any parts I needed; he'd bring them to the races. And I could sell them to other Triumph racers there too." Eventually, Coates told Fisher that Triumph wanted to set him up as a bike dealer.

"Well, that sounded good to me because now I could get my parts wholesale!" he said. "The agreement was I had to buy one new Triumph motorcycle plus $500 worth of parts and a small Triumph sign for outside my gas station shop. Suddenly, I was a Triumph dealer."

Fisher, already an astute businessman, had sold the new $900 twin even before he bought it.

I went down to Baltimore and paid Rod for the bike and the parts. Davey Jones and I assembled the bike right out of the crate and I rode it back home; they shipped me the parts. But now I was a dealer without any bike to sell, so I bought a new Thunderbird, which was the hottest model we had then.

He rode the new 650 twin for a few months, then sold it to his brother. "Now, I had two Triumphs in customers' hands but still no Triumphs to sell or to ride! Time to buy another one. This went on for some time—buy a new bike, sell it, buy another and some more parts—while I built up some savings."

By that time, Fisher was TriCor's top sponsored AMA professional rider, competing across the eastern states and traveling with Coates as his "factory tuner." He won the 1952 Langhorne 100-mile amateur dirt-track race and the 1953 Laconia 100, two marquee events. "I was racing every weekend, so keeping the shop going at the same time was a challenge!" he explained.

In 1954, Coates encouraged Fisher to build a motorcycle shop behind his house in rural Parkesburg, near Route 30. "It started out with about 800 square feet, then, a couple years later, we added a showroom. That was my first 'real' Triumph dealership," he recalled.

Scores of US Triumph agents began the same way, buying a bike or two at a time and a few boxes of parts, keeping a local hot shoe (or themselves) equipped for action on the local TT scrambles track or half-mile oval in between wrenching on and selling new bikes. Many of these pioneers were "enthusiasts first and businessmen second," admitted JoMo's Don Brown, who saw early Triumph and Ariel shops in rural southern California with dirt floors and wood stoves for heat.

As they often are today, the dealers were supported by their wives, who often kept the books, ran payroll, and quietly brought a vital dose of decorum to the enterprise. Some, such as Carol Baver at Hermy's Tire & Cycle in Port Clinton, Pennsylvania, ran the parts counter with encyclopedic precision. Her husband Hermy started his Triumph business in 1963 working out of a Willys Jeep pickup, from which he also sold snow tires.

"Mom-and-pop dealerships make the US motorcycle industry go 'round and were key to Triumph's success," JoMo's Pete Colman told the authors. He added that, for many of them, their annual profits were based not on selling new motorcycles but on accessories, service, and repair—and steady revenue from the ubiquitous Coca-Cola machine in the showroom. At smaller shops, such as DeHaven's Cycle in rural Sunnyside, Virginia, near Winchester, the owner's personality often set the tone for customer relations.

"Howard DeHaven was a good ol' country boy, with a huge barrel chest. He was a very religious man, with his radio tuned to Christian music stations," noted local Triumph rider Jay Cohen. "His Triumph shop was behind his house and I used to take my 1966 Thunderbird and BSA Rocket 3 in for annual state inspection. Howard took a *long* time to feel you out before he liked you. He complained a lot but always liked working on my bikes. I remember the soda machine in the shop well."

The arrival of Honda and Yamaha in 1959 and 1960 greatly expanded opportunities for the Triumph dealers, some of whom were World War II combat veterans with no prejudices against the Japanese newcomers. Ed Fisher continued to race and sell bikes until 1957. He took on Yamaha in 1960,

Winchester, Virginia, dealer Howard DeHaven balances his 1958 Tiger 110 demo bike clad with period TriCor accessories while his daughter spins a Hula-Hoop. Note the Coca-Cola machine inside the shop door. *Gaylin archive*

Welding, steam cleaning, and Lambretta scooters supplemented Duane Worden's Triumph sales in Akron, Ohio. Worden (at left) has just sold three new Buco-equipped TR6s. He started with Triumph in 1951. *Gaylin archive*

ABOVE: TriCor road man Jack Mercer shot J. R. Ewing's shop in Lafayette, Indiana, with new 1957 models out front. Note the thin-section Trophy-style front fenders fitted to one of the T110s and the Aztec Red Thunderbird. *Brooke archive*

RIGHT: Legendary Triumph racer and dealer Ed Fisher behind the counter of his tiny Parkesburg, Pennsylvania, showroom, with a newly arrived 1958 3TA "bathtub" in the foreground. *Brooke archive*

then Honda and Datsun cars in 1963. By then, he was adding employees; he had purchased land and a building adjacent to Route 30, where he moved his store, now featuring Triumphs, Hondas, and Yamahas. Two years later, he added a Toyota car franchise 25 miles away in Lancaster.

"I actually went to Lancaster with Toyota, just to get a Triumph store for that area!" Fisher exclaimed. "Lancaster was a good place to sell Triumphs, and I figured I'd get it before somebody else did."

The famous "family" atmosphere fostered by TriCor among the eastern US dealers during the 1950s and 1960s kept many allied with the brand when the competition got tougher. It also helped dealers keep a local distance between each other. Fisher recalled a customer named Ray Miller from Reading, Pennsylvania, about 30 miles away, whose love for his Triumph twin inspired him to become a dealer.

"I told Ray that I'd help him out to get started," Fisher said. "But the Triumph dealer in Pottstown, Frank Kiss, didn't want a new dealer in Reading so close to him. Kiss carried some 'weight' at TriCor, so they told Miller that he couldn't get the dealership. He took on Yamaha instead and that was probably a better deal for him anyway when Triumph got into trouble around 1970."

Triumph lust! Spot the new 1967 models in John Esler's packed Grand Rapids showroom. *Brooke archive*

The Hunting Yellow paint on this new 1965 Mountain Cub and a Jack Pine Enduro trophy got plenty of attention at a Michigan bike show organized by a local dealer group. *Brooke archive*

Mobiles from TriCor and JoMo showing Triumph's racing stars spun from dealer ceilings through the 1960s. *Johnny Greene/Ton-Up*

The level of financial commitment that is needed in 2017 to start a motorcycle dealership is "frightful" to old-school Triumph dealers like Fisher. He noted that a friend who has sold the new-generation Triumphs since 2003 was told by the US distributor that he had to upgrade his store—a $90,000 investment. Another Triumph dealer who opened a new Florida store in a lavish former Harley-Davidson facility took on an $18,000 monthly lease.

"You've got to sell a lot of bikes to cover a lease that enormous," he reported. "Despite Triumph pushing us to make it work, we exited the new bike business within three years." His company reverted to selling parts and accessories online. "You've got to be really, really smart to make money selling motorcycles today," he opined.

A stock Trident and one customized à la Bonneville are focal points in the Triumph-Detroit showroom, early 1969. The mannequin in the background wears Belstaff apparel. *Bob Leppan*

Originally founded by Bonneville speed king Bob Leppan and his business partner Jim Bruflodt in the late 1950s, Triumph-Detroit is among the brand's most famous dealerships. Upwards of one thousand new Triumphs per year were sold from the southeastern Michigan store during the 1968 to 1972 heyday, thanks to the high wages paid by the auto industry and the area's decades of British bike fandom. That history helped attract Dave Canu and his wife Sue to purchase the business in 2005 from Sue's brother Paul Lasco. Under the Canus' ownership, Triumph-Detroit became America's number one Triumph store in annual sales in 2008, earning Dave a seat at John Bloor's dinner table during that year's global dealer meeting.

Looking to retire, the couple sold the business in 2016, but Dave agreed to remain part-time to help the new owners for three years. He sat down with co-author Brooke to share his recollections on "a fantastic" decade.

Q: Most motorcyclists who think being a bike dealer must be a "dream job" don't realize the commitment that's required.

No doubt about that. But it is a great job if you love it. Sue and I had no intention of getting into the motorcycle business. I had just retired from a career in the printing industry when her brother, Paul, who previously owned Triumph-Detroit, left for service in Iraq. So, we purchased the store in February 2005 and moved it to a new, more modern location. Five years later we moved it again to the current facility. We've been successful because we ran it like a business and took care of customers.

Q: What's the best-selling Triumph model in Motown?

The Bonnevilles are the core of our business; they represent about 40 percent of sales. The Thunderbird and the other cruisers also are very good sellers. The Sprint ST was a great seller for us.

When the 800 Tiger came out in 2011, we couldn't get enough of them. The following year, we placed the same order, but demand had tapered off. The big Trophy? We sell a few.

Q: A "good" sales year for Triumph-Detroit would be how many units sold?

The 140 bikes we sold in 2008 made us the number one American Triumph store. That was about twenty motorcycles more than in 2007. When we took over the business in 2005, it was doing about sixty new bikes per year. Currently, we average about a hundred bikes per year, and it's going up.

Q: Triumph in recent years developed a 300cc single aimed at global markets, but the bike wasn't produced. Would that have been good for the US?

Absolutely! We still need a sporty, small-chassis single—a bike for learners. The smallest model we currently offer is 675cc, and that's not a small machine. Hopefully they have something in the works.

Q: What are the ongoing challenges of running a modern Triumph dealership?

Keeping good techs! We went through four of them, two of whom we trained. It's hard to keep the good ones. Dealerships steal them from each other. In Michigan, the hardest part of keeping good techs is our four-month winter, when business slows down. In the off-season, we do maintenance, performance tuning, and even restoration work on the vintage stuff.

Q: Triumph-Detroit only sells Triumph. What's the advantage in being a single-brand store?

You have greater margins with a single brand. We've been contacted by other brands to take on their lineups, but Triumph sold us on being a single-line dealer, so that's what we stayed.

Q: What should Triumph build that it's not currently building that would really drive your business?

They just did it with the new Bonnies! We need a sport tourer, a new Sprint ST. We need an entry-level bike, maybe a single. And, if the Rocket III Tourer had a full fairing and a passenger seat with armrests, we'd steal a lot of Harley customers, no question.

Dave Canu in 2016. *Brooke photo*

12

TRIUMPH STRIKES OUT
THE TUMULTUOUS YEARS: 1973 TO 1983

The impact of Triumph's product crisis during the late 1960s and early 1970s on the company's US dealers cannot be overstated. Veteran *Cycle World* columnist and author Kevin Cameron witnessed the tumult while he was a partner at Arlington Motor Sports, a Boston area multibrand dealership.

"We had become the [Triumph] R&D Department, the Testing Department and the Warranty Department," awash in fragged five-speeds, out-of-the-crate rebuilds, and parts shortages, Cameron recalled in *Vintage Bike*, the Triumph International Owner's Club magazine.

Of the new 650cc twins, "we tried to explain to Triumph-seeking customers why they could not have the time-honored 'sausage' mufflers and black-painted fork bottles that looked 'right' to them," Cameron recounted. "What's the oil doing in the frame? Where's the . . . you know . . . the oil tank? How come my feet don't touch the ground? Young men sat on the bikes, adjusted the mirrors so they could see their faces, murmured among themselves, and walked away."

By late spring 1972, however, Americans who entered their local Triumph shop were sticking around to see more. Meriden had been on a crash course to undo the Umberslade missteps and get the 650s back to traditional Triumph form. The 1972 ¹/₂ Bonneville and TR6 models lost their 3.5-gallon fuel tanks and now featured slimmer 2.5-gallon vessels. Gone were the "chopped" seats used as an emergency measure while the lowered Series C frames were being readied; they were replaced by a redesigned saddle. Also new were one-piece rockerbox covers. These finned castings replaced the knurled caps that had unscrewed themselves on Triumphs for years.

Glimmers of hope, but the havoc of 1971 had caused BSA's share price to drop by half. By early 1972, the group's bank credit was at its limit. And increasingly frequent work stoppages at Meriden kept new bikes from being shipped to the US during March. Reportedly, the plant only worked fourteen days in March instead of the regular twenty, resulting in a $500,000 loss for the month instead of the expected profit. Trident output was notably curtailed just as the newly styled T150 was catching a second wind in the US market.

Despite more "industrial actions" by the eight unions in the factory in April and May, Triumph profits briefly jumped back into the black. July passed with no break-even for BSA Group, though. Jim Greening reported in *Cycle* that, by November 1972, BSA was paying

LEFT: **1978 was a transition year for the 750 Bonnie. It carried over the seat and side covers from the 1977 Silver Jubilee model, then at midyear added the straight-port "E" head and MkII Amals. The early '78 T140 shown here still wears the splayed-port head and MkI Concentrics, along with incorrect K70 tires.** *Timothy Remus*

$48,000 in weekly interest on corporate bank overdrafts as high as $63 million. The increasingly regular work slowdowns and stoppages at Meriden torpedoed Triumph's production plan. A year-end report to shareholders predicted significant losses.

Little of the impending crash was mentioned in the American motorcycle press. Duarte tried to maintain American dealer confidence, which meant that the less everyone knew about the calamity in Britain, the better.

As 1973 neared, Triumph's product situation brightened considerably. The 1973 model range was the company's most promising since the 1960s. It was spearheaded by a 750cc twin-cylinder engine and revamped styling plus a couple of interesting new models.

US and Canadian dealers had been requesting a larger displacement twin for years—since 1944, in the case of Nicholson Bros., as detailed in Chapter 3. The 200 "homologation" T120RTs distributed in 1970 had helped spur demand for more "cubes," as did brisk aftermarket sales of Routt and Chantland big-bore kits. But competitive pressures were creating the need for a larger machine.

The CB750 Honda's incandescent success ignited the US 750cc market. Unfortunately, the Trident's rocky start and high price weren't helping Triumph's market share. Norton's Commando was one of the hottest 750cc rides, and rumors swirled about it being punched out to 850cc. Kawasaki launched its devastatingly quick H2 triple and Yamaha was readying an all-new 750cc parallel twin, while its hugely popular 650 twin gained an electric starter and disc brake—two important features the Bonneville still lacked. Triumph needed to up its game to meet these challengers.

As soon as he took over Triumph's US operations after Peter Thornton was fired, Dr. Felix Kalinski sent Pete Colman on a mission to Meriden. His orders were to impress upon engineering director Bert Hopwood the urgent need for a 750cc twin for America and to help finalize specifications.

Doug Hele's experimental team was working on new OHC twin designs, but the projects were in early stages. Given BSA Group's acute cash shortage, any project requiring extensive tooling would be prohibitively costly. Market demands thus dictated a factory-built 750cc version of the current 650cc engine. Colman told the authors that Hopwood initially stalled, then outright refused to pursue the project. In his essential book, *Whatever Happened to the British Motorcycle Industry?*, Hopwood defended his resistance to rushing the 750 twin into production. He reasoned that it needed further development. Hele agreed.

There was indeed a negative attitude within Meriden about stretching the old 650cc lump out another 100cc—but without a new, clean-sheet engine ready, there were no other options. "He [Hopwood] never had any intention of this 750 twin seeing the light of day," Colman said. The T140 project was given the green light only after Colman bluntly suggested

that Hopwood telephone his boss, BSA Chief Executive Brian Eustace, and explain to him "why the Americans won't be getting their 750 twin." It was then that Hopwood grudgingly agreed, claimed Colman.

The first T140V (twin-carb Bonneville) and TR7RV (single-carb Tiger) twins were built in September 1972. Early engines displaced the 724cc with a 75x82mm bore-and-stroke. On December 14, 1972, the first 744cc engine was built with 76mm bores. Visually, the 750's barrels were shorter than the old 650's, as were the connecting rods (by .406 inch). The rods were carryovers from the rare BSA A70 750cc twin built in 1971 for AMA racing homologation. American tuners have since referred to the T140 as the "short rod" engine.

The 750 twins featured new cylinder heads, held down with ten bolts rather than the old nine, and a lower 8.6:1 compression ratio. A milder exhaust camshaft with 1⅛-inch-radius tappets was also fitted in the interest of midrange torque and longer life. To handle the extra grunt, a triplex primary chain was used and the now-standard five-speed gearbox was strengthened considerably. Triumph's Duarte headquarters, wanting to put to rest forever the 1972 gearbox debacle, began distributing a kit (CP1000) to update the earlier five-speed gearboxes with the more robust 1973 parts.

Along with the larger engine came styling changes that transformed the Bonneville and Tiger (and the Trident too) into downright fetching motorcycles. Meriden brought back the classic bullet-shaped headlamps and added full-radius fenders and a polished aluminum taillamp housing. The bikes' overall symmetry provoked admiring glances wherever a Triumph was parked. "One of the best finished machines to come from England in a long time," beamed *Cycle World* in its May 1973 road test of the T140V Bonneville.

Best of all, the 1973 twins felt and performed as good as they looked. *Cycle World* gushed over the Bonnie's handling and gave equal kudos to the stopping power of the new 10-inch Lockheed hydraulic front disc brake. This was also the quickest standard Bonneville yet tested in the US. The magazine's best drag strip run—13.65 seconds at almost 94 miles per hour—outpaced the five-speed 650. Midrange throttle response was improved, and the engine itself was more pleasant at highway speeds due to a higher final drive ratio.

Nits on the T140 were mainly limited to the high "Western" handlebar (magazine testers hated them, though most US buyers preferred them) and the carryover Lucas handlebar switches. "Better quality control. More power via displacement. And one of the best-balanced chassis available anywhere. All told, the T140V is the best Bonneville to date," the editors concluded.

The same year, the single-carb TR7RV Tiger 750 was wrung out by *Cycle* editor Cook Neilson, who rated the front disc brake "one of motorcycling's best" and gave similar marks to the bike's steering, shifting, and roadholding. The Tiger's stiff suspension made for a harsh ride, but, in combination with the

The 750cc twin launched in late 1972 wasn't what Triumph's engineers wanted. For Americans, though, it fit the bill perfectly. *Brooke photo*

The Meriden siege spelled the end of production for the classic T100R Daytona. This unused and never-registered early 1974 model was saved by legendary Maryland dealer Bob Myers. *Gaylin photo*

1-inch-lowered Series C frame, it contributed to "handling you can bet your life on."

Vibration was objectionable compared with the smooth new Japanese multis or Ducati's 750 V-twin. In the quarter mile, the Tiger 750 tested by *Cycle* was also quicker and faster (13.51 seconds at more than 95 miles per hour) than the T140V Bonneville tested by *Cycle World*, and its 112-mile-per-hour top speed was about equal.

The 750cc Bonnie may have lost the old T120R's fire-breathing image, but it was, along with the Tiger, a genuinely quicker and far more livable machine. Overall quality was up—Meriden was now using an 8-psi static air check on every engine before it left the assembly line. Air was injected into the sealed engines through the breather, and the unit was rejected if any oil leaks were visible. And the bikes were vastly better value for the dollar: at $1,550 for the Tiger and $1,599 for the Bonnie, the 750s were priced about par with 1972 four-speed 650s, thanks to a favorable shift in the dollar/pound conversion rate and aggressive pricing by Duarte.

"The 750cc twin was what we'd been asking for, for years—we couldn't get enough of them!" exclaimed Bob Leppan. Said John Healy, proprietor of Triumph of Wellesley (Massachusetts), "A 1973 Tiger 750 is not only one of the best Triumphs, it's also a good motorcycle." *Cycle World* opined, "Triumph should have built the 750 Bonnie five years ago."

The T140V and TR7RV clearly proved the British anti–750-twin critics wrong. In truth, the displacement bump was late to markets that had been crying out for more oomph. They were barely sufficient to keep Triumph alive in America's ultracompetitive 750cc segment, where the technology, performance, and quality bars were rising each year.

TRADITION VERSUS PROGRESS

Keeping Triumph in the superbike hunt was the Trident's job, an assignment that was getting tougher by the month. Kawasaki's 903cc Z-1 ushered in a new era of DOHC inline fours with devastating horsepower. But Japan's early superbike multis still lacked good handling, so the Trident hung on. It was blessed with the new 10-inch Lockheed front disc, standard five-speed gearbox, K81 Dunlops on both ends, and the same classic styling cues that had rejuvenated the Bonneville and Tiger.

The 1973 Trident was the realization of what Doug Hele and Bert Hopwood had envisioned back in 1965 before BSA management and Ogle ruined the picture. The T150V continued to acquit itself well when facing road test competitors. In December 1972, *Cycle* again pitted the seven quickest, fastest, best-handling, hardest-stopping 1973-model production bikes against one another in the magazine's second "Superbike Comparison Test." Including the Trident, five of the players were 750s—Ducati 750GT, Honda CB750K2, Norton Commando, Kawasaki's Mach IV triple and powerhouse Z-1, and Harley-Davidson's new 1000cc Sportster.

When the stopwatches clicked for the last time, the Trident landed commendably in third place—behind the two Kawasakis and a step ahead of the Commando. Down 11 horsepower against the winners, the Trident benefited from exquisite preparation by Duarte's technical director Bob Tryon and tuning wizard Bob Ellison. It did everything very well and won the editors' vote as the best-looking motorcycle in the test.

All eight of the Trident's quarter-mile runs were in the 12.7-second range, with a best terminal speed of 106 miles per hour. The upgraded five-speed gearbox's shifting and ratios were deemed "fabulous." On the Orange County International Raceway road course, the Triumph lapped third-fastest, hindered only by its low footpegs and goofy high handlebar. Still, it offered "the best combination of cornering ability and low scare factor." *Cycle*'s editors even commented that the Trident was much smoother than in previous years.

Where the 1973 Trident lost big was in its price. At $1,930, the Triple now cost Americans over $200 more than the Norton or Honda, was about equally priced with the Ducati, and was slightly less expensive than the big Z-1. The writing was on the wall. How much longer could Triumph's aging, 750cc pushrod Triple remain in the superbike club?

Unknown to most American Triumph watchers, Triumph's developmental pipeline was filled with promise during the early 1970s. An 830cc (T180) version of the Trident was readied for production in 1973, the same year engineering boss Hopwood hoped to have his first modular-engined prototype running. The proposed modular range comprised a SOHC 200cc single, 400cc twin, 600cc triple, and 1000cc V-5, all sharing many common components and engine dimensions.

Also in the works since 1968 was the BSA/Triumph Rotary, which years later became a Norton. By 1974, Doug Hele had two air-cooled, twin-rotor Wankel prototypes undergoing testing. One of them was sampled in Britain by *Cycle*'s Cook Neilson, who described it as "a revelation: smooth, torquey, light, responsive, pleasant in every way, and capable of jerking the eyes out of a good-running 750 Trident." Other projects included counterbalanced Bonneville twins, overhead-camshaft and Isolastic-mounted Tridents, and the prototype Quadrent 1,000cc four.

In the end, all except the Rotary bit the dust, victims of BSA Group's collapse and the later uncertainties at Norton-Villiers-Triumph (NVT). In March 1973, BSA shares on the London Stock Exchange crashed again, from 20p (48 cents) to 5p (12 cents). This sent the company's market value plummeting and forced it to suspend share trading. Some observers felt that the stock crash was due to leaks of a merger with the still-profitable Norton-Villiers, owned by Dennis Poore.

In April, Triumph laid off 300 workers, reduced costs, and reportedly made a £390,000 profit for the month, thanks to strong US demand for 750cc twins and the Trident. The 500cc Daytona suffered from lack of development, however, having remained basically in 1969-spec throughout the Umberslade

years. Still a solid machine, it was fast becoming an anachronism. Because of this, *Cycle* pitted the $1,395 Daytona against Yamaha's new TX500 twin. The resulting eleven-page cover story was headlined: "Progress Takes on Tradition."

The $1,365 Yamaha bristled with the latest features—double overhead-camshafts, four valves per cylinder, a counterbalancer, electric starting, and a front disc brake. That the venerable kick-start, drum-braked, four-speed T100R could even keep the TX500 in sight was remarkable, but the Daytona slugged it out surprisingly well. It proved itself equal to the newcomer in handling and near par in stopping power. And the full-metal Daytona, with its cast-iron cylinder barrel and iron frame lugs, weighed 60 pounds less than the TX500—a triumph of simplicity over complexity.

But in terms of smoothness, starting convenience, and oil-tightness, the engine that won Daytona in the 1960s was trumped by state-of-the-art technology. *Cycle*'s editors concluded that "everything the Triumph does, the Yamaha does better—except be a Triumph."

TR5T: THE ISDT MEDALIST

The Daytona's high-pipe brother, the Trophy 500, had been dropped at the end of 1971 followed by the legendary TR6C a year later. For the first time since 1948, Triumph was left without even a street scrambler, let alone a true dual-purpose motorcycle—at a time when America's market for dirt machines was booming.

That is, until the marriage of the single-carb T100 engine with BSA's stout P51 oil-bearing frame from the B50 family. The resulting 1973 to 1974 TR5T Trophy Trail was a 344-pound mongrel that *Cycle World* labeled "a very pleasant, do-everything bike with equal shades of mediocrity and brilliance, depending on the situation at hand." It was best described as a capable fire-roader, but the little twin was given a chance to prove it could do more. In early 1973, Bert Hopwood assigned BSACI's Duarte facility the task of modifying a group of standard TR5Ts into suitable mounts for the International Six Days Trials, held that year in western Massachusetts.

Colman handed the project to Bob Tryon, who was Triumph's top US service man and tech center manager. The plan called for the Californians to prepare fourteen ISDT machines—six Triumphs for the British Trophy team, four Triumphs for an American Manufacturer's team, and four Rickman 125s for a second American Manufacturer's team. This was cut short by the aggressive timetable.

"We just went to the warehouse and picked out six crated TR5Ts to rebuild from the frame up," Tyron said. "The only involvement Meriden had was supplying the bikes in the first place. We got zero assistance from the factory. Also, there was friction between the American and British staffs over the project: I got a super-cold reception when I flew to Meriden to discuss the ISDT program."

With no previous ISDT experience, Tryon's six-man team gathered all the magazine articles they could find on Six Days motorcycles. Tryon then cut out photos of the best features on the winningest bikes and superimposed them onto a photo of a stock Trophy Trail. This rough paste-up gave the crew a basic direction forward.

Space for a small "assembly line" was cleared in the Duarte warehouse. Once stripped down to their bare frames, the TR5Ts were heavily modified. Spanish-made Betor forks replaced the stock Triumph legs. Quick-detach Rickman Enduro (front) and BSA B40 (rear) wheels were also added. Tyron's team machined close-tolerance backing plates for the brakes as a waterproofing measure. Plastic fenders, waterproofed airboxes with Filtron filters, special seats that incorporated a tool compartment, and simple, lightweight taillamps were fitted.

The 500cc engines were "blueprinted" at Duarte and given a 0.040-inch overbore. Tryon's team fabricated and fitted a new exhaust system with a tucked-in, high-level muffler. A clever dual ignition system resided under the seat to give backup sparks if needed. "We ran standard Lucas ET ignitions," Tryon explained. "Many people thought we were crazy, but the electrical systems only gave us one failure in the entire event. Otherwise, the engines ran faultlessly."

The first completed bike was tested in California by scrambles ace Chuck "Feets" Minert. Eventually, eight machines were built at Duarte, including those for the British team. Tryon later regretted that he could only get the bikes' weight down to 306 pounds—30 less than a stock TR5T but up to 60 pounds heavier than the factory Maicos, Husqvarnas, and CZs that were favored in the 500cc class. He believed that, with Meriden development support, the weight could have been pared to the 280-pound target.

Still, Triumph's American Manufacturer's Team of Frank Diaz, John Greenrose, Ken Harvey, and Dave Mungenast did a fantastic job. They emerged as the high-point team during AMA-sponsored ISDT qualifying rounds. Their only mechanical failure in the Six Days itself was a broken fork stem on Mungenast's TR5T. The British Team won a Silver Medal, bringing their TR5Ts in second behind factory CZs. Considering that the project was done on a limited budget at whirlwind speed, it was a remarkable finish.

X75 HURRICANE: FUTURE SHOCK

One of the most controversial, collectible, and "American" Triumphs nearly ended up as a BSA. And, given BSA Group's precarious financial situation when the bike was finally introduced, it's lucky that the three-cylinder X75 Hurricane saw the production line at all.

The concept for a factory-built "custom" machine occurred to BSA Inc. vice president Don Brown when he was returning from a late-1967 business trip to Britain. Brown was thinking about the popular "café racer" specials made by Paul Dunstall and others, as well as the US custom bike movement. He particularly remembered his first motorcycle—a 1952 6T Thunderbird customized by Vern Gardner, an Oakland, California, Triumph dealer. Brown reckoned that high-profile bikes aimed at specific market niches might boost his company's sales and image at a time when the Japanese were marching steadily toward the big bike market.

He also believed that, in developing US-specific models BSA, not Triumph, should be the brand to spearhead new styling. When sales of the 1969 750cc Trident and Rocket 3 fell far short of expectations, it was clear to Brown and the company's dealers that the triples' quirky Ogle styling helped squash a lot of their excitement.

"The only way we were going to sell the triples was by restyling them—I was convinced of that," Brown told the authors. "And I knew that, because BSA Group executives approved the original Rocket 3's styling, I'd have to get the bike restyled on my own, in the US—and in secret."

In 1969, Brown asked Harry Chaplin, BSA Inc.'s sales manager, if he knew a designer who could work on a styling project and build a prototype. "Craig Vetter," Chaplin replied at once.

Vetter, a hip young motorcyclist/designer from Rantoul, Illinois, had caught Chaplin's attention at the 1969 Daytona Bike Show. Vetter had displayed two interesting products from his fledgling fairing company: a slick fiberglass tank/seat unit mounted on a Suzuki 500 twin and an early Vetter S1600 fairing—predecessor to the Windjammer—that TriCor's Rod Coates had tested on a Trident. On Chaplin's recommendation, Brown telephoned Vetter and described his idea—creating a sportier, more "American" version of the Rocket 3. Vetter agreed to fly to BSA headquarters in Nutley, New Jersey, for further discussion.

"I liked Craig's mind right away," Brown said later. "Sure, he was a long-haired, hippie-type guy—a free spirit—but he was a keen thinker and ambitious. He brought some drawings with him for the project, and they intrigued me. So, I asked him right away whether he'd be interested in doing it."

Brown confided that there wouldn't be much fame involved, because Vetter would have to work clandestinely. And he would be forbidden to share details with anyone—the prototype had to be built without the corporation's blessing. BSA Group chairman Eric Turner and managing director Lionel Jofeh knew nothing about the project.

After establishing the project's design parameters, Brown loaned Vetter a stock Rocket 3. He was asked to invoice BSA on a weekly basis and include updated drawings and photos. Brown would pay Vetter out of petty cash at a rate of $15 per hour. The two men communicated secretly by telephone each week.

There was a lot of give-and-take between them in the beginning, but Brown later admitted that "once I began to see

Marred only by its US market handlebar, the 1973 T150V was the Trident that should have come in 1969. *Bill Delaney photo/Brooke archive*

his [Vetter's] interpretation of the idea I had given him, I realized that he was cutting new ground and I got excited about the direction he was taking."

Vetter certainly had a clear vision of what his custom Rocket 3 should look like. An unabashed fan of late 1960s Triumph Bonnevilles, he incorporated Bonnie-like curves while reaching into another all-American design idiom—the chopper—for inspiration.

"Look at a lion: Deep chest, paws forward, the rear-end light. There's something primitive in us that we associate with that and transfer into motorcycles. I think there are some lean animal proportions in some choppers today," Vetter told *Cycle World* for its September 1970 cover story on the project.

Offered with a yellow tank flash in 1973 and a red one in 1974, the TR5T Trophy Trail was named Adventurer in the UK. *Brochure image*

"Chopper ideas are pointing in some direction; I feel that the BSA is an assimilation of some of these ideas, some of the stimuli around me—it is what is happening today."

With the assistance of a few trusted colleagues at Vetter Fairings, Vetter threw himself into the project. Untold hours were consumed sculpting the tank/seat into the flowing final version. From his initial sketches, Vetter planned the integrated tank/seat as a major design element for the BSA.

"I'm part of the early generation of designers who worked primarily in plastics rather than stamped metal, so I had no reservations about doing a one-piece tank-and-seat unit," Vetter told co-author Brooke. Adding svelte plastic bodywork thrust the big three-cylinder engine into the spotlight. But Vetter felt the cylinder head lacked visual authority, so he formed cylinder fin extensions out of plastic and fitted them to the prototype. Later, when the bike was released for production, BSA's Small Heath factory cast a special big-fin cylinder head specifically for it.

Custom details abounded. Some were subtle, like the Velcro strips attaching the seat to the plastic molding. Others were outrageously brash, including a trio of upswept megaphone exhausts on the bike's right side. "Those three pipes were difficult," Vetter recalled. "I used real megaphones taken from Jim Rice's BSA dirt-tracker without any thought of their actually 'muffling' anything."

Ceriani forks with 2-inch extended stanchions and blazing Chevrolet Camaro "Hugger Red" paint completed the now iconic look. The pseudo-tank's gold striping was 3M's new Scotchlite reflective tape. Vetter also sketched a unique fairing for the machine, but it was not pursued.

"Functionally I wanted my design to look American, not British," Vetter reflected in 2002. "I wanted it to get its rider noticed by women and I wanted the overall form to be enduring." The bold prototype was completed in early September 1969. Vetter had truly transformed the Rocket 3, creating a lithe, 422-pound custom that still turns heads nearly fifty years later.

About the time the concept was finished, Don Brown was preparing to leave BSA in the aftermath of the BSACI reorganization. Despite the project's secrecy, BSACI boss Peter Thornton caught wind of it. He immediately demanded to see Brown's file on the effort and ordered the actual machine to be shipped to Nutley. So, Vetter loaded the machine into the back of a friend's VW Microbus and drove to New Jersey.

"We unloaded the bike at BSA headquarters and everybody went nuts," recalled Brown. "It was like, 'Yeah, that's what we ought to do!' Myself, I was ecstatic." Thornton also gushed over the custom triple. "He walked in, gasped, and exclaimed: 'My God, it's a bloody phallus! Wrap it up and ship it to England!'" Vetter said. Included with the bike were instructions to build it "as Craig Vetter had created it." This was apparently taken so literally that the excellent Lockheed front disc brake used on the 1973 Trident and 750cc twins was not added.

According to Brown, BSA's conservative British bosses were shocked when they found out the custom Three had been built in the US without their knowledge. Some were mad at him for having kept it a secret. "The reason I did the project was because I knew BSA in England would never have done it, let alone done it the way we did it," he noted. The time from Brown's first meeting with Vetter to the day the finished bike was unveiled in Nutley was only one year.

When Brown departed BSACI in 1969, Eric Turner asked him to refrain from granting interviews to the motorcycle press once he left the company. Brown knew much about the shaky financial condition of BSA Group at the time, something Turner didn't want publicized. Brown agreed, then got Turner to agree that, if the Vetter Triple ever went into production, it would remain honest to Craig's original.

In the meantime, BSA Inc. and *Cycle World* cut a deal for an exclusive cover story on the wild machine. Vetter's notes revealed that *Cycle* also had been approached to do the feature, but only *Cycle World* publisher Joe Parkhurst agreed to print BSA's spin on the facts—that Vetter, not Brown, dreamed up the bike. When the article was published (September 1970), "I had to gulp when I read some of that stuff," Brown recalled, "but I stuck to my agreement with Eric Turner and said nothing."

The saga didn't end there. Since his main contact at BSACI was gone and Thornton didn't return his telephone calls, Craig Vetter wasn't paid for another five months. Page after page of Vetter's logbook contains frustrated notes on how Thornton and other BSACI executives stonewalled him on payment. During one phone conversation noted in the log, a BSACI official asked Vetter if he'd accept less than the full amount they owed him! Finally, Vetter contacted Brown, who appealed directly to Eric Turner. The BSA Group chairman intervened, and Vetter was paid the full $12,000 owed him for his trendsetting Triple.

The Vetter BSA was in England from October 1969 to May 1970. During this period, Colman spotted the prototype during a visit to the Umberslade Hall R&D center, where it apparently was being dimensioned for production. BSA originally planned to build 500 units of the custom Rocket 3 in 1971 to test the market. The bike would be premium priced, at about $2,100.

According to Parkhurst's book, *A Hurricane Named Vetter*, Thornton's replacement, Dr. Felix Kalinski, christened the bike "X75 Hurricane." As BSA sputtered toward bankruptcy, though, the X75's production plans were delayed. The first preproduction prototype assembled at Meriden (and still wearing BSA tank badges) was viewed by American dealers at a February 1972 sales meeting in Houston, Texas.

The original Ceriani forks had been replaced with standard BSA/Triumph sliders, 2-inch longer stanchions, and special, polished aluminum triple clamps. Meriden's parts shelves also contributed a BSA/Triumph conical brake hub and wire-mounted front fender. Vetter's novel tank/seat unit (a one-piece molding) was not exactly replicated by the factory.

TR5Ts for the American and British ISDT teams being assembled at Triumph's Duarte race shop in early 1973. *Bob Tryon photo/Brooke archive*

Instead, Triumph engineers used a two-piece mold that added a seam down the middle of the fiberglass "tank."

The first production Hurricanes left the factory on June 2, 1972, and were designated 1973 models. None of the 1,175 bikes produced through January 12, 1973, were burdened with the turn indicators BSA and Triumph had used on all bikes since 1971. Most Hurricanes were fitted with five-speed gearboxes, though some four-speed versions are known to exist. Engines were coded both TRX75 and V75V: the latter designation is believed to have been for an aborted BSA version.

The Hurricane "will do more to boost Triumphism than anything since Gary Nixon was Number One," said a headline in *Motorcyclist's* April 1973 road test. But the magazine criticized the Hurricane's top-heaviness and truculent steering. Fuel mileage barely reached 30 miles per gallon, giving an 85-mile range per tank of gasoline. The testers balanced the Hurricane's easy starting, comfortable seat, exciting engine performance, "bitchin' sound," and "amorous plastic look" against its handling peculiarities and $2,300 price tag.

Triumph's Duarte technical staff and many dealers were also not pleased with the way their custom Triples handled. Triumph-Detroit's Bob Leppan labeled the combination of a ribbed front tire and extended fork "treacherous." Duarte sent dealers a fork kit with shorter springs along with each new Hurricane, to be retrofitted as requested by owners.

BONNEVILLE TT: VETTER PENS A TRIUMPH TWIN

While the first Hurricanes were entering production, Craig Vetter was working on another Triumph design concept. In the wake of their excitement over the stylish X75, he had been contacted by Duarte to apply his talents to the not-so-handsome 1971 and 1972 650cc twins. The Americans' main focus was their franchise product, the Bonneville.

Vetter later described the "Bonneville TT 750" design as being "as fulfilling to create as the Hurricane in many ways, because it embodied ideas for the twins that I'd thought about for years." A prototype TT 750 was constructed to show Triumph dealers and recent Bonneville buyers and solicit their reactions.

Triumph-Detroit's Bob Leppan attended the TT 750 Bonneville's private showing in Dearborn, Michigan, and liked the overall design. So did Ken Grzesiak, a veteran Triumph rider who had bought a new Bonnie in 1971. At the Dearborn hotel display, Vetter's newest creation was attractively illuminated. With it were company sales officials who asked everyone attending for their thoughts. Did they like the bike?

"It incorporated many of the little things we were doing to our own bikes," noted Grzesiak, who later founded the world-famous British Only parts emporium. "It had the old-style pre-'71 mufflers, and air cleaners that stuck out like the aftermarket K&N filters we'd put on our Triumphs. It had a lot of nice touches. When they asked me, I told them they should build it."

Vetter built the Bonneville TT as if he were personalizing a Triumph for himself. It was part flat tracker, part tastefully customized standard Bonnie. The bike's 750cc top end was a harbinger of the T140V. Yet despite favorable reactions from dealers and customers who viewed it, the Bonneville TT 750 was not green-lighted for production. Its beautifully proportioned fuel tank went on to inspire the T160 Trident tank. As of 2017, the bike was still owned by Vetter.

The Bonneville TT soon after completion, 1972. *Craig Vetter photo*

Still beautiful and outrageous in 2017, this unrestored 1973 X75 Hurricane has had its controversial ribbed front tire replaced by a Dunlop K81. *Brooke photo*

THE MERIDEN BLOCKADE

Ironically, just as Triumph's revamped 1973 model line was earning widespread praise from American customers, dealers, and the motorcycle press, BSA Group's financial crisis became a matter of intense national discussion in Britain. According to the company's official statements, it had lost £15 million each year since 1971. Through this train wreck, however, the Triumph Engineering Co. Ltd. remained consistently profitable.

In March 1973, the British government approved proposals for a merger between BSA and Dennis Poore's modestly profitable Norton-Villiers. Two months later, BSA Group sold off its non-motorcycle subsidiaries to Norton parent company Manganese Bronze for a mere £3.5 million—thought by many to be less than half their true value. The flip side of the deal was that Norton-Villiers and Triumph would be combined into a single motorcycle manufacturing company, and the government would inject £4.87 million into the new Norton-Villiers-Triumph.

The optimism of Triumph's 1973 model range was clouded by shortages of machines and spare parts throughout the year. American dealers were beginning to display hostility toward their distributor and factory. Many openly declared their belief that this latest shortfall was contrived only to pressure them into selling the glut of remaining 1972 models then jamming US warehouses. The "family" congeniality that had been the hallmark of Triumph's US business—something that had served as inspiration for Honda and other motorcycle importers—was dissipating.

So limited was the supply of 1973 street models that an April BSACI memo advised dealers that they had only five days from the time of notification to collect their new arrivals, or the machines would be immediately assigned to another shop! It was a wicked trick to play on the once-loyal dealer network—offering them an oversupply of unattractive product for two years, only to ration the hot-selling 1973 machines.

There were, however, plenty of TR5Ts to go around, and US dealers were given an official blessing to convert them to street specification to spark sales. The X75 Hurricane supply was more than adequate as well: the bikes' high price, long forks, and small tanks made the radical Triples showroom dust-collectors for years. But road-going twins were at a premium.

BSACI attempted to lessen the problem by announcing the arrival of Triumph's 1974 models early, in July 1973. This head start, the US distributor claimed, would prevent the product shortfall of the previous year. The 1974 six-model range, still including the Daytona 500, was finished in slightly more conservative colors and revealed further refinements to the much-improved 1973 models. The Hurricane was dropped; in its place appeared a Triumph-badged B50MX called the TR5MX Avenger. The big thumper was made downright potent by the addition of a 580cc kit with ForgedTrue piston developed by Bob Tryon's small Duarte staff. The bike impressed magazine testers in nearly every regard—especially its attractive $1,159 base price.

There was reason to be bullish about Triumph's 1974 fortunes—until September 14, 1973, when US dealers received an ominous British press release. It announced details of BSA's financial collapse along with Dennis Poore's plan to close Meriden in February 1974 and move Triumph manufacture to BSA's old Birmingham plant. A shocked American Triumph dealer body inundated Felix Kalinski's office with inquiries about Triumph's apparent bankruptcy.

Exactly one month earlier, on August 14, Edward Turner had died, the victim of a heart weakened by diabetes. It is a merciful God that prevented Turner from seeing what was about to happen to his beloved motorcycle company.

Kalinski issued a BSACI memo dated September 25, denying Triumph was going out of business and explaining the NVT decision to consolidate manufacture. But no mention was made of the Meriden workers taking control of the factory and locking out management following Poore's September 14 manifesto. In fact, it wasn't until October 16 that US dealers were officially told about the blockade! They could only watch the unfolding debacle in horror. No one then knew that Triumph twin production would cease for the next eighteen months and not resume until May 1975.

The BSACI president had done an extraordinary job of candy-coating the news. Clyde Earl recalled the effort to control the bad news within the Duarte complex. "We'd get the British magazines in every week, but management would pull them from the mail during this period," Earl said.

Kalinski couldn't keep the sour developments at Meriden from reaching his dealers. Labor taking over a factory was big news, and word of the Triumph siege spread quickly, finally making the front page of the *Wall Street Journal*. To American small businesses trying to make a living selling Triumph products, this could be the last straw—and Kalinski knew it.

Much emphasis has been put on the unavailability of new motorcycles during this period, but it was the acute shortage of spare parts that strangled Triumph's US national dealer body. Many of them had become dealers not for the slim margins in new bike sales, but because an official Triumph agency gave them access to profitable factory-made spares at wholesale prices.

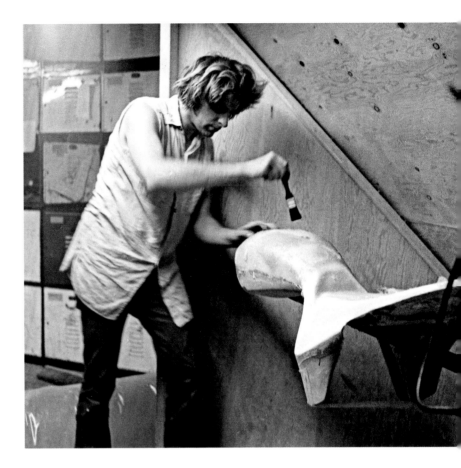

Craig Vetter lays up the original bodywork mold for his groundbreaking BSA Rocket 3 concept, July 1969. *Craig Vetter photo*

Since the late 1960s, the Meriden factory had preoccupied itself with making and turning over as many motorcycles as possible. Giving priority to spares manufacture interrupted motorcycle output and delayed immediate returns. This situation grew worse between 1971 and 1972, when Triumph rushed out the oil-in-frame models as it attempted to salvage the fleeting US riding season. There was simply no time for parts, only complete bikes.

Dealers needed spares for their very survival. All they got, however, were back-order memos from BSACI, stating that better days were just around the corner. The situation got so bad that some dealers had to strip parts from showroom models. For Meriden, the shift of focus away from serving the vital and profitable US spares market later proved to be a nail in Triumph's coffin.

AMERICAN ADVICE

BSACI had such a stockpile of leftover 1971 and 1972 motorcycles that it had to cut prices by nearly 50 percent and dump machines on the US market. Dealers who moved the most units were awarded a trip for two to England and France in fall 1973. More than 100 American shop owners qualified; many had never been to the Triumph factory and decided to go on the trip just for the opportunity. Imagine the group's surprise when, during the last week of October, they weren't allowed anywhere near the chained-and-picketed factory gates!

There was little that the US distributor or its dealers could do about besieged Meriden. Still, the Americans couldn't passively accept the prospect of bankruptcy. Veteran Maryland dealer Bob Myers was a member of Triumph's National Dealer Advisory Council. His personal efforts to break the factory deadlock went far beyond his duties as council member. Myers made twelve trips to Coventry between 1973 and 1976, spending an estimated $40,000 of his own funds in the process.

Dennis Poore tried to convince the British government that the US dealers did not want Triumph twins. This was completely the opposite of reality, of course, but Poore aimed to save the Commando and Trident at the expense of the Bonneville. Led by Myers, a group of twenty American Triumph dealers met with UK Minister for Industrial Development Christopher Chataway and members of the House of Commons to convince them of the ongoing American demand for Triumph's twin. At the meeting, Myers presented firm orders from over seventy-five US dealers for 5,000 new Triumph twins. "Few of us ordered Tridents," noted John Healy.

The authors have reviewed two dozen of these orders (scans of the dealers' original letterhead) from the late Bob Myers's files. They clearly show that the commitment from America, worth an estimated $8 million (retail) in new Triumphs, was sincere and powerful. This is an example, from Pontiac, Michigan, dealer Andy Anderson, dated March 18, 1974:

Dear Bob,

Pursuant to our recent telephone conversation, I wish to make the following commitment for purchasing 1974 Triumph motorcycles.

For the period ending December 1, 1974, and based on the original price schedule of July 1973 for Triumph motorcycles, this is our order:

200 T140V

200 TR7RV

100 T100R

Terms: Net Cash on Delivery

Congratulations on getting this together and best wishes for speedy delivery of motorcycles. Had Triumphs been available this year we could have sold at least 2000.

Andrew C. Anderson, President

"We were 'all in' on this," Healy asserted.

We were itching for a fight. In less than three years we'd seen Peter Thornton spend $3 million on the racing program when the company owed us hundreds of thousands in warranty money. Then when BSA production stopped, the Triumph dealers had the BSA dealers jammed down our throats. And now we had to absorb the Norton dealers into the Triumph family, often placing competitors a few blocks from each other.

To top it all off, Felix Kalinski and I had a meeting with Poore and his wife, where they told us verbatim: "We're not going to do any business with the f - u - c - k - i - n - g Communists," as he called the Meriden workers.

And when I asked him about continuing to make the Bonneville, Poore looked at me and said, "I have a twin, why would I want another?" This was communicated to Felix and myself in no uncertain terms.

Myers was also part of a more ambitious plan: to buy the Triumph factory. His partner in the proposed deal was Elyria, Ohio, dealer Bill Kennedy. The plan, however, never got off first base. "I was interested in buying the factory, but once we found out what a mess it was, with the unions and all, we decided against it," Kennedy told co-author Brooke. "The floor sweepers had a union; the people putting the spokes in the wheels had a union. If one union had a problem, they'd all just sit down."

Kennedy then envisioned made-in-the-USA Triumphs and even selected a site in Gassaway, West Virginia. He would ship only the Meriden tooling back to the US, leaving the factory's leaky roof and squabbling unions behind. Such an uprooting was, of course, out of the question, but it shows the extent to which American Triumph dealers were prepared to go to save their beloved brand.

Even Denis McCormack's counsel was sought on how to get things going again. In a letter to Myers, dated November 19, 1973, the former TriCor chief cut to the chase, criticizing both British and US management. He noted that "the magic Triumph name, flavor, product and reputation in the US Market coupled with US Triumph Dealer loyalty, is the major—and I believe vital—asset."

McCormack's last piece of advice from the letter was prophetic: "The delay in delivery of machines and parts for the essential US spring market of 1974 will be fatal and catastrophic" for the "loyal Triumph dealer organization."

In December, the effects of the Norton-Villers and BSA merger in Britain finally landed stateside when it was announced that the US Norton-Villers Corporation and BSACI would be amalgamated as well. The new company (the third in the US in four years) was called Triumph-Norton Inc. (TNI) and would be headquartered in Duarte. Although Norton's Paramount, California, location was closed and its operations moved in with Triumph, this still left the new organization with three points of distribution: Duarte, Baltimore, and the Berliner Corporation in New Jersey.

Early in February 1974, Dr. Kalinski resigned. In his place, Roger Stange from the US Norton distributor took over as TNI president. And Pete Colman, the canny technical wizard who had joined Johnson Motors in 1948, was given early retirement. The few Triumph diehards remaining at Duarte now worked in what was clearly a Norton-based organization. Sad irony abounded: even in its brief Commando heyday, Norton sold a fraction of Triumph's volume in the US. Its brand was barely known outside the enthusiast clique.

In late April, Trident manufacture resumed, this time from the old BSA works in Birmingham. Although the three-cylinder engine units had always been manufactured there, the rest of the T150's cycle parts and final assembly were by Meriden. At great expense to NVT, and without any cooperation from the picketing workers, an assembly line was laid out at

Small Heath and all-new tooling installed in time to meet the spring riding season in the US.

The new T150 differed only in mufflers and paint scheme from the 1973 version. Allocation of the 1974 Tridents to US dealers was based on past sales histories, but no one was beating down showroom doors for the triples. Likewise, the 1974 TR5T Trophy Trail was a carryover, except for its red paint. Neither machine could substitute for the Bonneville. A 1974 750cc twin would have been the US dealers' salvation; unfortunately, their future was still being held hostage by the Meriden occupation.

In a lengthy policy statement to US dealers dated April 26, NTI's national sales organization revealed much about the parent company's future plans, including the upcoming electric-start Trident and a new-generation twin being

The handsome and expensive T160 Trident was available with two gas tank capacities and two paint schemes. This one was photographed right out of the crate at TriCor in 1975. *Gaylin archive*

Presenting
The Bonneville Special

TRIUMPH

Built by British craftsman to your American taste.

RIGHT: The **T140D Special** seemed like a winner in 1979, but it was a sales failure that helped sink Triumph. *Brochure image*

BELOW: The US-tanked version of the 1977 Silver Jubilee was a high-bling Bonnie that sold poorly, 201 years after America rejected the British monarchy. *Brooke archive*

developed (presumably the Cosworth Twin). It was also revealed for the first time that a workers' cooperative planned to purchase the factory and continue Bonneville manufacture. Although the idea had surfaced earlier, it was the first time that US dealers had been clued in.

American dealers saw these latest promises as propaganda to keep the US sales network from disintegrating completely. One longtime Triumph man opined that the dealers still hanging on at the time were only doing so because the once-proud Triumph marque had provided much of their past success. They hoped the trend would reverse.

In August, the name of the US sales organization was changed yet again, this time to Norton-Triumph Inc. (NTI). Many Americans believed that Poore ordered this change, as he'd had enough of Triumph and Meriden headaches and wanted to showcase Norton as much as possible.

One of NTI's first acts was to offer a price list for 1974 models. In September, a small batch of motorcycles held since the start of the factory siege was released and sent to America. As it turned out, these were mostly 650cc T120Vs, originally intended for other markets. Tridents continued to arrive even after the peak sales and riding season had ended; by October, the warehouses were crammed with unsold T150s. To liquidate these and other leftovers (including unsold Rickman and AJS two-stroke dirt bikes), NTI offered dealers free floor planning for six months.

The company did offer an early Christmas present to the stalwart Triumph dealers: a limited-support program for dirt-track racing. The gift came with a catch, however: the sponsorship was only available for Norton riders because of a lack of Triumph spare parts!

A SELF-STARTING TRIUMPH

In January 1972, US availability of the long-awaited, redesigned Trident was announced. Originally intended to be an 830cc (T180), NVT's new offspring was still a 750, but now it featured the forward-slanting cylinder of the old BSA Rocket 3 and X75 Hurricane. The 15-degree cylinder angle allowed easier installation of an electric starter, which was fitted directly under the carburetors.

The revamped T160 Trident also met new US federal regulations, which standardized all motorcycle controls per common (Japanese) practice. Thus, the foot shifter was transferred to the left side of the machine. The frame benefited from lessons learned on the factory's Production racing T150s to give improved cornering clearance. The bike's exhaust system employed a splitter manifold at the central exhaust port that fed two additional header pipes. The visual effect was that of a four-cylinder engine—the current rage. New "annular discharge" silencers (also used on the Commando) looked like plugged-up megaphones, but the net result was 84.4 decibels and a much quieter Trident, albeit at the expense of performance.

This slight emasculation was more than offset by the Triple's fresh styling, developed by the master, Jack Wickes. The swingarm was lengthened and the front forks shortened slightly, giving a lower, leaner look to the machine. The fuel tank was resculpted per Craig Vetter's Bonneville TT concept. The T160 was definitely a looker. But while the T160's widely praised handling and styling "attracts admirers like ants at a picnic," as one tester put it, its $2,870 price was more expensive than a Z-1 and only $100 shy of a Honda GL1000 Gold Wing.

The slick new triple wasn't enough to stem NTI's cash-flow problems in early 1975, which spurred a reduction in staff and facilities. The once-proud Triumph Corporation in Towson was turned into a warehouse. The field sales force was dramatically downsized and, in May, Norton-Triumph Inc. became the sole US distributor of Norton Commando motorcycles when it bought out Joe Berliner's operation. At the time, NTI was barely liquid and held only property and inventory. Berliner was given the Baltimore warehouse property in compensation for the takeover of his Norton business.

In the UK, the enormous expense of operating two old and inefficient factories, coupled with the Trident retooling at Small Heath and its simultaneous T160 redesign, sapped the company's capital. Projected US sales of both the 1974 and re-engineered 1975 Trident failed to materialize. In August 1975, NVT's plea for additional assistance from the British government was turned down. Losses mounted.

Poore argued that, if the UK government hadn't intervened and he'd been allowed to reestablish Triumph production in Birmingham, NVT's financial performance would have been much better. In hindsight, there's no way to know if his prophecy would have come true. But those in Parliament holding the pursestrings knew all about US warehouses piling up with new Tridents, AJSs, and Commandos. With poor domestic sales generating little revenue—and a foundering parent company overseas—NTI was in dire straits. Drastic action was needed if the US distributor was to survive to handle the Bonnevilles that were promised from Meriden when the blockade ended.

All NTI sales reps were immediately eliminated and the still-substantial former TriCor parts inventory was sold off; eleven semi-trailers of new-old stock parts were purchased by Cycle Hub, a Portland, Oregon, motorcycle dealership. More cash was raised in the "Jam Breaker Sale," a price-slashing program that effectively dumped Tridents and Commandos on the US market. Machines that had a wholesale price of $2,280 in January were knocked down to dealers for as little as $1,320. Public response, even during the dead of winter, was strong enough to clear almost 100 percent of NTI's unsold motorcycle stock. Along with the consolidation and staff reduction, the "fire sale" gave Triumph's US organization a slight reprieve.

THE BONNIE RETURNS!

The best news that US Triumph dealers could hear came in late October 1975: the Meriden factory lockout had ended and production of 750cc twins resumed. After a nearly two-year absence, the Bonneville was back! The 1976 T140V (and TR7RV Tiger) were virtually identical in specification and appearance to the machines announced for 1974, except for the new left-hand gearshift lever and rear disc brake. The Bonnie's retail price was $1,895, which was more than some dealers asked for an electric-start Trident during the Jam Breaker Sale.

With overall quality that was superior to the early 1970s versions, the revised T140V would have been a viable competitor had it been introduced a few years earlier. But in America's Bicentennial year, Triumph's "franchise" twin was a dated design that no longer enjoyed its former road-burner reputation. "The big, bad Bonneville is back, only it's not so big or bad anymore," reported *Cycle Illustrated* in its March 1976 road test.

Cycle Guide's twelve-page cover story of Triumph's resurrected legend was objective (yes, the bike did still leak oil) and concluded that the Bonneville 750 was "definitely not everyman's motorcycle." Most riders weaned on Japanese bikes would shun it. But the editors went on to state that "what the Bonneville has to offer is light weight, dead-accurate steering, telepathic handling, low-rpm torque and stone-ax simplicity" with styling "strong enough to get a certain kind of rider interested and a personality vivid enough to keep him that way."

As the Meriden worker-managers mapped out Triumph's future, they decided to drop the 500cc twins despite the disc-brake front end added to the Daytona (T100D) prior to the factory takeover. Triumph's fortunes now rode on a 750cc market niche, and NTI assumed that demand for the reborn twin would be high. This was reflected in the hard terms given to dealers on the T140V: payment in full was required upon receiving delivery of the new models.

Dealers were informed that all new bike certificates of origin would be held by NTI until final payment was satisfied. If a Triumph dealer couldn't float his own paper locally, he simply would not be allotted Bonnevilles. This put a greater chill on the dealer-distributor relations that had once made Triumph the envy of the industry.

To proclaim the Bonnie's return to America, NTI turned up the marketing. For several years, the US Norton distributors had monopolized the inside front covers of the major US bike magazines with the popular "Norton Girl" campaign.

That coveted space would now be occupied by various Triumph Bonneville ads for the next two years. They aimed to differentiate the light, simple, good-handling, and, increasingly, hand-built British 750 twin to a motorcycling public that had grown used to push-button starting, appliance-like reliability, and warp-speed performance.

By January 1976, there were more units than orders. The company's unsold stock included yet more T150s and Norton Commando Mk 3s, which Duarte had acquired from Canada. When it was discovered that the fledgling Meriden Co-Operative wasn't making profit on its products, NTI had to raise the bike's price $100—no boon to sales. It also announced that a limited number (120) of European-spec Bonnevilles, designated T140 B/T, would be available. Fitted with UK-market 4.8-gallon "breadbox" fuel tanks, lower handlebars, and rubber fork gaiters, these sporty, longer-range B/Ts carried the same price as a standard US-spec T140 and were snapped up quickly.

In March, NTI admitted to Triumph dealers that a perpetual parts shortage was anticipated and that the company intended to seek alternative sources within the US. At the same time, the final shipment of new Tridents was on its way to the US, the last motorcycles produced at the former BSA Small Heath works.

The 1976 name of the US organization changed to NVT-America. According to Roger Stange, this was related to the liquidation of Norton-Villiers in England. Little more than a year remained of NVT's exclusive contract to market the Co-Op's product, and US Triumph dealers had to sign a new franchise agreement. Stange's claim that Triumph had 600 dealers nationwide during this period seems unlikely. With a $2,000 price tag on Bonnevilles and no financial assistance on floor planning, a Triumph dealership had lost its luster. Many US dealers decided to drop from the withering tree.

A new, smaller headquarters was leased in Anaheim, California; the reduced volume of motorcycles being handled no longer justified the larger Duarte facility. By November, the relocation to 1261 State College Parkway was complete. Company staff had been slashed to less than thirty employees. Stange admitted to *Cycle Guide* in 1976 that "the days of glory, of $100,00 dealer conventions, of $300,000 carpets for this place are gone"—the latter reference was likely directed at Felix Kalinski's extravagant efforts to decorate Duarte.

The 1977 models were introduced in November with few visible changes other than paint. To keep the T140V's retail price at $1,995 NVT-America asked dealers to absorb a $50 price increase while a new NVT-developed moped was announced. The Italian-made, Franco-Morini-powered "Easy Rider" ER1 and ER2 were late to the cheap-mobility game and ill aimed at a market that never really accepted Triumph's Tina and Tigress scooters, and rejected outright Ariel-3 trikes. US Triumph dealers who wanted to handle the Easy Rider had to order in quantities of five or more.

The fresh direction that Craig Vetter had proposed with the Bonneville TT five years earlier was re-explored by the Co-Op in 1977. Meriden stylist Tom Higham enlisted Jeremy "Jez" Bradley, a local university student doing his internship at Triumph, to present new themes for the Bonneville. Higham and Bradley loved the purposeful look of America flat-track racing Triumphs and, like Vetter, recognized the influence of US customs. Working offsite in secret, they developed the dirt-track–inspired 750FT and a more chopper-like custom. When unveiled at Meriden, the FT750 was well received and gained the support of John Rosamond, one of the Co-Op's directors and a welder in the plant's frame shop.

Both concept bikes were shipped to the US for dealer evaluation; the hope was to sell 200 units of the FT at a premium price, according to Rosamond's insightful 2009 book, *Save the Triumph Bonneville!* Company management rejected both proposals but Higham and Bradley's work wasn't in vain. Some of their design cues were incorporated into the 1979 Bonneville Special.

NEW COMPANY, BUT NO PARTS

Norton-Villers-Triumph's two-year contract to market the factory's product in the US was due to expire in July 1977. The Co-Op, Triumph Motorcycles (Meriden) Ltd., believed they could do a better job, so did not renew the agreement. Instead, they set up their own sales corporation. With additional assistance eked out of the British government, the Co-Op severed its relationship with Dennis Poore and continued independently. This triggered the final reorganization of Triumph's US subsidiary.

Triumph imported a few UK-spec T140Es in 1979, appealing to the big-tank, low-handlebar rider. Co-author Brooke found his to be a well-mannered, reliable machine. Drilled brake rotors are non-stock. *Brooke photo*

A 1982 T140ES Executive with standard Brealey-Smith cockpit fairing and Sigma touring luggage. *Press kit image*

Brenda Price, an accountant, had worked at Meriden since she was seventeen years old; now she was one of the Co-Op's directors. She traveled from England to establish the new company, Triumph Motorcycles America (TMA), and took over as interim president. Price secured a new facility in Placentia, California. All NVT-America Inc. senior staff members except Roger Stange were retained to smooth the transition and avoid interruptions in dealer service.

Spare parts availability had become such an acute problem in the US that TMA pledged to make it their top priority. A spring 1977 TMA memo to dealers trumpeted, "By the time you read this, Meriden will be packing enough Triumph T140 parts to fill your back orders. Shortly, thereafter, they will commence staging a year's stocking order for the US."

Old-timers had heard this before. At a special Triumph dealer meeting with Price and other TMA officials held that year during the annual Cincinnati motorcycle trade show, true believer Bob Myers again grabbed the torch. He stood up to show the new regime his parts backorder list. Raising the computer printout high over his head, Myers let it unfold—

all the way to the floor! The room erupted in cheers, hoots, and hollers. To Price, accompanied by British MP Geoffrey Robinson, a Co-Op supporter, the scene must have looked like a restaged Boston Tea Party.

While the factory and its US distributor appeared to address the T140 spares emergency, they dictated a draconian policy regarding replacement parts for the classic 650cc and 500cc models. "We are currently in the business of making and selling 750 Bonnevilles," asserted a 1978 TMA memo to dealers. "These units are our major concern. Triumph's fortunes over the next few years depends on them. Therefore, our parts and service efforts will be oriented towards these models from 1973 to date. We will not, at present, be concerned with models now out of production."

To say this mandate puzzled and angered the American dealer body is an understatement. Selling parts and service for thousands of older Triumph twins still in use nationwide was the lifeblood of those US dealers who hung on. "Discontinuing the pre-1973 parts was the biggest mistake they made," said Big D Cycle's Jack Wilson, echoing the view of a dozen former dealers interviewed for this book. "Boy, that really hurt those of us who stuck with Triumph and still deeply believed in the products."

Many of Wilson's colleagues who could afford to drop the British franchise and fall back on Japanese lines did so. Many Triumph-exclusive shops packed it in after TMA's indiscriminate move. In his book, Co-Op board member John Rosamond admitted that there was big money to be made in parts for old Triumphs. He indicated that the company's neglect here was a mistake. When the factory abandoned the spares market for its legacy twins, it supported those who wanted to enter the Triumph parts scene. An entire aftermarket industry—some honest, some pirates, and all offering varying degrees of quality—emerged to fill the space. Meriden's short-sightedness had caused it to lose out on the profits.

The factory worker-managers did, however, seize on a uniquely British event—the twenty-fifth year of Queen Elizabeth's reign, her "Silver Jubilee"—to market Triumph and the Bonneville. Conceived as a prestige model to commemorate Her Royal Highness's tenure, the Silver Jubilee (T140J) was a standard T140V with a glitzy finish: chromed engine covers, a reshaped twinseat in blue vinyl with red piping, and a vibrant paint scheme in silver, red, and Royal Blue with white pinstriping. Even the wheel rim centers were painted and coach-lined.

Special badges on the new, larger side covers and on the fuel tank mounting bolt declared the Silver Jubilee to be "One of a Thousand." However, with a thousand units made for both the UK and US markets, as well as additional quantities for Australia and New Zealand, the actual total was around 2,400 units. Ownership status was conferred by a personalized, numbered certificate. Despite the extra bling, though, the Jubilee was priced at only $125 more than a standard T140. While some were purchased by speculating dealers who kept the bikes "in the crate" as future collectibles, most Silver Jubilees in the US collected showroom dust for months, despite classy magazine ads that ran in fall 1977.

By this time, the Co-Op's new American distribution arm was established. Trans-Atlantic frequent flyer Price returned to Meriden and was replaced as TMA president by thirty-five-year-old Robert Wells, formerly a California banker. His tenure lasted only three months; Wells was terminated along with BSA-Triumph veteran Tom Cates and longtime Duarte service boss Bob Tryon in the next round of austerity cuts. Wells was replaced by Jack Hawthorne, who left American Honda to join a floundering Triumph.

By December, TMA's inventory of one thousand unsold 1977 models caused the company to contract with Borg-Warner's finance arm to offer free floor-planning on all leftover 1977 machines through June 1978. Dealer acceptance of this "freebie" financing for the cheaper 1977 bikes (when compared to the 1978s) was so vigorous that a hopeful Meriden dispatched another shipment of unsold 1977 twins to its US distributor.

REAL MOTORCYCLES DON'T HAVE TO LEAK OIL

Meriden was anticipating sales of twelve thousand new 1978 machines in the US, but the initial shipment was delayed by an East Coast dock strike in October. When the Bonnevilles and Tigers finally did land, they carried the inevitable price increase: $123 more to dealers, while their suggested retail was only bumped up $100. Single-carb TR7RVs increased by only $80; few of these were sent to America and surviving 1978 examples are rare today.

Besides the addition of gas-charged Girling rear shocks, standard K81 Dunlops on both wheels, and a new seat design, the year's initial "hit" feature was the expanded selection of fuel tank finishes. Three main-color scallop combinations were available on the Bonneville, and the paint option helped breathe new life into Triumph sales that year. *Cycle World* tested a T140 in its April 1978 issue; their overall review was quite favorable. Writer Henry Manney III subtly noted that the Bonnie's dragstrip runs of 13.8 seconds at 93 miles per hour were simply noncompetitive in the 750cc class, adding that wasn't a big issue to many riders.

"At least you know you have a motorcycle underneath you, and not a golf cart," he quipped. Best of all, the test bike didn't leak oil anywhere.

By the time the road test appeared, however, Triumph had already announced significant technical changes to the Bonneville. These were driven by more stringent US federal emission requirements that took effect on January 1, 1978. The 1978 1/2 T140E—the "E" designating EPA certified—featured a completely redesigned cylinder head fed by a pair of 30mm Amal MkII carburetors. The Mikuni-like MkIIs and the new parallel-port head allowed a leaner fuel mixture per EPA regulations. Unfortunately, the need for the MkII in the US meant that the single-carb Tiger 750 could no longer be sold here. Unlike the smaller Amal Concentric, a single MkII would not package within the oil-bearing frame. This also meant that future models, such as the TR7T Tiger Trail and the 650cc TR65 Thunderbird, were nonstarters for the US.

In their T140E test, *Cycle* concluded that the Bonnie was still "legitimately fun." However, riding it above 55 miles per hour for extended periods made the machine "almost unbearable" due to engine vibration and a stiction-prone fork. But even these negatives didn't deter editor Bill Stermer from appreciating the T140E's fine handling qualities. *Cycle Guide*'s December T140E road test drew similar conclusions while noting that the new MkII-carbureted bike was 0.79 seconds quicker and 3.5 miles per hour faster than the '76 version. "No threat to the Honda Six (CBX), to be sure, but respectable enough to keep the men in black and white alert," the testers reported.

Triumph's overall quality during the 1977 to 1980 period was deemed by many former dealers to be the best from Meriden in a decade. "The Co-Op workers really were conscientious; they just had little money to work with," offered

John Healy. Briefly, things were looking up for Triumph and its US organization. Confidence by the middle of 1978 was such that a limited number of field representatives were hired, this time headed by TMA's Gene Cox.

Triumph's US market share even increased enough by late summer to bump BMW out of sixth place, behind the four Japanese brands and Harley-Davidson. The achievement coincided with the first-ever magazine comparison test pitting the Triumph Bonneville against its Milwaukee archrival, the Harley Sportster. Both machines were considerably more refined, mellow, and heavier than in their heyday, noted the August 1978 issue of *Motorcyclist*. The Harley even had an electric starter and displaced a full liter, while the Triumph remained a kick-start 750. But any motorcyclist who had fallen asleep in the mid-1960s and awakened in 1978 would instantly recognize both legendary machines.

Not surprisingly, the two 1978 models tested were quite similar dynamically to their Kennedy-era predecessors. In handling and drag strip performance, the T140E topped the XL. And, with its 50 percent displacement advantage, the Sportster would walk away from the Bonnie during top-gear roll-ons unless the Triumph rider downshifted. Even in 1978, the storied Limey versus Hawg rivalry still burned.

CATALOG OF MISFORTUNE

Under Jack Hawthorne's guidance, Triumph's revitalized US sales organization managed a brief spike in prosperity during 1978. An attractive product helped, of course, but Hawthorne's nine years with Honda had taught him much. He established an "800" telephone number at Placentia for dealer orders and customer inquiries. He also plowed all he could afford into advertising, putting Triumph motorcycles in more places and publications than had been done for years.

But the optimism was short-lived. Triumph's worldwide sales that year were dismal, down 39 percent in the UK during the fourth quarter of 1978. According to the same report, US sales were also off 30 percent during the first quarter of 1979, typically the peak sales period. This was due to more fluctuations in the dollar–sterling relationship: the pound was approaching $2.40. So slim was Meriden's margin on each motorcycle that the currency factor alone would have negated any expected profit for the Co-Op, even with better results in other markets.

Triumph Motorcycles (Meriden) Ltd. posted 1978 losses at near $1.5 million. The factory had to cut the workforce, first by 20 percent and later more severely. Stories surfaced about the Cooperative seeking a waiver on the more than $2 million interest payment due on their initial government loan. Leaving no stone unturned to find much-needed capital, the Co-Op engaged Kawasaki, Suzuki, Britain's Armstrong Equipment, and even Harley-Davidson as potential partners. Feelers were also extended to BMW, according to Rosamond. Nothing materialized.

If Triumph was to have a future, much of the Co-Op's minuscule capital would have to be spent on the development of new models. EPA testing and certification of the T140E model cost hundreds of thousands of dollars—a good chunk of the limited "quid" at the company's disposal. A T140 with counterbalanced crankshaft was prototyped; it showed significantly reduced engine vibration, but the £500,000 tooling costs were prohibitive. Ditto for an aluminum cylinder barrel and belt-drive primary (see sidebar). Upgrades that did enter production during 1978 to 1979 weren't cheap; these included Lucas Rita electronic ignition; new handlebar switchgear; a redesigned instrument console and side covers; reversion to a negative-ground electrical system; a locking hinged seat; and a standard handrail/luggage rack. But all these features made the 750 twin a much more robust and livable machine.

The 1979 Bonnie's retail price was $2,615, which included both the teardrop-tanked US models and a smaller batch of T140E UKs—home-market models fitted with 4.8-gallon "breadbox" fuel tank, low handlebar, and rubber fork gaiters. These became cult bikes in the northeastern states, but Triumph dealers elsewhere often had difficulty attracting buyers to the sportier bars and nontraditional tanks.

The biggest news for 1979, however, was the T140D Bonneville Special. Like the X75 Hurricane six years earlier, the Special was primarily a restyle of an existing model. It was Triumph's play to capture a slice of the booming "factory custom" segment that Yamaha had spawned the year before, led by its XS650 parallel twin. The Specials featured pseudo-custom tanks, seats, exhausts, and trim that, ironically, mimicked the modifications that American riders made to their Triumphs, BSAs, and Harleys.

Honda, Suzuki, and Kawasaki jumped on the bandwagon with varying degrees of taste and success. It took longer for Triumph to join the fray. To create the T140D, stylist Tom Higham at Meriden leveraged features from the 750FT and Lowrider concepts. The "D" shared all the standard T140 upgrades, plus a beefier swingarm and rear brake caliper mounted above the rotor. Cosmetic changes exclusive to the D included US-made Lester seven-spoke cast wheels, an abbreviated front fender, a wider section rear tire, slightly stepped twinseat, and new cast tank badges. And the Bonnie Special also wore a unique two-into-one exhaust system with TT-style head pipes.

The overall look, with Norton-esque black-and-gold paintwork, struck a nice balance between a tracker-like custom and a standard Triumph twin. *Motorcyclist* and *Cycle Guide* tested the T140D during 1979, and neither liked the stepped seat, the peg location, the harsh ride—nor did they approve of Triumph's flattering a Japanese bike by imitation. The T140D was "a knee-jerk reaction to Yamaha's Special series," argued *Cycle Guide*. Its greatest hurdle was the unfavorable dollar–pound exchange rate that also plagued the standard T140E. The Special retailed for $3,225—about $600

MR. OSWALD GOES TO MERIDEN

Bob "Ozzie" Oswald ran a small Triumph dealership and machine shop in southeastern Pennsylvania surrounded by cornfields, a rural location that spurred Oswald's creativity. He was no fan of the leak-prone, maintenance-intensive, roller-chain primary drives on British twins. In the early 1970s, he designed and tested a rubber-belt primary drive on a BSA A65 mule. Its success encouraged Ozzie to convert a 750 Bonneville with his Quiet Power Drive (QPD) and show it to Triumph's US management for possible production. Soon, Ozzie and his wife Betty were flying to Meriden at the factory's invitation.

"We had to sell all our Black Angus [cattle] to pay for the trip," recalled the former part-time farmer and self-taught machinist whose love affair with Triumph began on an early 1950s TR5. Oswald's journey, the first of three he made to the UK, had been partly arranged by Bill Lapworth, then secretary of Britain's Transport and General Workers' Union, a body that represented Meriden's hourly workers. Lapworth was a key negotiator during the bitter eighteen-month blockade. He empathized with the American dealers who "bled Triumph blue" and just wanted new motorcycles to sell again.

The two weeks of Oswald's first trip to England were spent divided between Triumph's Engineering Department and meetings with the managers, union reps, and Midlands politicians then steering Triumph's precarious course. The QPD belt drive was fitted to a factory T140 mule and thoroughly tested at the MIRA proving grounds and on public roads, delivering faultless, durable performance. But Oswald could not get anyone to give him a straight answer regarding Triumph's interest in purchasing his design. "Someone would propose buying 1,000 kits one day and another would tell me 50 the next," he recalled. As a high school graduate, Oswald couldn't get the ear of some Co-Op directors who would only listen to a graduate engineer—such was the professional elitism in British industry at that time.

Oswald also designed a compact electric-start system for the T140 based on an American Bosch snowmobile starter motor. It used a 14 amp-hour battery and Bendix drive to spin the primary side, rather than the timing side as seen later on Norton Commando and Triumph Electro starters. Triumph opted to cut costs on the T140ES by fitting a cheap sprag-clutch drive. Oswald was asked to prototype his electric start system but, after evaluation, it was rejected by Chief Engineer Brian Jones as having an "obsolete" Bendix drive.

"I was flabbergasted," Ozzie recalled. "Every car starter in the world uses a Bendix drive and anybody can replace one when it goes bad. It's far superior to that junk on the ES." T140ES owners whose sprag-clutch issues are well documented on Triumph internet forums regularly wish their bikes had Bendix starter drives. That doesn't surprise Ozzie Oswald, who sunk over $20,000 of his own money into time and tooling for the e-starter and belt-drive systems he prototyped for Triumph. As of 2017, he was still selling them to T140 owners.

Triumph rebel "Ozzie" Oswald in 2015, still selling his QPD belt drive systems. *Brooke photo*

The small batch of T140LE Royal models shipped to America were finished in all-black tanks, gold pinstriping, black frames, and Morris wheels with twin front discs, as shown on this unrestored, unregistered example. *Brooke photo*

more than the high-tech 1979 Suzuki GS750 Four. It would take Triumph three years to clear US stocks of T140Ds.

All unsold Triumphs were now suffering the same fate: the cost of British biking in America had finally become too expensive. Meriden had geared up for projected sales of eight thousand machines in the US during 1979, but actual sales by the remaining 454 dealers fell far short of Hawthorne's forecast. Ultimately, it was TMA's inability to liquidate these models within their sales season that contributed heavily in Meriden's demise. The factory, having operated hand-to-mouth on a week-by-week basis, had committed all resources to the success of 1979 model production.

NEW MODELS CAN'T SAVE TRIUMPH

Crated motorcycles were again accumulating in TMA's warehouses. When Triumph realized that actual sales would be about half of the eight-thousand-unit forecast, Meriden had no choice but to scale back production—but not before twelve thousand machines had been built.

This was a deathblow to the Co-Op. With the pound then hovering at $2.40 and the Bonneville's price tag approaching $4,000, the factory could do little except cut expenses. More layoffs reduced the plant's workforce to approximately two hundred by year's end. Those who remained had their work hours trimmed severely. These measures ensured that, by the end of 1980, Meriden would produce only about one quarter of the motorcycles built in 1979.

The increasing belt-tightening naturally extended to Triumph's US subsidiary. Gene Cox's field representative program was dissolved and the Placentia staff sliced to a skeleton crew of about a dozen, according to the ever-valuable Ruth Furman. She had started at Johnson Motors in 1963 as Pete Colman's secretary and survived the concurrent alphabet soup of BSACI, TNI, NTI, NVT-A, and TMA.

The TMA exodus included Jack Hawthorne, who had failed to move his promised eight thousand machines in 1979, even though the overpriced motorcycles were not his doing. Once again, Brenda Price returned to California as temporary head of TMA while searching for a new CEO. Ruth Furman later told co-author Gaylin that TMA was "very fortunate to have Brenda Price" and that, without her experience in international finance, the American subsidiary—and Triumph as well—wouldn't have soldiered on for as long as it did.

Price's exec search led to Wayne Moulton. No stranger to Triumph or its US organization, Moulton had been a Utah Triumph dealer and regular at Bonneville Speed Week for thirteen years before becoming a district manager for BSACI from 1968 to 1971. He left the Triumph family "because the company adhered tenaciously to tradition and proved unyielding to suggestions of change," according to a 1981 *Rider* magazine interview. He then joined Kawasaki's US organization and was instrumental in developing the highly successful Z-1R and LTD custom models.

Moulton was available; by April 1980, he was installed as vice president and sales manager while Price continued to head the overall operation. A few months later, Moulton was given full reign and Price returned to the UK. Moulton's first duty was to move the mountain of leftover 1979 models that were eating Triumph alive in interest and warehouse rental fees. To do this, Moulton resorted to a proven incentive: he offered trips to Acapulco and London to the dealers who moved the most T140D Specials. The trick worked, even though most of those who won the vacations were already Triumph's top US retailers.

Next in the pipeline was the Co-Op's latest limited-edition model, the Bonneville Executive. It was a standard T140E upfitted with a Brealey Smith quarter fairing and Sigma hard luggage, following the sport-tourer trend established by BMW's R100S and RS models. The German marque's influence was also seen in the Bonnie's red "smoke" paint finish. To complete the touring package, a quasi-King and Queen twinseat was fitted in place of the standard butt-numbing bench.

The overall package, combined with the earlier UK market fuel tank, made a handsome machine. *Rider* tested the Executive purely on contemporary terms, directly against other sport-tourers from Japan and Germany. The balanced review contained its share of criticism while praising the Executive's broad powerband, accurate handling, and reduced vibration.

Given Meriden's dire financial straits, it seems incredible in hindsight that Britain's surviving motorcycle factory could find resources to develop and introduce new models in 1980. Whereas the Executive consisted mainly of bolt-on items and a paint job, however, the electric-starting Bonneville involved considerable engineering and expense. Announced in June, the T140ES Electro had been anticipated for a long time. The model used the same India-made Lucas M3 unit as the 1975 Norton Commando, fitted in the old pre-unit magneto location. It spun the engine to life via a sprag clutch through the timing gear train on the engine's right side and was fastened directly to a reinforced timing case with a pronounced bulge.

The first US magazine to wring out a Bonneville Electro was *Rider* in February 1981. They found the new starter to be "remarkable, fuss-free, and reliable." *Motorcyclist* followed

in July with a six-page, in-depth feature outlining many of the new refinements that had been made to the entire Triumph range. Changes included the strengthened swingarm and reconfigured rear brake from the T140D, a new four-valve oil pump, and American Standard fasteners.

The editors highlighted well-known T140 sore points (stands grounding, uncomfortable seat, fork stiction) while delighting in the machine's quality finish, handling, and classic appearance. "The polishing of all plated parts is exceptional," they reported. "The pin-striping is done by hand, of course, and the paint is deep and will last much longer than that done on early Seventies Triumphs."

Cycle World's November test, written by editor Peter Egan, was more analytical. It found the Electro's top speed and quarter-mile performance "not blazingly fast" at 94 miles per hour and 14.96 seconds, respectively. The bike's handlebars proved comfortable, but editors found the seat to be like "upholstered plywood" toward the end of a day of riding. They admired the finish quality and pointed out that the "other ghosts from the Limey past"—such as oil leaks, vibration, and faulty electrics—appeared to be exorcised.

When the magazine's time with the T140ES concluded, Egan noted that the Electro was difficult to part with because it really was "a good, all-purpose bike . . . fun to ride and convenient at the same time." He dubbed it "the Handy Bike of the Year."

Where the Electro truly shocked was in its $3,995 retail price, double that of a Yamaha XS650 Special. Both the ES and the Executive were introduced late in the US riding season as 1981 models. TMA still had large stocks of unsold 1979s to move, and they believed introducing the new machines would make the leftovers a harder sell. The need to liquidate the glut of T140D and T140E Bonnevilles in America was essential if Triumph was to have a shot at fiscal health.

The company's financial "window" was narrowing. In September 1980, the British government finally wrote off the £8.4 million (then $20 million) owed to it by Triumph Motorcycles (Meriden) Ltd. The Conservatives, then in power, realized they weren't going to see the money anyway and understood that this enormous liability was scaring potential investors away from Triumph.

This financial lifeline still left the Co-Op with approximately £2 million owed to Britain's Export Credit Guarantee Department. Amazingly, the ECGD was also persuaded to waive repayment if Meriden could sell its stockpiled US inventory, valued at almost $10 million. Co-Op chairman John Rosamond knew that, if this could be accomplished, the factory would be (for the first time) free of all financial obligations, apart from the normal extensions given to any manufacturer by their suppliers.

The need to turn those unsold 1979s into cash was critical at a time when Triumph's prospects in the US were increasingly bleak. With an economic recession and a strong pound, demand was weak for Triumphs, let alone "reheated leftovers." Wayne Moulton acknowledged the problem. "Nineteen eighty-one will have to be a coasting year," he told *Rider* magazine. "We'll have to get rid of our '79 models to get the money we need to pay off the remainder of the loan." Adding to the pressure on Moulton were rising concerns over US product liability exposure that could decimate a small manufacturer like Triumph without millions in insurance coverage.

In July, a third version of the electric-start Bonnie was announced, this one to commemorate the nuptials of Prince Charles and Lady Diana Spencer. In the tradition of the Silver Jubilee, the new Bonneville Royal (T140LE) model involved only a special finish and little change in technical specs. Few examples of the 250 units made reached America. New slab-sided fuel tanks made in Italy carried 4 gallons. Machines imported into the US were finished in black, with double-lined gold pinstriping and carrying the larger "swooping R" Triumph emblem. The use of this new tank extended to the whole Triumph range, including the Executive and Electros.

Morris cast wheels made by Performance Machine in California were fitted to some units, traditional laced-up spoked wheels to others. Twin Lockheed disc brakes graced the Royal's fork. The engine's top end was painted black, while the crankcases remained bare aluminum, looking like a job half-finished.

As all Triumphs were by then being hand-assembled in batches of fifty to eighty, faithful adherence to any stated specifications was often waived. This situation resulted from Meriden's willingness to build a one-off to customer order and the necessity of using whatever components were stocked at the time. The quality of the machines remained remarkably good while more non-British parts were sourced: German Bing CV carburetors made under license in Spain; Bosch turn indicators and Magura handlebar switchgear; and Marzocchi rear shock absorbers and French Veglia gauges.

Few of the Royal editions (or any other Triumphs) made it to America in 1981. No more than five hundred machines were imported during the year. Triumph was definitely on the ropes, and the atmosphere at Placentia was one of deep gloom.

In 1982, Ronald Reagan's economic policy was affecting the international currency market. The US dollar strengthened against all others. A single British pound that cost Americans $2.35 in 1981 could now be had for $1.75. The dollar's 25 percent rebound was good news to anyone trying to peddle a British product in the US.

To meet the ECGD requirements, Meriden had been willing to liquidate its bloat of old-stock 1979 models (including 300 T140Ds, now three years old) in the US at a loss. Now, with a stronger dollar, the reduced price on these models no longer represented a fiscal loss. In spring 1982, Meriden announced that it was finally free of government debt obligations. Much was made of this fact abroad as well as in the US, but the

$2 million still owed to the British Government's export agency was simply taken over by a private bank.

The Co-Op, with fewer than two hundred workers, was floundering without a savior on the immediate horizon. This severe crisis caused TMA to downsize further, leaving a bare-bones staff at Placentia. Only an overseer and a handful of shipping clerks remained. Among the stalwarts who felt the axe were Ruth Furman and sales manager Gene Cox. It was Furman who had recommended Wayne Moulton to the Cooperative; the two had worked together in the wildly profitable 1960s and early 1970s. Now, Moulton had the unenviable task of dismissing her.

SAVING THE BEST FOR LAST

Somehow Meriden kept going, with enough ambition to announce two new models in spring 1982. Although neither machine was exported to the US in great numbers (fewer than two hundred of each), they deserve mention as motorcycles aimed specifically at American riders.

The first, designated TSX, was a further attempt to capture a slice of the "factory custom" market that the Japanese were milking. The bike was Moulton's brainchild: a standard Bonneville fitted with the classic Triumph teardrop tank and a 16-inch rear wheel shod with a fat Avon Roadrunner. Other unique-to-TSX cues included a stepped twinseat; 1971-style wire mounts for the headlamp; 1.75-inch diameter exhaust pipes feeding two stubby megaphone silencers; and shortened fenders. A trippy multicolor paint scheme completed the factory-custom look.

It is questionable whether the TSX would have significantly boosted Triumph's fortunes in the US had the marque survived. The model's sheer garishness offended those who worshiped Triumph's classic lines. The TSS (T140W, the W standing for Weslake), unveiled in March 1982, was a completely different story.

During 1980 and 1981, Meriden engineer Brian Jones, in collaboration with Weslake Engineering and Big D Cycle's Jack Wilson, developed an eight-valve cylinder head for the 750 twin. This was actually the fifth-generation version of the Weslake head first marketed in 1969 by the Rickman brothers as a bolt-on kit for 650s. The new head, combined with flat-topped pistons, gave greater valve area and improved airflow. Compression was bumped to 10:1. All of this spelled 20 percent more power for Triumph's forty-four-year-old design, boosting its power rating to a claimed 60 horsepower.

The eight-valve head crowned a long-overdue cast-aluminum cylinder barrel fitted with pressed-in steel liners. Big D's Wilson led "field development" of the new top end, successfully running it on his shop's thundering Battle of the Twins race bike that was clocked at over 152 miles per hour in Daytona qualifying. To cope with the more rev-happy top end, Jones redesigned the Bonnie's crankshaft with bigger, wider journals and beefed-up outer webs. Big D's rider Jon Minonno spun the eight-valver to its 10,000 rpm peak in race testing. The added crankshaft rigidity also made the TSS the smoothest 750cc twin ever offered by Triumph until a few rubber-mounted AV-framed models were released in the UK.

The TSS used the standard T140ES chassis and cycle parts, but American versions came with Morris cast wheels, triple disc brakes, a low Euro-spec handlebar, and EPA-compliant Bing carburetors. In its February 1983 issue, *Rider* conducted the only TSS road test to appear in an American publication. Test rider Joe Minton's verdict on the new twin was declared in one sentence: "This new Triumph, the best ever, is fully capable of being compared with the latest from across the other ocean."

It was perceptively smoother than the T140ES, with overall vibration levels at "about as much as a Honda [400cc] Hawk—not enough to talk about," Minton opined. During his

The standard Bonneville Electro with traditional Triumph tank, now made in Italy. *Press kit image*

ABOVE: **TMA president Wayne Moulton conceived the 1983 TSX Custom, a handful of which were imported prior to Meriden's closure.** *Press kit image*

RIGHT: **A Triumph dealer in Pennsylvania since 1963, Hermy Baver kept the sole TSS model that he received new in 1982 and displays it in his current showroom. Note the Weslake eight-valve head and electric-start timing covers.** *Brooke photo*

test on the roads around Coventry, he saw no evidence of any oil leaks—though some TSSs left Meriden with porous engine castings and imperfect head-to-barrel sealing that tainted the model's reputation.

Minton's plaudits extended to the eight-valver's superior brakes and handling, coupled with criticism of the usual suspension stiction and ill-placed footpegs. However, the *Rider* cover story was a strong vote of confidence for Triumph's latest twin. It is regrettable that Triumph didn't survive long enough to give the TSS a fair outing. The bike was released in the US on November 1, 1982, six weeks after the TSX. The two retailed at $3,895 and $3,695, respectively—hefty sums for 750s in 1983.

THE CLOCK RUNS OUT

Regardless, Triumph's time was up. Sales data from the final five model years of production taken from the Five Year Plan that was submitted to creditors just prior to Triumph's bankruptcy shows the decline:

	1978	1979	1980	1981	1982
USA	5,299	5,020	2,060	2,202	674
UK	3,028	2,951	1,741	1,176	336
Europe	694	922	725	360	245
Australia/Japan	914	784	180	258	232
Rest of world	752	739	1,175	137	103
Totals	10,667	10,416	5,881	4,133	1,590

By early 1983, production had ceased completely, although it was hoped only temporarily. The Meriden premises had been listed with real estate agents since 1981, but the recession had hit the UK particularly hard. There were no takers until April 1983, when a developer offered the equivalent of $1.5 million for the site. The Co-Op accepted the bid with plans to relocate in a vacant building once used by tire maker Dunlop. However, any money realized through the sale of the factory was already spoken for by the bank holding the note on the ECGD loan.

Destiny had closed in on Britain's most famous motorcycle maker. Even arrangements for the Co-Op's new facility collapsed when its owners were outbid; now they had no place to go. Many rescue plans were formulated, only to come crashing down, while the zombie-like shell of a factory piddled out spare parts with a thirty-person crew. Finally, it was the workers themselves who voted to end it all. On August 26, 1983, bankruptcy was declared; by November, it was all over.

The famous Triumph logo, patents, and manufacturing rights were secured by forty-year-old real estate developer John Bloor. The Meriden works, home to Triumph since 1944, were eventually bulldozed and turned into a housing development. Spares and motorcycle inventory eventually ended up with Andover Norton.

In America, the death of Triumph caused few waves beyond the faithful, since the organization no longer figured prominently in the motorcycle industry. When the money ran out in Britain at the end of 1982, so did the subsidies to TMA. Early in the new year, Wayne Moulton and his remaining staff were out of work, leaving only a couple of custodial people in Placentia.

Incredibly, some US dealers were still hanging on, willing to sell anything Triumph could make available. But most realized that it was over and that even their tireless enthusiasm couldn't overcome the uncompetitive prices. In a 1983 interview in *Motorcyclist*, veteran Pasadena, California, dealer Bill Mason pronounced the cold, hard truth:

When we ran out of the '79 models in 1981, they were selling for $2,295 which wasn't too bad. But the next batch went up to $2,895, and the electric-start eight-valvers—when they finally got here—were priced at $3,690. That's ridiculous for an old-fashioned bike that isn't even reliable. No one's going to pay that [money] when he can get a Japanese bike that will outperform it for half the price.

TMA closed, owing dealers their warranty credits and the factory for sold inventory. In the summer of 1983, remnants of the venerable US Triumph organization were auctioned to satisfy the many creditors who had been left holding an empty bag. On sale were records and hardbound ledgers dating back to the Johnson Motors days. Also among the memorabilia were several signs, including the electrified logo that hung outside the Placentia warehouse. Naturally, a small number of unclaimed machines were available to be sold off, including six T140D Specials, two Bonneville Royals, one Executive, one TSS (reportedly the last T140 made at Meriden), and several machines that had been cannibalized by TMA.

The day that Triumph lovers hoped would never come was unfortunate and in many ways tragic. Perhaps it was avoidable. At least the motorcycles had remained true to the form that, at one time, made them America's most popular imported machines. The last Meriden-built Triumph twins were straightforward, light, simple, beautiful, and exhilarating to ride on a winding road—just like those from the days of Reggie Pink, Johnson Motors Inc., and the Triumph Corporation.

"Triumphs are more than eccentric links to the past," reflected journalist Joe Minton in early 1983. "They are an embodiment of a philosophy—traditional if you will—that motorcycles should serve the rider, and not the opposite."

13
REBIRTH OF THE LEGEND
TRIUMPH AMERICA IN THE HINCKLEY ERA

Soon after the doomed Meriden Cooperative built its last 750cc Bonneville in 1983 and the old factory was demolished, a plan was devised for Triumph's resurrection. It came from a savvy thirty-nine-year-old British businessman named John Bloor. A former plasterer's apprentice, Bloor had no motorcycle industry experience. Nor was he a "biker." Bloor was a self-made millionaire who built his fortune in construction and real estate. As he watched fate catch up with Meriden during the early 1980s, Bloor recognized that the only asset certain to survive, Triumph's great name, was also the most valuable.

ABOVE: A well-used 1995 Sprint 900, Triumph's bulletproof sport touring triple. *Brooke photo*

LEFT: Triumph's outrageous 2300cc Rocket III is the ultimate muscle bike, as Andy Smart's customized 2015 Phantom Black model attests. *Brooke photo*

Launched in 1994, the Super III was a 115-horsepower Cosworth-tuned version of the Daytona 900 triple. Triumph built 805 examples, 179 of which were sold in the US. *Triumph photo*

The first 885cc T309 Speed Triples created a serious buzz for Triumph in the US when they launched in 1994. *Triumph photo*

Triumph Motorcycles America's first CEO Michael Lock. *Russell Hightower photo/Brooke archive*

Following the Co-Op's demise, he purchased the Triumph name, logo, and manufacturing rights from the liquidators for a reported £120,000—about $300,000 at the time. The package included all of Meriden's final R&D projects, the most intriguing of which were blueprints and a full-scale mockup of the Phoenix—a DOHC, liquid-cooled parallel twin with a monoshock frame and angular bodywork. The Co-Op had hoped to produce this bike as the Diana in 600cc, 750cc, and 900cc versions. Some observers saw it as the future Bonneville.

Competing with Bloor for rights to the famed marque was L. F. "Les" Harris, an independent Triumph parts manufacturer and importer in the British Midlands. Harris's company, Racing Spares, had been making Triumph components since the 1960s. More than anything, Harris's interest was in keeping the air-cooled Bonneville alive. He ultimately lost out to Bloor in the bidding, but not without realizing part of his dream.

With Triumph's assets officially in hand, Bloor granted Harris a five-year license to assemble kick-start T140V Bonnevilles at his small Devon plant. The deal accomplished two things: it kept the Triumph name alive, and it gave Bloor time to secretly develop both a range of new Triumph motorcycles and the company with which to produce them. The license also prohibited Harris from using the TSS head or the anti-vibration engine mounts employed on a handful of Meriden's final bikes.

The first Harris-built Bonnies hit the road in 1985, but none were imported to the US due to America's strict liability-insurance rules, and emissions and noise regulations. In late 1988, Bloor chose not to renew Harris's license after some two thousand bikes had been produced. The air-cooled Bonnie died again.

NEW HOME IN HINCKLEY

By this time, Bloor had quietly established a new company: Triumph Motorcycles Limited. He now owned a 10-acre, green-field site at Hinckley, Leicestershire, not far from Triumph's original Coventry works. There, construction began of a 90,000-square-foot factory to be filled with state-of-the-art manufacturing equipment and a new, mostly young work force.

Bloor financed the early steps of Triumph's rebirth out of his own pocket. His small team of engineers saw no future potential in the Phoenix twin or other last-grasp Meriden projects. Working in secrecy, the team designed a modern range of three- and four-cylinder, liquid-cooled, DOHC four-valve motorcycles. Their strategy was not to directly fight the Japanese—a costly battle tiny Triumph could not win. Instead, they chose a "modular" strategy for the entire model range—just as Bert Hopwood had envisioned for Triumph in the mid-1970s.

The modular approach is widely used by motorcycle and car makers today. It shares common engine dimensions and

The aluminum-framed, fuel-injected 955cc Daytona 955i in its 1999 killer black livery. *Triumph photo*

Originally sold in both four- and three-cylinder versions, the Trophy-3 gained slick new bodywork in 1995. An excellent tourer, the Trophy's sales have always underwhelmed. *Brooke photo*

RIGHT: The 885cc Thunderbird spawned multiple variants, including the now-collectible Sport shown here in its 1999 debut year. *Triumph photo*

BELOW: Speed Triple gained its now-iconic twin headlamps when the all-new T509 generation launched in 1999. *Triumph photo*

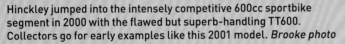
Hinckley jumped into the intensely competitive 600cc sportbike segment in 2000 with the flawed but superb-handling TT600. Collectors go for early examples like this 2001 model. *Brooke photo*

The still-lamented T595-based Sprint ST was a popular sport tourer. *Triumph photo*

components, and basic chassis and cycle parts among different models. This greatly reduces investment costs, minimizes spare parts inventory, and simplifies service training. By going modular, Triumph proved that it learned from the excesses of the Japanese makers, whose motorcycles rarely shared as much as a mirror.

Triumph's design engineers were influenced by Kawasaki's groundbreaking GPz900R in creating an architecture for the new engine "family." They chose a 76mm cylinder bore and either 55mm- or 65mm-stroke crankshafts (sourced in Germany), depending on specified displacement. Three-cylinder engines were 749cc and 885cc, while the fours measured 1180cc. The triples featured 120-degree crankpin spacing, just like the classic T150 Tridents. Twin-cam four-valve cylinder heads fed by 36mm flat-slide Mikuni CV carburetors also were a common design. Compression ratio and camshaft profiles were different to give the various models distinct "personalities."

To quell vibration, both the triples and fours incorporated balance shafts in their horizontally split crankcases. The wet-sump triples employed a single shaft ahead of the crankshaft, while the dry-sump fours used twin counter-rotating shafts below it with oil carried in a reservoir below the gearbox.

Depending on the model, gearboxes featured either five or six ratios with a beefy 6-inch multi-plate wet clutch. By every analysis, the new Triumph powerplants were as robust as any in the industry. In fact, they were over-engineered and delivered healthy power—from 90 horsepower at 10,500 rpm for the 750 triples to 147 horsepower at 9,500 rpm for the hottest 1200 four.

Modularity also extended to the new Triumphs' chassis, which featured a large-diameter tubular steel "spine," the engine serving as a stressed member for extra rigidity.

Swingarms were aluminum and featured large, eccentric chain adjusters on the axle end. Triumph went shopping in Japan for its Kayaba suspension units and Nissin disc brakes.

The "platform" supported a variety of models—from "naked" standards to hot sport bikes and sport-tourers, and even a big "dual-sport" and a classically styled "cruiser."

TRIUMPHS ON THE ROAD AGAIN

Amazingly, John Bloor managed to keep his bold, new venture secret for almost two years after the first prototype engine was run in May 1987. Then his cover was blown. In March 1989, American Triumph enthusiast John Hubbard, an engineer with Ford Motor Co., spotted a table full of new motorcycle engine castings on display at the Society of Automotive Engineers annual Expo in Detroit. All parts, including a cylinder head, carried an embossed Triumph logo. The logo was a stylized version of Jack Wickes's 1930s "swooping-R" masterpiece.

The excited Hubbard immediately sped home, grabbed his camera, and hurried back to the SAE event. He sent his "spy" photos with descriptions to *Classic Bike* magazine in Britain, where they became an international scoop—the first real evidence that Bloor's project was well underway.

Finally, in fall 1990, Bloor launched Triumph's new range of 750cc and 900cc triples and 1200cc fours at the Cologne Motorcycle Show. The official 1991-model lineup evoked some of Triumph's most famous model names, from the standard Tridents to the fully faired Trophy sport-tourers and Daytona sport bikes. Britain, and its famous two-wheeled marque, were back in the volume motorcycle business!

Triumph started out methodically, taking small, calculated steps. The company initially targeted the UK and

Immediately after its 2001 debut, the new 60-horsepower Bonneville twin became Triumph's bestseller and one of the bike industry's most profitable "platforms." *Triumph photo*

Germany, countries with the most demanding motorcyclists. In both, anything less than a world-class motorcycle would not be accepted. The great name was nothing if the product didn't measure up. Luckily, it did. By the end of 1991, Triumphs were Britain's bestselling large-capacity motorcycles. Three years later, the company had set up sales operations in Japan, Australia, and Canada.

It was a Cinderella saga; after just four years of business, Bloor had recouped his original investment. Triumph was operating in the black. The factory more than doubled in size in order to meet worldwide demand, and annual

Sold from 2002 to 2006, the 600cc Speed Four was the "naked" version of the TT600. *Triumph photo*

production increased from 3,098 bikes in 1992 to 6,512 in 1993. A bulletproof, "overengineered" reputation preceded the motorcycles wherever they were sold, and a few early quality issues were quickly rectified. The new Tiger "adventure bike" sported the first-ever plastic fuel tank on a Triumph, which was trouble-free.

By 1995, Hinckley's production reached 13,525 machines. Engine castings were now made using the Cosworth pressure-sandcast process. Now came the final beachhead: America. As in the glory days, the US market represented Triumph's greatest potential. It also enjoyed the most residual affection for the marque.

BACK IN THE USA

Triumph finally returned to the US in late 1994, bringing ten 1995 models—the entire UK range except the 750 Trident, which carried no real price or insurance advantage over its 900cc big brother. US prices ranged from $7,900 for the Trident 900, to $14,000 for the limited-production 900cc, 115-horsepower Daytona Super III fitted with Alcon 6-piston brake calipers and some carbon fiber bodywork. The company aimed at a conservative 2,000 to 2,500 total sales the first season.

From the start, Triumph's new triples became favorites of magazine road testers. "The engine cranks out prodigious torque, which makes it very easy to ride, yet when a blast of power is needed for sport riding or passing it's readily available," reported Mark Tuttle Jr. in an early 1995 *Rider* test of the 900cc Trophy 3. The magazine added that the big triple's "song and feel are what begin to separate the Trophy 3 from the Universal Japanese Sport Tourer."

In the first full US road test of the screaming yellow Daytona 900, *Cycle World* noted that "the engine pulls like a team of oxen from right off idle," while the bike's six-speed gearbox "clicks between ratios with the short-throw precision of a rifle bolt. No missed shifts here."

Most of the 1995 US reviews concluded that the new triples brimmed with personality, despite their conservative chassis design and large proportions. Praise was unanimous for the bikes' finish: "Paint is right and thick, with no orange peel," reported *Cycle World*. "The bodywork is of very high quality and it all fits together as if it was designed and built in Japan."

Adding a double shot of espresso to the 1995 lineup was the Speed Triple. Available in black or Fireball Orange, the bike was Triumph's take on the Laverda Jota triples of the late 1970s. Its name was also a clever play on the legendary Speed Twin. Basically, a Daytona 900 devoid of fairing and with five, not six, cogs in the gearbox, the 100-horsepower Speed Triple was a badass-looking café racer with punchy-but-civilized performance, according to Mitch Boehm's late-1994 *Motorcyclist* test.

But, due to the bike's extreme ergonomics, Americans didn't warm up to it as quickly as Triumph had hoped. As in the past, resourceful dealers stepped in: At Big D Cycle, Keith Martin began swapping the Speed Triple's top fork clamp with a Kawasaki item that allowed a tubular handlebar to be fitted above the clamp. The result was a more upright riding position that helped sell Speed Triples in Dallas. Soon, US aftermarket firms began offering handlebar kits too. By 1996, the factory had fitted a raised clip-on to American-spec Speed Triples.

THE US SALES NETWORK

Returning to America had been a key to John Bloor's strategy since 1984. He closely watched as the US market evolved into two basic segments: high-tech, blindingly fast sport bikes dominated by the Japanese, and laid-back cruisers, dominated by Harley-Davidson and Japanese clones. For Triumph's entry, Bloor initially considered developing an in-between custom model heavily influenced by Craig Vetter's pioneering Hurricane triple, according to the late Don Brown, who served as Bloor's US market consultant during the early years. But such a machine was not pursued.

As Triumph systematically laid its US groundwork, various distribution plans were considered. One involved a link with Kawasaki that was to be dissolved once Triumph was firmly established. Another proposed a joint sales deal with Ducati's distributor, Cagiva North America. Both ideas were eventually nixed in favor of a wholly owned US distributor, Triumph Motorcycles America, Ltd. A 20,000-square-foot headquarters was established in Peachtree City, Georgia, an Atlanta suburb.

Michael Lock, a young ex-Honda UK marketing executive, spearheaded the US return. Extremely focused

The Tiger adventure bike range has been in Triumph's US lineup since 1994. It's evolved from 885cc to 955cc (2004 version shown), 1050cc, and 800cc engines in increasingly capable chassis. *Triumph photo*

The 2004 Thruxton ushered in the 865cc twin engine in a handsome café racer package. *Triumph photo*

Cruiser variants of the Bonneville include the America, shown in its 2008 Pacific Blue paint. *Triumph photo*

Triumph's US management contracted San Diego–based custom bike builder Richard Pollock's Mule Motorcycles to build this 2010 concept street tracker to show potential directions for the 865cc Bonneville. Mule is one of dozens of custom shops working with Triumph's twin. *Brooke photo*

and creative—he even wrote and helped design Triumph's hip, provocative sales catalogs that immediately became collectors' items—Lock had spent most of the early 1990s as Triumph's international marketing manager, where he set up Triumph's global sales network. Now, he turned his attention to America. For twelve straight months, Lock crisscrossed the country as he interviewed prospective dealers.

He aimed to sign only those agents who shared his energy and enthusiasm for the sport. "We're looking for dealers who love motorcycling and are motorcyclists," he told the authors in

1995. His total dedication to putting his company back on the US map compared with that of early Triumph giants Bill Johnson and Denis McCormack.

By spring 1995, Lock had become president of TMA. He'd signed sixty American dealers from Alaska to Florida who formed the core of Triumph's new US network. Only a handful among them had sold Triumphs in the past, including Fay Myers in Denver; Carl Donelson in St. Louis; and perhaps the most famous American Triumph dealer of all, Jack Wilson's Big D Cycle in Dallas.

Most of the new stores were multi-line outlets selling the Japanese Big Four, or Euro-centric shops specializing in BMW or Ducati. A few open-minded Harley stores were in the mix. Harley-Davidson at the time assisted Triumph in homologating its US models for EPA certification, while Triumph helped Harley certify its European lineup.

"In our choice of dealers, it wasn't about what they've got. Its whether they care about people," said Lock. "Do they get involved in rides on Sunday morning, or are they glad to be home? They've got to be enthusiasts."

Lock was barely finished setting up the original US network when he came under fire for what some midwestern dealers called "the Home Depot approach" to store location. That meant concentrating multiple dealer points in a metropolitan area and then watching those stores "claw each other's eyes out," as one described it, in a battle for customers and their own survival. Early US dealers also recall that Hinckley was painfully slow in delivering the Triumph-branded "Triple Connection" apparel they'd been promised as a vital revenue-driver.

During its first few years in the UK and Europe, the reborn company was, Lock admitted, "a bit cold-hearted toward the old establishment"—the ardent fans who never abandoned

The Street Triple leverages Triumph's high-revving 675cc triple and nimble chassis. This 2008 model wears a Triumph factory accessory exhaust. *Triumph photo*

Triumph. As word of this treatment reached American Triumph enthusiasts, including parts vendors and restoration shops, they wondered if they'd fare any better.

"It was vitally important for us, as a new company, to maintain some distance with the past—perhaps it was more distance than we would have liked," Lock later explained. Particularly in Britain, where the public wanted to forget the failed Meriden "industrial experiment," Bloor had to prove that his new enterprise was bringing a high-quality, competitive product—and didn't require the drip-feed of government assistance.

Outside the UK, however, motorcyclists told Lock that they wanted Triumph to embrace its rich heritage. That desire was most apparent in America, where the name always held the most magic.

"Without any shadow of doubt, the Triumph name is stronger [in the US] than anywhere else," Lock told co-author Brooke at the 1994 Toronto Motorcycle Show. For proof, he noted an independent survey of non-motorcyclists, commissioned by Triumph to gauge brand awareness. Survey results showed Triumph to be the third best-known motorcycle brand in America, after Harley-Davidson and Honda. And this was a decade after the last new Triumphs were sold!

THE T-BIRD SOARS AGAIN

Hinckley's first reconnection to Triumph's heritage was the 1995 Thunderbird—a star of Triumph's American rebirth. With its curvaceous black side covers, wire wheels, polished engine cases, authentic chrome Burgess mufflers, and "traditional" Triumph fuel tank (complete with 1957 to 1965–style "harmonica" badge and optional scalloped paint scheme), the 900cc triple was a thoroughly modern classic. However, the new machine nearly failed to make its US debut.

Launched in 2010, the 1600cc Thunderbird was the first parallel twin to enter the US midsized cruiser market dominated by Harley and the Japanese V-twin clones. *Brooke photo*

For months leading up to the bike's introduction, the US Office of Patents and Trademarks refused to grant Triumph rights to the Thunderbird name. The agency noted only one trademark standard covering automotive products, both two- and four-wheeled. Ironically, the feds recognized Ford Motor Company as having exclusive rights to Thunderbird. Ford had used the name on its car since 1955—but only after Triumph had granted them permission to use it.

The popular Tiger 800 adventure-bike range was expanded to include the 2016 XRT, a more road-biased model. *Triumph photo*

The lifestyle media fell in love with the Bonneville Scrambler. *Men's Journal*

Unfortunately, Triumph last re-registered the Thunderbird name in 1971, and rights to it lapsed when Meriden collapsed in 1983. Negotiations between Hinckley and the Patent Office dragged on to winter 1994. The bike, badges and all, was ready to go. The name had been leaked to the press. Dealers were taking orders; Daytona Bike Week was fast approaching and a big debut in Florida had been planned. Triumph management became nervous.

Finally, on the eve of Daytona, the Patent Office resolved the issue to Triumph's satisfaction. The T-Bird flew again in the US and would comprise roughly 25 percent of Triumph's 1995 US model mix. Overnight, it was Triumph's most popular model worldwide.

"Our guess is that Triumph will sell a lot of these," enthused *Cycle World* in its May 1995 T-bird test. The magazine's review generally praised the bike, giving highest marks to its gearbox and sharp engine performance. Fuel economy was poor, however: an average 35 miles per gallon.

"When it comes to Saturday nights, the Thunderbird takes its styling cues from the history books," reported *Motorcyclist* in August 1995. "But there's enough rip in the torquey 885cc triple to leave the average V-twin wheezing in the rearview."

The magazine dubbed the $9,995 T-bird "a bloody good motorcycle." It went on to name the entire 1995 Triumph range as "Motorcycle of the Year." The Thunderbird platform went on to underpin spinoffs Adventurer (1996), Thunderbird Sport (1998), and Legend (1999).

For its rookie year in the US, the tiny company reckoned that only a low-key, low-budget marketing program was

Brand strategists would have a tough time pinning down Drew Winter. The veteran Michigan-based automotive journalist cut his motorcycling teeth on various dirt bikes in his youth. He lusted after Honda's CB750 when it debuted in 1969, but like many off-road-centric riders didn't make the transition to road machines due to college, family, and career.

"For years, I wanted to get back into motorcycling with a road bike," Winter explained. "When I started shopping in earnest in 2008, I knew very little about the Triumph brand. But the minute I threw a leg over the Bonneville at the Cycle World show, everything clicked for me. The narrowness, the peg position, seating, everything about the bike and its ergonomics seemed perfect."

Winter admitted some initial resistance to the Bonnie: Did he want a "retro" bike? And in the height of the Great Recession in 2009, he felt drawn to buy American. But after back-to-back test rides on a new 883 Sportster ("unacceptable vibration") and a Bonneville, and brief review of a Suzuki Gladius, the choice was clear.

"It was only after the [Bonneville SE] purchase that I started reading up on Triumph. Then I truly understood why I chose the Bonnie. Now I doubt I'll buy any other brand."

Winter and his Bonneville Black with cast wheels. *Brooke photo*

necessary to spark America's pent-up excitement for Triumph's return. Unlike the halcyon era, Triumph's magazine ads throughout the 1990s were dull, with inconsistent messaging. Still, the T-bird and a steady stream of customers at the more than 100 US dealerships helped make Triumph the most talked about motorcycle company of 1995.

BRINGING BACK BONNIE

The first of Hinckley's second-generation triples arrived in 1997: the fully faired T595 Daytona sports bike and the iconic bug-eyed T509 Speed Triple. The T595 code was ill-considered, as it led some to believe the new 955cc engine was a 600. This was rectified two years later when the updated Daytona was renamed 955i. Still, the 1997 engines were co-engineered by Lotus and marked Triumph's first use of fuel injection made in France by Sagem. They delivered 108 horsepower (Speed Triple) and 120 horsepower (Daytona).

Also new were novel-design aluminum tubular frames and single-sided swingarms. The first hundred Daytonas off the Hinckley production line were recalled due to reported cracking issues; their frames were replaced under warranty.

In 2016 heroic Danell Lynn set a Guinness record for the world's longest motorcycle journey in a single country. Her 53,000-mile odyssey in all US states and three Canadian provinces aboard her Bonneville named "Amelia" took nearly two years to complete. *Keith May/Triumph photo*

Sophisticated electronic chassis control and a new 1215cc engine give the 2017 Tiger Explorer XCX globe-trotting capability. *Triumph photo*

The remaining spine-frame US models (Trophy tourer, Tiger adventure bike, Sprint sport-tourer, and standard Trident) would evolve or, in the case of the Sprint and Trident, be dropped eventually. The final spine-frame Triumph was the 2003 Thunderbird Sport. Even in 2017, US dealers were still lamenting the loss of the Sprint and Sprint ST, arguing that Triumph never really replaced the handy, quick, and popular sport-tourer.

The irrepressible Michael Lock left Triumph's American operation in 1997. He was briefly replaced as CEO by Ross Clifford, the company's global marketing manager. Within a year, Bloor hired the widely respected Kawasaki USA veteran Mike Vaughan as general manager, then promoted him to CEO. The US dealer body at that time numbered about one hundred stores but had only six district managers to serve them.

"Just about everyone wore several hats" in the thinly stretched organization, Vaughan wrote in a 2014 *Dealernews* column. When he took over, Triumph's model line "with few exceptions was behind the curve in terms of styling and development. Other than that, the mechanicals were good, and the quality and finish were excellent. Pricing, however, was out of line with the market."

A 1998 Thunderbird listed for $8,995, when a new Kawasaki Vulcan 1500 retailed for $7,699 and a Honda CBR900RR for $8,999. Vaughan noted that compared to other European bikes, Triumph was on the low end of the price scale, but the brand at that time "was more frequently compared to the Japanese than Ducati or BMW."

As Triumph was re-entering the American market, Hinckley engineers had a modern twin-cylinder engine under development. Its long gestation was due to Bloor's design and engineering team being adamant about getting it "just right," explained Michael Lock. In the process, Triumph re-secured rights to the Bonneville name, through a legal arrangement with General Motors. The giant automaker originally registered the Bonneville name in 1955 and continued to renew its trademark. When the Triumph Engineering Company launched its twin-carb 650cc twin in 1959, it was with GM's approval.

But, in the late 1990s, the two companies struck a simple deal: Triumph will never build a car named Bonneville, and GM won't make a bike with the same name. Finally, in fall 2001, Triumph unveiled the machine for which every Triumph fan and dealer had been waiting. The new Bonneville, now displacing 790cc, was air- and oil-cooled and sported a DOHC four-valve top end. Potential vibration from the traditional Triumph 360-degree firing order was kept nicely in check by counter-rotating balance shafts.

Independent motorcycle designer John Mockett, who had a long relationship with Hinckley, ensured the bike would capture the overall style and proportions of classic-era Bonnies. The born-again twin was a sensation. It quickly became Triumph's worldwide bestseller and soon accounted for up to 40 percent of the brand's US sales.

"To this day, the Bonneville and its variants remain the 'point of the sales spear' for the company," Mike Vaughan noted. Its overwhelming popularity and robustness—some owners racked up more than 100,000 trouble-free miles, a fantasy in the Meriden era—helped convince a new crop of dealers that Triumph was a desirable brand to sell. Perhaps more compelling, the Bonnie was a "platform" for upgrades and variants: Scrambler versions with a 270-degree crank; Thruxton and T100 versions that brought the 865cc engine;

ENGINEERING THE NEW TWIN

Stuart Wood joined Triumph in 1987 as a rookie engineer, four years before Hinckley built its first motorcycle. Since then, he had a hand in developing virtually every Triumph model. By 2011, Wood had earned one of the most sacred jobs in the motorcycle industry: chief engineer on the next Bonneville. On the eve of that machine's US introduction in late 2015, Wood gave Lindsay Brooke some insights on the new Bonnie's birth.

Q: You're chief engineer of a motorcycling icon. Talk about the responsibility of having to get the new Bonnie absolutely right.

Yes, it is a responsibility, but it's also an opportunity. That's how we felt going into this project. It was great to be able to design the new range from the ground up. It's a bike for current riders but still very definitely a Bonneville.

Q: The 2001 Bonneville will have had a fifteen-year life cycle when it finally exits production. During that time, it was bumped up to 865cc and gained fuel injection, the 270-degree crankshaft, and a big-fin cylinder barrel on the cruisers. Did you guys envision that long a model run?

I wouldn't have bet that it would've been fifteen years, but we knew it would be a longer product cycle than, say, a sports bike. It's a very solid architecture. The style of the bike and what we could do in terms of derivatives ensured that it would be a large proportion of Triumph's business from that point [2001] on. Since then, the Bonneville's attractiveness has only increased.

Q: The Triumph twin since 1938 has been a natural for iteration and personalization. What role did the "platform" success of the 2001 Bonnie play in developing the 2016 model?

Our goals with the [2016] Bonneville were to keep it rider-focused, clean, and uncluttered. We have added a lot of technology that makes the riding experience better. Some of it, like ABS brakes, is required by law. But the technology hasn't detracted from the Bonneville's visual simplicity, which is very, very important. It's still a bike that people can strip pieces from and add other bits to it. They can customize it. We've launched over 470 accessories with the 2016 model. The Street Twin is the most stripped, purist version and there are over 150 parts just for it.

Q: Many people won't understand how your engineers sweated the details in developing such an aesthetically clean engine.

When you get really close to the Bonneville, you don't see coolant hoses and electronics and antilock brake units. We've got ride-by-wire and standard traction control, but as a rider you don't need to see those things. It's in the background. It is quite a tough job to package all those bits so you don't see them; they're not just hidden under a cover. What you do see is all understandable. The bike describes itself visually.

Q: At what point during the previous Bonneville's fifteen-year run did Triumph Engineering commit to liquid cooling for the new engine?

Four years ago, when this project began, we decided we were going to do a whole new motorbike range. And from day one there was discussion on how much liquid cooling, or water cooling, would be required. There was the option of

Stuart Wood, chief engineer of the 2016 Bonneville program. Triumph photo

not moving to water cooling at all. One concern was how it was going to look. Very early on, we built our first mockup to ensure the bike's beautiful looks would not be spoiled by a big radiator. That was our greatest concern. From our engineering analysis, we knew we could package the coolant lines internally and use very simple centerline water inlets.

One thing that helps a lot is that we've got actual cooling fins that aren't just cosmetic. Our early designs looked at how much we could cool via the fins and how much through water. We use both. The fins actually help reduce the size of the radiator. And with water cooling we've optimized engine response and performance far better than with the previous oil-cooled strategy. Water cooling also enables fast warmup times for improved emissions performance. It gives us headroom to meet future global rules and regs while the theme of "honest motorbike" shines through.

Q: How about the 270-degree crankshaft?

It also was decided very early on, based on going to an engine platform that must support both 900cc and 1200cc versions. The experience with our 360-degree crank is excellent in terms of the exhaust sound quality, but you've always got second-order vibrations that are hard to isolate from the rider. The 270 crank gives natural second-order balance. The bikes have got twin primary-balance shafts anyway so going to the 270 crank wasn't a hard decision. We got bigger and it was just the tipping point, enabling us to create a bike you can literally ride all day.

A snarling pair: 2017 Speed Triple RS. *Triumph photo*

America and Speedmaster "factory customs." Hinckley filled the pipeline with a mind-boggling number of special editions and an enormous aftermarket rose up to serve the bike some have dubbed "the Ford Mustang of motorcycles."

Electronic fuel injection came in 2008 on UK models then arrived in 2009 on US bikes. Brilliantly, Triumph and Keihin developed an injection throttle body that resembled a carburetor to retain the classic look. Unfortunately, the new fuel system required an injection pump located in the fuel tank, which made the tank slightly bulbous. The first-generation Hinckley Bonnies suffered from a few cheesy cost-saving tricks, including lack of a standard tachometer, a screwed-on seat, and no tool kit. The ignition key was poorly sited next to the headlamp rather than facing the rider, and the center stand was a $200 option. But Bloor's team got far more right than wrong on their new "franchise" product.

Originally produced exclusively at Hinckley, the Bonnie was shifted to Triumph's new plant in Thailand in 2014 to save labor costs. "That plant's tooling is newer and the workforce is top-notch," reasoned Don Brown, after co-author Brooke had discovered a "T" (for Thailand) in his 2007 Bonnie's VIN number. "You likely have a better-made machine than the English ones," he counseled.

In 2003, a year after a fire devastated the Hinckley factory, Triumph built its last four-cylinder (Trophy) model and moved to a twins-and-triples-only market strategy. While it prototyped a liquid-cooled 300cc single aimed at Asian markets, that machine was not produced as of 2017. An ATV-like four-wheeler was also considered as Triumph, now managed by John Bloor's son Nick, looked at new growth opportunities.

The company's model range by 2013 was comprised of twenty-five motorcycles covering a wide swath of market segments, from 675cc triples to the 2.3-liter Rocket III colossus.

Triumph enjoyed a record sales year, selling about 13,000 machines in the US out of 52,089 units sold worldwide. By early 2014, the American distributor counted 230 dealers in the US and Canada and was aiming for 300. It was the fastest-growing motorcycle brand in the US, moving from 1.5 percent market share to 3 percent. Overall sales jumped ahead of BMW and Ducati for the first time in the Hinckley era, and some Triumph dealers were selling one hundred new bikes or more per year.

The 2011 to 2014 growth in North America came under new CEO Greg Heichelbech, who was hired by Bloor in 2010 after a twenty-year career at Harley-Davidson. Heichelbech revamped many of Triumph's inventory and logistics processes and instituted a twenty-four-hour service and parts hotline. He also aimed to inject a new enthusiasm into the company by pushing hard to connect Triumph's racing heritage with the modern era.

A collaboration with Castrol, Carpenter Racing, and Hot Rod Conspiracy created the Castrol Rocket streamliner with the goal of being the first motorcycle to break the 400-miles-per-hour barrier. Heichelbech also increased Triumph's US support of Pro Road Racing that led to a Daytona 200 victory for the 675R triple. He partnered with two AMA American Flat Track teams, one led by Oregon Triumph dealer George Latus and the other by Bill Gately, head of Florida-based Bonneville Performance. More links with customizers and café-racer builders showed the limitless potential of the Bonneville platform.

"No question, Greg raised our collective profile in the industry and got Triumph back into moto sports, which was neglected for a long time," said one California dealer. "But he also really came under pressure from the UK to 'move the metal' as the factory increased output. Unfortunately, by doing this he put many of us under the same pressure too."

In mid-2014, Nick Bloor arrived in Georgia and fired Heichelbech. While no official reason was given, some dealers and industry watchers believed that Triumph was "channel stuffing" (forcing more inventory on dealers than could be sold, in order to inflate annual sales and earnings figures), an unethical and reviled practice once used by automakers to "cook the books."

Heichelbech was replaced by the joint team of chief operating officer Matt Sheahan and financial boss Don Carleo in the Georgia HQ. Under their management, Triumph in America enters a new era armed with the all-new, second-generation Bonneville range that debuted in late 2016. Developed over a three-year period, the new SOHC, liquid-cooled engines (to meet new global emissions and noise regulations) use a 270-degree crank, by-wire throttle control, and offer a choice of 900cc and 1,200cc displacements. The big engines feature a six-speed gearbox, a first for Triumph twins.

US dealers were thrilled; the 2017 Bonnies were sold out as of early May that year. Along with a reinvigorated dual-sport/adventure range of Tiger 800 and Explorer models and the ever-popular Speed and Street Triples, Triumph marked its eightieth anniversary in North America with a product line, distribution network, and reputation that were second to none.

In its design details and overall execution, Triumph's 2017 Bonneville Bobber was the year's top factory custom. *Brooke photo*

The 2017 Street Cup is the first of many niche iterations of the liquid-cooled Bonneville to come. *Triumph photo*

Half Mountain Cub, half Ski-Doo, the Sno-Go kit was a pioneering American concept that attracted few customers. *Joel Alderman photo*

Johnson Motors' famous 11 x 11-inch, fifteen-page prestige brochure from 1965 is a top collectible of the post–World War II Meriden Triumph era. Sales boss Don Brown spent most of his $30,000 ad budget that year on creating this beautiful color booklet. *Brooke photo*

King of the collectible Triumphs: Bud Ekins' 1962 Trophy-Bird used in the actual jump for *The Great Escape*. But where is this bike today? *Promotional photo, Brooke archive*

Triumph-Detroit owner Bob Leppan built this transverse-dual-650 machine in the 1960s as a testbed for a four-engined version of the Gyronaut streamliner. It made the cover of *Cycle* magazine and was still in existence in 2017. *Brooke archive*

APPENDIX:
TRIUMPHABILIA

The collectability of Triumph motorcycles is perhaps only equaled by that of Triumphabilia—the accessories, high-performance goodies, sales literature, dealer signage, and memorabilia that comes with a world-famous 115-year-old brand. More than eighty of those years selling bikes in America and Canada have generated ongoing collector demand for anything with the iconic "swooping-R" logo.

Need proof? Unopened pint cans of Triumph "Cycle Bath"—repackaged Gunk engine degreaser that retailed for 30 cents in 1960—typically sell for $45 and up in 2017 online auctions. Such humble artifacts have become desirable period art. Their whimsical cartoon label showing a gleaming Triumph twin in a bathtub next to its proud owner still gets smiles today.

Item CD358 in the early 1960s TriCor catalog was this 20-inch-diameter "Triumph Fun Time" lighted wall clock. Original price: $16.49. One of many Triumph catalog clocks. *Ken Grzesiak collection; Brooke photo*

Far rarer is the Cycle Sno-Go sled attachment, which Johnson Motors marketed in magazine ads and dedicated flyers in 1966. Manufactured in Sacramento, California, the Sno-Go rig was aimed at Mountain Cub owners looking to transform their little trail bikes into winter fun machines, although Triumph dealers could also fit it to any lightweight motorcycle. JoMo claimed that forty minutes and a few hand tools were all that was needed to replace the Cub's rear wheel with the Sno-Go tracked bogey mechanism and fit the front skis. The 130-pound assembly used a dedicated rear axle supported by ball bearings and fitted with a 48-tooth final drive sprocket, which was driven from the gearbox sprocket. The axle also carried a secondary sprocket, which provided chain drive to the caterpillar tracks.

On paper, the Sno-Go seemed well designed. The rubber tracks provided nearly 1,000 square inches of contact area with minimal ground force. However, without a differential the machine was difficult to maneuver away from a straight line, particularly in snow. (The rig could also be used without the front skis, turning a Tiger Cub into a "Panzer Cub," as some dealers jokingly called it.) And with the front skis fitted the machine had no brakes, only compression braking, so deceleration from the advertised 20-miles-per-hour top speed could be thrilling.

Few Sno-Gos were sold by JoMo, according to Clyde Earl. Their $304 retail price was nearly half the cost of a new Mountain Cub. In their forty-five years in the British motorcycle hobby, the authors have seen only one complete unit, and it is pictured here.

Showing even a fraction of the "Triumphabilia" that interests collectors would require a book of its own. Both the Triumph Corporation and Johnson Motors used various ad agencies, jobbers, and local manufacturers to create literally hundreds of items for their dealers to help sell motorcycles and accessories. The following pages provide a glimpse of the cool stuff that's in circulation—and even some gems that have yet to be found.

The Most Exciting Motorcycle Ever!

TRIUMPH
Thunderbird

LEFT: This original 1950 Thunderbird dealer poster evokes the excitement of the new 650cc twin. *Ken Grzesiak collection; Brooke photo*

BELOW: Copies of Triumph's inaugural 1903 sales brochure are rare and a must-have for serious collectors of historic motorcycle literature. *Gaylin archive*

TRIUMPH CYCLES.
Coventry 1903.

Johnson Motors operated six custom-bodied Chevrolet 3100 series trucks for dealer deliveries during the 1950s. Three were from Chevy's 1949 to 1954 "Advanced Design" era and three from 1955 to 1957. Do any exist today? *Brooke archive*

LEFT: Triumph's lighted 4 x 6-foot dealer signs like this one from Hermy's Tire & Cycle in Port Clinton, Pennsylvania, were part of the American roadscape for many years. They are worth many times their original $169 price today. *Brooke photo*

BELOW: Among the most collectible "American" Triumphs is the late Pat Owens's amazing, unmolested T120RT prototype on which he and wife Donna clocked over 500,000 miles of riding from Alaska to Central America. *Brooke photo*

Massachusetts-based Warren Leather Goods supplied TriCor with its classic tank bags, which fit perfectly on the stock Triumph parcel grid. They look great on restored bikes. *Brooke photo*

Period racing equipment such as this cast-aluminum slimline primary cover made by Carl's Sport Shop in Oklahoma City are a must for vintage dirt-track bikes and restorations. Other sources included Kosman, Trackmaster, ACK, and Smitty of Rock Island. *Brooke photo*

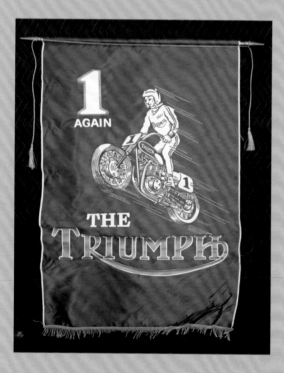

Hollywood Banners based in New York City produced iterations of this velour hanging drapery for dealers. This 1969 one celebrates Gary Nixon's 1968 AMA championship. *Ken Grzesiak collection; Brooke photo*

One of Triumph's winningest desert racers, Buck Smith, built sets of super trick "Traveler" forks that offered 8 inches of travel. They were briefly marketed through JoMo and now prized by desert sled restorers. *Brooke archive*

ABOVE: Original paintings that once hung in the Meriden factory are rare, such as this one of Jess Thomas's 1958 record runs in the Texas Ceegar at Bonneville. *Ken Grzesiak collection; Brooke photo*

BELOW: Anything touched by custom pinstriper and fabricator Von Dutch, a.k.a. Kenny Howard, carries a premium value—including this 1959 Thunderbird, built in the early 1960s and displayed in 2017 in the National Motorcycle Museum in Iowa. *Courtesy of Mark Mederski*

ABOVE: **Some of the many TriCor desk items given to dealers during the 1950s and 1960s. Unlike today, all were made in the US.** *Ken Grzesiak collection; Brooke photo*

LEFT: **Minichamps' series of 1:12-scale Triumphs included this 1938 Speed Twin, a 1939 Tiger 100, 1959 Bonneville, 1964 Trophy, and even a 1973 X75 Hurricane. All are out of production and have nicely gained collector value.** *Brooke photo*

TOP 25 COLLECTIBLE AMERICAN-MARKET TRIUMPHS

MODEL	YEARS	COMMENTS
5T Speed Twin and T100 Tiger	1938–40	First years for the pioneering modern parallel twin
Grand Prix 500 racer	1948–50	Scored Triumph's first Daytona win, 1950
Tiger 100c	1953	With factory-fitted Speed Kit, one year only
6T Thunderbird "Black Bird"	1953	Triumph painted this one for its American customers
TR6/A and TR6/B Trophy	1956–60	The do-it-all 650 that spawned the Desert Sled
TR5R, T100/R, and T100/RS production racers	1955–57	Rare Meriden-built dirt and road racers for US dealers
TR5AD Delta-head twin-carb 500	1959	The ultimate pre-unit 500, only a handful built and sold
T120 Bonneville	1959–70	Whether pre-unit or unit, a solid and fun investment
TR7 and T120C Bonneville Scrambler	1960–65	1960–62 are the rarest of these lovely high-pipers
TR5AC and TR5AR	1961	One year only/US-only comp and roadster 500s
T120C TT Special	1963	First year of the firebreather
T100S/C and T100C "Jack Pine" Tiger Competition	1965–66	Hard to find comp 500s with unique small fuel tanks
TR6C Trophy 650	1966–70	1966 models are rare
T150 Trident	1969	First year triple with Ogle styling is finally appreciated
X75 Hurricane	1973	Factory custom pioneer still turns heads
T140V and TR7RV Bonneville and Tiger 750	1973–74	Underrated "wet frame" 750s with few vices
T140W Bonneville 750 TSS 8-valve	1983	114 units imported to US
TT600	2001–02	Middleweight four is gaining value; avoid 2000 model
Speed Triple T309	1994–96	Big, brutish, and collectible from the start
Daytona Super III	1994–95	150 examples built; 115 horsepower, Cosworth engineered

If Dave Gaylin and I had a dollar for every time we've been asked, "What's the most collectible Triumph model?" we'd have enough money to afford at least one of the machines listed here. This table is the summation of not only our opinions but also those of a half dozen respected Triumph collectors, restorers, and longtime enthusiasts. Truth is, there are many factors that establish a motorcycle's desirability, including its rarity (one year of production, low volumes), its aesthetics, technical significance, racing success, and its inherent "cool" factor when new. Desirability and value are indeed a reflection of the collector base's demographics. Which, of course, only partly explains why late 1960s Bonnevilles are solidly blue-chip collector bikes. Their inarguable coolness and visual appeal are somewhat offset by their relative ubiquity. As motorcycles for everyday use, however, a strong case can be made for various "wet frame" T140s being better overall machines that are quicker, faster, and better mannered than the revered "oil tank" models. The 750 twins typically get less respect from the "Triumphs don't get any better than a 1970 Bonnie" crowd, but we believe the T140's value will continue to grow in the long term. And as this edition was completed, a few of the early Hinckley triples and fours had already reached collectible status. In another ten years, the models listed here will likely be different. *Lindsay Brooke, April 2017*

INDEX